My Journey Through Life

Autobiography of Chief Sir,
Prof. Alexander D. Wozuzu Acholonu

First Published in 2017
by University of Lagos Press and Bookshop Ltd
Unilag, P. O. Box 132
University of Lagos
Akoka, Yaba – Lagos Nigeria
Copyright by Acholonu, Alexander D. W.

Second edition
With a few corrections and additions 2019
by Dorrance Publishers,
585 Alpha Drive, Suite 103
Pittsburgh, PA 15238

Reprinted and first published as a paperback 2021
by Author's Note 360
10228 Nicolls Avenue, Corona, Queens,
New York 11368

All rights reserved.

Copyright by Prof. Alexander D. Wozuzu Acholonu 2021

ISBN: 978-1-951670-41-2 (Paperback)
ISBN: 978-1-951670-42-9 (Digital)

Library of Congress Control Number: 2021917621

No part of this book may be reproduced or transmitted, downloaded reverse engineered, or stored in or introduced into any information storage and retrieval system in any form or by any means including photocopying and recording, whether electronic or mechanical, now known or hereinafter invented without permission in writing from the publisher.

My Journey Through Life

Autobiography of Chief Sir,
Prof. Alexander D. Wozuzu Acholonu

First Published in 2017
by University of Lagos Press and Bookshop Ltd
Unilag, P. O. Box 132
University of Lagos
Akoka, Yaba – Lagos Nigeria
Copyright by Acholonu, Alexander D. W.

Second edition
With a few corrections and additions 2019
by Dorrance Publishers,
585 Alpha Drive, Suite 103
Pittsburgh, PA 15238

Reprinted and first published as a paperback 2021
by Author's Note 360
10228 Nicolls Avenue, Corona, Queens,
New York 11368

All rights reserved.

Copyright by Prof. Alexander D. Wozuzu Acholonu 2021

ISBN: 978-1-951670-41-2 (Paperback)
ISBN: 978-1-951670-42-9 (Digital)

Library of Congress Control Number: 2021917621

No part of this book may be reproduced or transmitted, downloaded reverse engineered, or stored in or introduced into any information storage and retrieval system in any form or by any means including photocopying and recording, whether electronic or mechanical, now known or hereinafter invented without permission in writing from the publisher.

MY JOURNEY THROUGH LIFE

AUTOBIOGRAPHY OF CHIEF SIR PROF. ALEXANDER D. WOZUZU ACHOLONU

Illustrated with Photographs
By

Alexander Dozie Wozuzu Acholonu
Ph.D., FNSP, FRAES, FAS, OON

My Philosophies:
Take time to work; it is the price of success.
He who stops being better, stops being good.
The Road to success is always under construction.

DEDICATION

To my beloved father, Mr. Wilfred Wozuzu Acholonu who saw in me a bright future; a father who called me early in my life "blessed Alexander"; a father who called me "the apple of his eye" and while in elementary four (4) gave me the impetus to aspire to go overseas for further studies by saying: "I will see that you go overseas for further studies even if I have to sell my house at Port Harcourt"; a father who, not only showered immense love on me but who also jealously guarded and protected me; and to my mother, Mrs. Esther Rose Ekwemma Acholonu, who gave me all the love I needed to succeed.

Table of Contents

List of Figures xi
List of Relevant Congratulatory Messages And Tributes xxvii
Foreword xxix
Preface xxxi
Acknowledgements xxxv

Chapter One
Background—Awaka My Home 1

Chapter Two
Early Days of My Life 23

Chapter Three
Going to America and My American Experience 47

Chapter Four
My Family—I am a Husband, Father and Grandfather 65

Chapter Five
Academics and Professional Development 115

Chapter Six
My Titles, Affiliations and Laurels 135

Chapter Seven
The Igbos and Their Neighbors (My Views 199

Chapter Eight
Philanthropy..219

Chapter Nine
Some Key Dates in My Life (1932–2017................................241

Chapter Ten
Profile and Curriculum vitae of Chief Sir Professor
Alexander Dozie Wozuzu Acholonu, PHD, FNSP,
FRAES, FAS, OON 247

Chapter Eleven
Some Relevant Congratulatory Messages and Tributes 283

Conclusion 319

Appendix..321
My Firsts..321
Countries Visited 322
Positions of Leadership Held...324
Awaka Constitution as Prepared by My Committee
and I in 1984 327

References..331

Index 333

About the Author 339

LIST OF FIGURES

Chapter One: Background—Awaka My Home

Fig. 1.1: Awaka Club One members and some wives, left to right sitting: Herbert Emezi (late), Alex D.W Acholonu, Gibson Nkwo, Henry Opara (late), Simeon Enwere (late), Manace Os`uagwu (Maco) Standing, (Men): John J. Amadi, John Njoku (Ose John), Victor Nwakuna (late), Alphonsus N. Onyebiri 13

Fig. 1.2: Mr. Alfred U. Acholonu. My most senior uncle a tailor who made clothes for all the priests in the old Emekuku Parish; one of those Awaka people who brought Christianity to Awaka; the man used as banker by many Awaka people because of his impeccable or transparent honesty; the grandfather of Rev. Father Valentine Acholonu, the first Awaka Priest. He died in 1961 14

Fig. 1.3: Obu Omumu (Ficus vogelii, Miq.) (Yoruba Name Obadan) in its majesty. It is 91 years old. Picture taken Aug. 2016 15

Fig. 1.4: Acholonu backing Obu Omumu (Ficus vogelii, Miq.) (Yoruba Name: Obadan) in his village, Ndegbelu (91 years old tree) 15

Fig. 1.5: A dry leave of Obu Omumu (Ficus vogelii, Miq.) (Yoruba Name Obadan) in Awaka, a. back of the leaf b. front of the leaf collected directly from the tree (91 years old), on Nov. 21, 201716

Fig. 1.6: A dry leaf of Obu Omumu (Ficus vogelii, Miq.) (Yoruba Name Obadan). This shows a bigger sized leaf; collected directly from the tree (91 years old), on Nov. 21, 2017 16

Fig. 1.7: Awaka Community Vigilante that ensures the peace and security of Awaka, Owerri North LGA people. From the left and standing: Chigbechemba Osuagwu, Florence Ngozi Nnadi, Smart Onwana, Anthony Mbachu, Ikechukwu Nnaemeka, Emmanuel Udeokporo (Coordinator), Donatus Obi, Kelechi Mbata. Squatting on the ground and from left, Christian Nwachukwu, Amaka Ugwuegbulam, Ukachi Ukwuoma................................... 17

Fig. 1.8a: Holy Trinity Catholic Parish Church, Awaka in its present form and location 17

Fig. 1.8b: Holy Trinity Catholic Parish Church, Awaka in its present form and location with identification signboard and church (mass) schedules... 18

Fig. 1.8c: Holy Trinity Catholic Church Awaka in its present form and location showing a big crucifix 18

Fig. 1.9a: Willy Wozuzu Acholonu Memorial Mansion, a 3 story building, built in 1978 in honor of my father and in fulfillment of his request before he died in August, 1976. Below, the Parish Church wall blocking it from the front. It was the biggest commercial house in Awaka at the time 19

Fig. 1.9b: Willy Wozuzu Acholonu Memorial Mansion a 3 story building built in honor of my father and in fulfillment of his request before he died in August, 1976 that I build a big house here in his honor.. 19

Fig. 1.10: Willy-Esther Foundation Diagnostic Laboratory located on the ground floor of Willy Wozuzu Acholonu Memorial Mansion officially launched on Aug. 21 2017... 20

Chapter Two: Early Days of My Life

Fig. 2.1: My dad, Court Clerk and Councilor, Wilfred Wozuzu Acholonu in his greener or youthful days, a man to whom I owe a lot! Died in August, 1976 37

Fig. 2.2: Uncle Cyril Manuba Acholonu (Late). Lived to be 103 Years. Died in 2012 38

Fig. 2.3: Dr. Ben Njoku (Late), my mentor, my standard six teacher, my benefactor; a distinguished Professor of English and former Vice President of Academic Affairs, Rust College, Holly Springs, Mississippi, USA. Died May 17, 1995... 38

Fig. 2.4: Prof. Acholonu (right) as a sports man at CKC wearing his college blazer. He, another student (Ezeoke) and their house master (Mr. Ukigwe) are holding 3 trophies which they won during intra college sports. They were in St. Michael's House. He was the best tennis player in his set among the boarders 39

Fig. 2.5: Clothes that I wore during the final year football (soccer) play when we, the graduating seniors, went to cheer the players (CKC team) in 1952 40

Fig. 2.6: Picture taken as a finalist in Christ the King College, Onitsha, 1952 41

Fig. 2.7: Alex Acholonu in CKC posing—but not really a smoker 42

Fig. 2.8: Sitting: Alex Acholonu and Joseph Nwaneri, final year in CKC, and 2 from Owerri in class 5 (following us), 1952. Standing, left to right, Felix Nze and T. Njoku............................ 43

Fig. 2.9: Acholonu with secondary school friends, 1950. Left to right, Anthony Njoku, Dominic Nwaturuocha, Anthony Manuba, Victor Anyaso and Alex Acholonu... 43

Fig. 2.10: Left to Right: My teacher, mentor, benefactor, Dr. Ben Njoku and me, Alex Acholonu... 44

Fig. 2.11: Picture taken in front of the gate of Christ the King College in 2016. Left to right is Rev. Father Dr. Charles Okwumuo, Principal of CKC, Prof. Acholonu and Some Executive Members of CKC Alumni Association (Old Boys) 44

Fig. 2.12: Picture taken near the Statue of Archbishop Heery in 2016 who established CKC in 1933.. 45

Fig. 2.13: Picture of CKC classroom building in the 40s and 50s while I was there as a student.. 45

Chapter Three: Going to America and My American Experience

Fig. 3.1: Late Mr. Benjamin N. Acholonu, my uncle, the immediate senior brother of my father, the man who contributed 100 pounds towards my travel to the US for further studies in Dec. 1954. He died in 1988 at age 96.. 58

Fig. 3.2: Barrister Raymond Njoku (Late), former Minister of Commerce and Industry, Transport and Aviation, 1954-1966. My benefactor who made it possible for me to go to America more than anyone else. He signed a waiver for me............................. 59

Fig. 3.3: Ship that took me from Lagos to Liverpool – M. V. Aureol Elder Demister Shipping Line, December 1954 (Two weeks journey) 60

*Fig. 3.4: Ship that took me from Liverpool to New York – Saxonia Cunard R.M.S Line, 1954-55 (Two weeks journey) 60
Virginia Lodge, Restaurant in Alexandria, Virginia.................... 61*

Fig. 3.5: First place I worked in the USA after arrival from Nigeria. I worked as a Busboy removing used plates and cleaning tables in the restaurant 61

Fig. 3.6: My job as a house construction worker in the US, working to subsidize my cost of education and send money home to dad for support of my family. This is a display of the dignity of labor and the fact that America is a land of opportunity for the strong, mentally and physically. I did two to three jobs at a time while going to school at Howard University to make ends meet; to help my father with three wives and 25 children and no longer working *61*

Fig. 3.7: Prof. Alex Acholonu singing as a musician in an African Band group of which he was the leader, Washington D.C., about 1957. Included is his late friend, Engr. Gregory Okafor to his right ... 62

Fig. 3.8 From left to right Agbim, Gregory Okafor, Olatunji and Alex Acholonu singing and entertaining women cosmetologists group in Washington DC in about 1960 .... *62*

Fig. 3.9: Dr. Nnamdi Azikiwe (Zik). Former premier of Eastern Region and 1st President of Nigeria. The person I wrote to help me find funds to go to America for further education but, got a courteous negative response *63*

Fig. 3.10: Picture of Acholonu (left) with Mrs. Flora Azikiwe (Zik's 1st wife) at Howard University in Washington, DC as fellow students *63*

Fig. 3.11: Dr. Mrs. Uche Azikiwe (second wife of Dr. Nnamdi Azikiwe) and Chief Alex Acholonu (right). On the left is my friend, Prof. Anya O. Anya. Picture taken after Zik's Memorial Lecture at Enugu in the 90s. I paid her hotel bill in one of the World Igbo Congress (WIC) Conventions in the US. *64*

Chapter Four: My Family – I am a Husband Father and Grandfather

Fig. 4.1: My grandparents, Acholonu Nwokoro and Nwanyiocha *82*

Fig. 4.2: My Father, Wilfred Wozuzu and Mother, Esther Rose Acholonu (called "Ekwe-mma" i.e. literally "gong of beauty", by her people because of her exquisite beauty) in their youthful days *83*

Fig. 4.3: My mother and her 12th and last child, Leonard Acholonu 83

Fig. 4.4: My mother, Esther Rose Acholonu (nee Onukwugha) in her CWO (Catholic Women Organization) uniform. Died Oct. 2000 at age of 92 .... *84*

Fig. 4.5: Family Picture with mom and dad: (Middle line left to right) Casimir, Uchenna's Wife, Victoria carrying Uchenna Jr., dad Wilfred W. Acholonu, Esther (first wife), Mary, my wife and baby Leslie, then myself Alexander. (Standing, left to right) Wilfred Jr., Uchenna, Raphael, Newton, Francisca, Joseph, Felix, Oliver (late), Maximian. (Sitting down, left to right) Ngozi, Cynthia, Anderson, Ijeoma, Sandra *85*

Fig. 4.6: Young Acholonus coming behind me after my departure for the United States for further education. (Standing left to right) Uchenna, Adolphus (Hitler) (late), Paulina, Francis (late), Jane, Anthony (late), and Sylvester. (Squatting left to right) Caroline, Isabella, Chinyere (late) *85*

Fig. 4.7: Joy, the first lady who wanted me to marry her *86*

Fig. 4.8: My First Fianceé, Alganish, from Ethiopia. I named a parasite after her (Cercaria alganishi; Acholonu 1968) *86*

Fig. 4.9: My younger brother, Sir Engineer Uchenna Acholonu next to my Financee, Alganish, from left, who lived with me at the time in Baton Rouge, LA. Next to her is Dr. Nicholas Onyewu (late) with whom I shared the same cabin in the ship while coming to America in Dec. 1954. On my right is the Priest who got Alganish and I formally engaged in 1965 .... *87*

Fig. 4.10: Chief Sir Engineer Uchenna C. Acholonu, my immediate junior brother, next to sister Philomina, when he was very young and who lived with me in Baton Rouge, LA. I brought him to America in 1960 .... *87*

Fig. 4.11: Wedding Picture Mary and Alex Acholonu *88*

Fig. 4.12: Wedding Picture Mary and Alex Acholonu. She joined me in Baton Rouge, LA on Jan 16, 1967. We married on March 27, 1967 .... *89*

Fig. 4.13: Wedding Picture Alex Acholonu *89*

Fig. 4.14: Wedding Picture – Mary Acholonu *90*

Fig. 4.15: Wedding Picture Mary Acholonu *90*

Fig. 4.16: Wedding Picture—my wife Mary and my sister, Mrs. Paulina Okpechi as one of the bride's maids *91*

Fig. 4.17: Wedding Picture Bride, and groomsmen with Dr. Ben Njoku (left) and my best man, Dr. Moses Nwulia on my right. The others are my Biology Dept. Colleagues *91*

Fig. 4.18: Prof. Acholonu 2nd from left. Dr. Benedict Njoku next to him, Dr. Moses Nwulia, my best man on the left *92*

Fig. 4.19: 2nd from left, Dr. Melvin Clark, the President of Southern University (SU), Baton Rouge L.A. and on the left of Acholonu, Dr. Lewis White, Chair, Dept of Biology, SU *92*

Fig. 4.20: My wife Lolo, Lady Mary E. Acholonu and I in our youthful days shortly after our wedding in 1967 .... *93*

Fig. 4.21: Chief Prof Alex D. W and Lolo Lady. Mary Acholonu. Picture taken after my 70th Birthday, Nov. 30, 2002 .... *94*

Fig. 4.22: Chief Prof Alex, Lolo Lady Mrs. Mary Acholonu and my seven Children. Picture taken after my 70th Birthday, Nov. 30, 2002 94
Fig. 4.23: Anderson Ukachi Akopoazu Acholonu (1st Son) 95
Fig. 4.25: Cynthia Onyemaechi Acholonu-Grant (2nd Daughter) 95
Fig. 4.24: Sandra Akunna Acholonu (1st Daughter) 95
Fig. 4.26: Leslie Onyemauchechukwu Acholonu-Okere (3rd Daughter) 95
Fig. 4.27: Esther Eberegbulam Acholonu-Streete (4th Daughter) 96
Fig. 4.28: Alexandra Kaonyeuyoaso Acholonu-Fashina (5th Daughter) 96
Fig. 4.30: Aaron (left) and Austin (right) (Anderson Acholonu's children) 97
Fig. 4.31: Urenna, Onu, Ugochi, Amaka (Chikodi) (Anderson Acholonu's children) 97
Fig. 4.32: Urenna (left), Ugochi (middle), Onu (right) and Amaka (Anderson Acholonu's children) 98
Fig. 4.33: Kelechi (right), Uchechi (middle), Chidumam (right) (Leslie Okere's Children) 98
Fig. 4.34: High Chief Kennedy Okere MD and Lolo Leslie Okere and their children 99
Fig. 4.35: Osinachi (left) Kelenna (middle), Nkechinyere (right) (Esther Streete's Children) 99
Fig. 4.36: (Esther and Kevin Streete's Children) 100
Fig. 4.37: Esther and Kevin Streete's 100
Fig. 4.38: Zion (left), Elijah (middle) Victoria (right) and below, Isaiah (Alexandra Fashina's Children) 101
Fig. 4.39: Prof. Acholonu in his prime of life, 1988 102
Fig. 4.40: My wife Mary Acholonu on her 50th birthday, April 12, 1999. (Adulthood) 103
Fig. 4.41: Wedding picture of my senior brother, late Architect Casimir and wife Josephine Acholonu. I brought him to the US in 1961 after the death of his wife at child birth in 1958. He died in May 26, 1991 104
Fig. 4.42: My immediate junior sister, Mrs. Philomina Osuji (1st daughter of my dad) and her husband, Mr. Ferdinand Osuji who wedded at Port Harcourt in 1956. She was nicknamed "Ego-ndu

Fig. 4.6: Young Acholonus coming behind me after my departure for the United States for further education. (Standing left to right) Uchenna, Adolphus (Hitler) (late), Paulina, Francis (late), Jane, Anthony (late), and Sylvester. (Squatting left to right) Caroline, Isabella, Chinyere (late) 85

Fig. 4.7: Joy, the first lady who wanted me to marry her 86

Fig. 4.8: My First Fianceé, Alganish, from Ethiopia. I named a parasite after her (Cercaria alganishi; Acholonu 1968) 86

Fig. 4.9: My younger brother, Sir Engineer Uchenna Acholonu next to my Finance, Alganish, from left, who lived with me at the time in Baton Rouge, LA. Next to her is Dr. Nicholas Onyewu (late) with whom I shared the same cabin in the ship while coming to America in Dec. 1954. On my right is the Priest who got Alganish and I formally engaged in 1965 87

Fig. 4.10: Chief Sir Engineer Uchenna C. Acholonu, my immediate junior brother, next to sister Philomina, when he was very young and who lived with me in Baton Rouge, LA. I brought him to America in 1960 87

Fig. 4.11: Wedding Picture Mary and Alex Acholonu 88

Fig. 4.12: Wedding Picture Mary and Alex Acholonu. She joined me in Baton Rouge, LA on Jan 16, 1967. We married on March 27, 1967 89

Fig. 4.13: Wedding Picture Alex Acholonu 89

Fig. 4.14: Wedding Picture – Mary Acholonu 90

Fig. 4.15: Wedding Picture Mary Acholonu 90

Fig. 4.16: Wedding Picture—my wife Mary and my sister, Mrs. Paulina Okpechi as one of the bride's maids 91

Fig. 4.17: Wedding Picture Bride, and groomsmen with Dr. Ben Njoku (left) and my best man, Dr. Moses Nwulia on my right. The others are my Biology Dept. Colleagues 91

Fig. 4.18: Prof. Acholonu 2nd from left. Dr. Benedict Njoku next to him, Dr. Moses Nwulia, my best man on the left 92

Fig. 4.19: 2nd from left, Dr. Melvin Clark, the President of Southern University (SU), Baton Rouge L.A. and on the left of Acholonu, Dr. Lewis White, Chair, Dept of Biology, SU 92

Fig. 4.20: My wife Lolo, Lady Mary E. Acholonu and I in our youthful days shortly after our wedding in 1967 93

Fig. 4.21: Chief Prof Alex D. W and Lolo Lady. Mary Acholonu. Picture taken after my 70th Birthday, Nov. 30, 2002 94

Fig. 4.22:Chief Prof Alex, Lolo Lady Mrs. Mary Acholonu and my seven Children. Picture taken after my 70th Birthday, Nov. 30, 2002 94

Fig. 4.23: Anderson Ukachi Akopoazu Acholonu (1st Son) 95

Fig. 4.25:Cynthia Onyemaechi Acholonu-Grant (2nd Daughter) 95

Fig. 4.24: Sandra Akunna Acholonu (1st Daughter) 95

Fig. 4.26: Leslie Onyemauchechukwu Acholonu-Okere (3rd Daughter) 95

Fig. 4.27: Esther Eberegbulam Acholonu-Streete (4th Daughter) 96

Fig. 4.28: Alexandra Kaonyeuyoaso Acholonu-Fashina (5th Daughter) 96

Fig. 4.30: Aaron (left) and Austin (right) (Anderson Acholonu's children) 97

Fig. 4.31: Urenna, Onu, Ugochi, Amaka (Chikodi) (Anderson Acholonu's children) 97

Fig. 4.32: Urenna (left), Ugochi (middle), Onu (right) andAmaka (Anderson Acholonu's children) 98

Fig. 4.33: Kelechi (right), Uchechi (middle), Chidumam (right) (Leslie Okere's Children) 98

Fig. 4.34: High Chief Kennedy Okere MD and Lolo Leslie Okere and their children 99

Fig. 4.35: Osinachi (left) Kelenna (middle), Nkechinyere (right) (Esther Streete's Children) 99

Fig. 4.36: (Esther and Kevin Streete's Children) 100

Fig. 4.37: Esther and Kevin Streete's 100

Fig. 4.38: Zion (left), Elijah (middle) Victoria (right) and below, Isaiah (Alexandra Fashina's Children) 101

Fig. 4.39: Prof. Acholonu in his prime of life, 1988 102

Fig. 4.40: My wife Mary Acholonu on her 50th birthday, April 12, 1999. (Adulthood) 103

Fig. 4.41: Wedding picture of my senior brother, late Architect Casimir and wife Josephine Acholonu. I brought him to the US in 1961 after the death of his wife at child birth in 1958. He died in May 26, 1991 104

Fig. 4.42: My immediate junior sister, Mrs. Philomina Osuji (1st daughter of my dad) and her husband, Mr. Ferdinand Osuji who wedded at Port Harcourt in 1956. She was nicknamed "Ego-ndu nwaolara iche" (that is, new money that is different) because of her beauty like my mother 105

Fig. 4.43: The wedding picture of my 2nd Sister Paulina and her husband, Prof. Simeon O. Okpechi who wedded in Baton Rouge LA on July 8, 1967. She joined me in Baton Rouge from Nigeria on Dec. 24, 1964 106

Fig. 4.44: Mrs. Paulina Okpechi, my second sister next to bother Uchenna who lived with me at Enugu, Nigeria before my departure to US in 1954 and in Baton Rouge, LA before she married in July 1967. I brought her to the US on Dec. 24, 1964... 106

Fig. 4.45: My Third and youngest sister with her wedded husband, Mr. Adolphus Onyeuche who wedded in New York in August 1986 in my presence 107

Fig. 4.46: My immediate younger brother, Chief Sir Engr. Uchenna Acholonu that I fully sponsored to come to the USA in 1960 and for whom I sacrificed a lot that helped make him what he is today; a brother on whom I demonstrated true love; a brother who on two occasions, publically, called me "the Christopher Columbus of the Acholonu family", and his wife, Lolo Lady Victoria N. Acholonu... 108

Fig. 4.47: Dr. Felix Acholonu, a misinformed brother I love so much, a brother I gave the name he bears, Felix; a brother I chose his field of study, medicine, and helped him to get into the medical school; a brother for whom I obtained Nigerian Federal Government Scholarship while in the medical school, among other things. A computer science person turned medical doctor, a man, with God on my side, I helped to make what he is today, and his wife Ijeoma 109

Fig. 4.48: Dr. Willie W. Acholonu Jr., a brother I love very much, a brother I brought to America in 1974, a brother I nurtured and helped shape his future and has openly and privately shown appreciation for what I did for him, and his wife, Ezioma........110

Fig. 4.49: Engr. Maximian Nnamdi Acholonu, my junior brother, who lived with me in Washington DC. He was the very first Acholonu son I brought to the US after he finished secondary school at Washington Grammar School, Onitsha where I put him. Fig. A (2nd from left) shows how little he was when I put him in secondary school at Onitsha. Fig. B shows him when he came *to the US in September 1959. He is the first son of my father's second wife, Grace, that I brought to the US to demonstrate unity and sincere brotherly love 111*

Fig. 4.50: Late Mr. Adolphus ("Hitler") Acholonu, another junior brother I brought to the US in 1962. He was the first son of my father's 3rd wife, Mezi. He became sick and had to be taken back to Nigeria where he later died... 112

Fig. 4.51: Dr. Kenny Uzoma Acholonu, President and CEO, Bioorganic Co, Lagos, Nigeria, the first son of Uncle Sir Cyril Acholonu. 113

Fig. 4.52: Chief Prof. Alex Acholonu and wife Lolo Mary E. Acholonu with his younger brothers and their wives during his 80th birthday celebration in Vicksburg, MS in Nov. 2012 namely: Felix Acholonu, MD and his wife Ijeoma (left), Wilfred W. Acholonu Jr. Pharm D and wife Ezioma (right).. 114

Chapter Five: Academics and Professional Development

Fig. 5.1: Research with Rev. Sister Mary Joy Haywood from Philadelphia, 1966, a summer program graduate student....... 125

Fig. 5.2: Alex Acholonu with Rev. Sister Mary Joy Haywood at a visit to her in Philadelphia... 126

Fig. 5.3: Alex Acholonu's visit to Rev. Sister Mary Joy Haywood and her fellow Sisters in Philadelphia 126

Fig. 5.4: Left to Right—Lolo Mary Acholonu, Dr. Clinton Bristow (late), 16th President of Alcorn State University (ASU) and Chief Prof. Alex Acholonu. Picture taken after ASU faculty and staff Xmas party, Dec. 2002. Acholonu as Chief and Professor at ASU and later, President of ASU Faculty Senate 127

Fig. 5.5: Professor Acholonu lecturing students at Huaiyin University in China. May 20–June 5, 2005 127

Fig. 5.6: Prof. Acholonu (3rd from right side) in conference with members of the Department of Biology of Huaiyin University in China answering questions from them. May 20–June 5, 2005 128

Fig. 5.7: Prof. Acholonu and some students from Huaiyin University where he taught and conducted research on water pollution in China. May 20–June 5, 2005 128

Fig. 5.8: Professor Acholonu doing research with students on the parasites of Cat Fish at Alcorn State University in October 2016.. 129

Fig. 5.9: Professor Acholonu on Ecology Education Workshop Field Trip as Director of Ecology Education Program Alcorn State University, summer of 2013.. 129

Fig. 5.10: COLONEL T.K. ZUBAIRU, FSS, psc Military Administrator, Imo State The person that appointed Prof Acholonu as the third ProChancellor and Chairman of Counsel, Imo State University 130

Fig. 5.11: Prof. Acholonu in academic graduation regalia as Pro-Chancellor of Imo State University and Chairman of Governing Council 1997-1999 appointed by the Military Administrator, Colonel Tanko K. Zubairu. Picture taken after the graduation exercise of 1998.. 131

Fig. 5.12: The Vice Chancellor Prof. Thomas Ndubuizu and another Prof. helping Prof. Acholonu to put on his Pro-chancellor Academic Regalia.. 132

Fig. 5.13: Acholonu as Pro-Chancellor and Chairman of Governing Council of Imo State University with Governing Council members including 2nd to my right, Eze Emmanule Njemanze of Owerri (late), next to me by the right, Prof. Ndubuizu, Vice Chancellor, 1997.. 133

Fig. 5.14: Found, described and named fourteen new species of parasites (8 from the hawksbill sea turtle) (Eretmochelys imbricata imbricata) and six from several species of snails)... 133

Fig. 5.15: Prof. Alex Acholonu doing what he does best working (doing research)... 134

Chapter Six: My Titles, Affiliation and Laurels

Fig. 6.1: Prof. Alex Acholonu being inducted as a chief for the first time by HRH Eze Nwosu of Amaigbo in Dec. 24, 1992 with the title Ogbuhoruzo 1 of Amaigbo... 155

Fig. 6.2: Picture after my first Chieftaincy Conferment, as Ogbuhoruzo 1 of Amaigbo Dec. 24, 1992.. 155

Fig. 6.3: First Chieftaincy Conferment Certificate as Ogbuhoruzo 1 of Amaigbo Dec. 24, 1992.. 156

Fig. 6.4: My Family after my First Chieftaincy title in Dec. 1992... 157

Fig. 6.5: Photo with my wife Lolo Mary E. Acholonu and my two sons Anderson Akopoazu Acholonu and Alexander Dozie Wozuzu Acholonu Jr. after my Induction as Chief Ogbuhoruzo 1 of Amaigbo in Dec. 1992.. 158

Fig. 6.6: My second Chieftaincy Conferment as Ekwueme 1 of Ihitta Ogada Dec. 24, 2002 159
Fig. 6.7: Second Chieftaincy Conferment Certificate as Ekwueme 1 of Ihitta Ogada Dec. 24, 2002.. 160
Fig. 6.8: Prof. Acholonu in his 2nd Chieftaincy regalia as Ekwueme 1 of Ihitta Ogada with his wife Lolo Mary E. Acholonu on Dec. 24, 2002.. 161
Fig. 6.9: Prof. Alex Acholonu's 3rd Chieftaincy Induction Ceremony as Omereoha, March 31, 2007... 162
Fig. 6.10: Prof. Acholonu and his wife, Mary E. Acholonu. Picture taken after his third chieftaincy title as Omereoha March 31, 2007.. 162
Fig. 6.11: 3rd Chieftaincy Title as Omereoha March 31, 2007 163
Fig. 6.12: Third Chieftaincy Conferment Certificate as Omereoha March 31, 2007 164
Fig. 6.13: Picture of Acholonu showing Chieftaincy red hat; taken after his 70th Birthday in Nov. 30, 2002... 165
Fig. 6.14: Induction as 4th degree Knight of Columbus Prof. Acholonu 3rd from left Feb. 26, 2009.. 166
Fig. 6.15: Prof. Alex Acholonu given a religious recognition. Induction as a fourth degree knight of Columbus in 2009. Picture with the grand knight (left) 166
Fig. 6.16: Induction as 4th Degree Knight of Columbus, Vicksburg Feb. 26, 2009 (Acholonu row 3 no 4 from left) 167
Fig. 6.17: My wife and I with 2 Bishops from the Jackson Catholic Diocese, MS who visited our church, St Joseph Catholic Church, in Port Gibson, MS, 1995... 167
Fig. 6.18: Plaque "Distinguished Legend Award" of Recognition from CKC Alumni Association in America, Aug. 6, 2016 168
Fig. 6.19: Photo after my Induction as a fellow of the Nigerian Academy of Science (FAS) in 1992... 169
Fig. 6.20: Prof. Acholonu inducted as a Fellow of the Nigerian Academy of Science (FAS), 1992.. 170
Fig. 6.21: Picture of Prof. Acholonu, (right) with Rev. Dr. Clement Amadi (uncle of my son-in-law, married to my daughter, Leslie, High Chief Kennedy Okere, MD) and wife who attended my Imo Diaspora Award Ceremony.. 171
Fig. 6.22: Picture of some Imo Diaspora Awardees (left or right) Engr. Marcel Anyanwu, Nze Gibson Chigbu, Chief Ekene Amaefule,

Atty Charles Onyerimba, Chief Ngozi A. Duru, Kingsley A Ogu, Chief Prof. Alex Acholonu 171

Fig. 6.23: (Left to right) Prof. Acholonu, Dr. Austin Orishakwe, Registrar of Gregory University, Uturu and Nze Charles Muruako, Secretary of Imo State Congress of America (ISCA) attendees of Imo Diaspora Award Ceremony Dec. 20, 2016 ... 172

Fig. 6.24: Eng. Uchenna Acholonu, brother of Prof. Acholonu and Dr. Austin Orishakwe, the person standing on the left is my junior brother Engr. Uchenna Acholonu attendees of Imo Diaspora Award Ceremony, Dec. 20, 2016 172

Fig. 6.25: The chairman of the occasion former Pro Chancellor of Imo State University presenting the Diaspora Award to Prof. Alex Acholonu 173

Fig. 6.26: HRH Eze Emmanuel Okoro shaking Prof. Acholonu after the Imo State Diaspora Award 173

Fig. 6.27: Picture of Prof. Acholonu 3rd from left with some key position holders in the PPSN which includes Prof. Chinyere Ukaga extreme right, President of PPSN (Parasitology and Public Health Society of Nigeria Sept. 21-24, 2016) 174

Fig. 6.28: A group picture with some members of PPSN who attended the Abeokuta Annual Meeting 174

Fig. 6.27-28: Recognition to Prof. Acholonu by members of NPPS as Foundation Fellow (FNSP) of the Society and former President (1980-81) 174

Fig. 6.29: MAS Distinguished Contribution to Science Award February 23, 2012 175

Fig. 6.30: MAS Contribution to Health Disparity Research Award February 18-19, 2016 176

Fig. 6.31: Prof. Voletta Williams, Chair, Dept. of Biology, Prof. Acholonu and Prof. Babu Patlolla of ASU 177

Fig. 6.32: Picture taken during the Health Care Disparity ward made to Prof. Acholonu in Feb. 2016 during the Annual Meeting of the Mississippi Academy of Sciences. Left to right are Prof. Babu Patlolla, Dean, School of Arts and Sciences, ASU, Attorney Esther Streete, daughter of Prof. Acholonu, and Prof. Acholonu, the awardee 177

Fig. 6.33: Picture with the Executive Director of MAS, Dr. Ham. Benghuzzi, after receiving a plaque for "Contribution to Health Disparity Research Award" Feb., 2016 178

Fig. 6.34: Group Picture, Zoology and Entomology Division of MAS and some ASU students and faculty with Prof. Acholonu (middle) after his Health Care Disparity Award. Picture includes Prof. Julius Ikenga, Vice Chair of Division (left of Prof. Acholonu) 178

Fig. 6.35: Executive Board Members of the World Federation of Parasitologists (WFP) 2010-2014. Prof. Acholonu (4th from left front line) was one of those elected to serve as a member of this highest governing body of the WFP, which took place in Melbourne, Australia, 2010 179

Fig.6.36: Chief Prof. Acholonu receiving award for "Distinguished Contribution to Science" from the Chair of Awards Committee of Mississippi Academy of Science (MSA), Dr. Kenneth Butler, February 2012.. 179

Fig. 6.37: Cruise in a boat on the Gulf of Mexico on the way to Ship Island to check damages done by the BP oil spill and damage done by Hurricane Katrina. Accompanying Prof. Acholonu are K-12 Teachers. (Summer Ecology Education Workshop Grant Program) Aug. 23, 2011 180

Fig. 6.38: Chief Prof. Alex Acholonu and Lolo Mary Acholonu on his 80th birthday with Hon. Mayor Henry Banks and wife (left). He chaired the occasion... 180

Fig. 6.39: Proclamation: Declaration of Chief "Dr." Alexander D.W. Acholonu Day in Hazlehurst, MS by Hon. Henry Banks, Mayor Hazlehurst, MS on 23rd of November 2002, Prof. Acholonu's 70th Birthday, as a special recognition for his accomplishments.... 181

Fig. 6.40: Acholonu given honorary citizenship to Hazlehurst, Copiah Country, Mississippi on the 23rd of April 2012 Earth Day Celebration at Alcorn State University by Mayor, Hon. Honorable Henry C. Banks Sr. for his achievements 182

Fig. 6.41: Recognition for Prof. Alex Acholonu for conduction of Earth Day Celebration at Alcorn State University for many years ... 183

Fig. 6.42: Mayor Henry Banks giving city key to Hazlehurst City, MS to Prof. Acholonu April 23 2012 184

Fig. 6.43: Mayor Henry Banks giving a proclamation to Alex Acholonu in recognition of his accomplishments April 23 2012.............. 184

Fig. 6.44: Chief Acholonu holding key to Hazlehurst City, given to him by Hon. Mayor, Henry Banks, April 2012 (Symbol of rare honor making him Honorary Citizen of the City) on Earth Day Celebration at Alcorn State University....................................... 185

Fig. 6.45: Picture of Prof. Acholonu with Hon. Darryl Grennell, Former member of the Dept. of Biology, ASU, former President of Adams Country Board of supervisors and now Mayor of Natchez, MS. Benefactor of Prof. Acholonu. He gave Prof. Acholonu a prominent recognition as President of Board of Supervisors when he received his distinguished contribution to science award in Feb. 2012. Picture taken during his retirement ceremony from ASU. Dec. 2016 186

Fig. 6.46: Resolution honoring Prof. Acholonu for his award from MAS for distinguished contribution to Science by Hon. Darryl V. Grennell President, Adams County Board of Supervisors on 16th April 2012 and currently Mayor of Natchez 187

Fig. 6.47: "Alexander DW Acholonu, PH.D., FAS, OON is recognized and honored for contributions made to the education of our nation's youth and is hereby acknowledged for excellence as a distinguished educator in WHO'S WHO among America's Teachers" (see above) 188

Fig. 6.48: Prof. Alex Acholonu with Mr. Agbaso Udeokporo ("Ababanna"), the famous top Awaka vocalist, who in his several records, recognized me for my accomplishments. Among other names, he called me "an international educationist by nature" Picture taken on May 2016 after Medical Mission at Awaka .. 189

Fig. 6.49: Chief Prof. Acholonu special dedication disk (front) by Mr. Tochukwu Oparah 2017 192

Fig. 6.50: Chief Prof Acholonu special dedication disk (back) by Mr. Tochukwu Oparah Special recognition of Chief Prof. Alex Acholonu by a Young and Rising Vocalist, Mr. Tochukwu Oparah from Awaka, 2017 193

Fig. 6.51: Recognition by the Editorial Board of Advances in Science and Technology Journal 194

Fig. 6.52: Prof. Acholonu recognized as one of the 2000 Intellectuals of the 21st century, May 2002 195

Fig. 6.53: Prof. Acholonu recognized as one of Top 100 educators of the year 2005 196

Fig. 6.54: OON (Officer of the Order of Niger) Certificate 10 December, 2003 197

Fig. 6.55: Prof. Acholonu being congratulated by the then President, Chief Olusegun Obasanjo of Nigeria after he was conferred a high award of OON (Officer of the Order of Niger) due to his academic and social accomplishments, 10 December, 2003 ... 198

Chapter Seven: The Igbos and Their Neighbors (My Views)

Fig. 7.1: Chief Sir Prof A D W, Acholonu poses as a triple chief with the following titles Ekwueme, Omereoha and Ogbuhoruzo 215

Fig. 7.2: Prof. Alex Acholonu receives World Igbo Congress (WIC) Chairman's Community Service Award. He was also a member of the WIC Council of Elders and Imo State Council of Elders under former Gov. Ohakim, representing WIC 216

Fig. 7.3: Late Mr. Nathan Ejiogu former Chairman, Civil Service Commission, Eastern Region, Nigeria. He gave me five pounds after my father and I visited him before my travel to US for further studies 217

Fig. 7.4a: Secondary school founded in 1965 by Dr. Benedict Chiaka Njoku of Azaraowala, Emekuku, Owerri North, LGA, my mentor. He deserves a special recognition for this achievement and others 217

Fig. 7.4b: Classroom building of Secondary school founded in 1965 by Dr. Benedict Chiaka Njoku of Azaraowala, Emekuku, Owerri North, LGA, my mentor, former Vice President for Academic Affairs, Rust College, Holly Springs, MS, USA 218

Chapter Eight: Philanthropy

Fig. 8.1: Free Medical Mission at Awaka by WEF in collaboration with Awaka Go Forward, NGO May 2016 225

Fig. 8.2: Medical mission and Willy Esther medical mission slogan D.E.L.T.A (Doing Everything Locally to Stop Aids) 226

Fig. 8.3: Prof. Alex Acholonu with HRH Eze Emmanual Sonde Okoro of Emii (left) and Pascal Nnadi, Chief Justice of Imo State going to cut the ribbon and declare the Medical Mission of May 2016 open 227

Fig. 8.4: Prof. Alex Acholonu with the individuals who officiated during the May 2016 Willy-Esther Foundation Medical Mission 227

Fig. 8.5: Prof. Alex Acholonu with Prof. Chidi Akujor of Federal Univ. of Technology (left), who chaired several of Willy-Esther Foundation Free Medical Missions opening ceremonies including the one of May 2016 and HRH Eze Godwin Merenini (right) of Umudibia, Nekde who attended the 2016 Medical Mission 228

Fig. 8.6: Anthony Omeni Njoku DJ (my bosom friend) and Prof. Alex Acholonu 228

Fig. 8.7: Prof. Alex Acholonu with Mr. Nwakolobi of Ihitta Ogada. At age 91, he was the oldest man that came to the May 2016 Willy-Esther Foundation Medical Mission held at the Ekeamma Elementary School Awaka Building behind Prof. Acholonu and Mr. Nwakolobi 229

Fig. 8.8: Prof. Acholonu (3rd from left) and his brother Dr. Wilfred Acholonu Jr. (4th from left) and student laboratory scientists from IMSU that officiated during the Medical Mission of 2010 230

Fig. 8.9: Prof. Acholonu flanked at both sides by his sons—Anderson Acholonu (right) and Alex Acholonu (JNR) (left) who worked with him during the Medical Mission of 2010. In the background is the Ekeamma Elementary School, venue of the Medical Mission.. 230

Fig. 8.10: Prof. Acholonu showing Laboratory Technology students from Imo State University how to test blood sugar in patients 231

Fig. 8.11: Flyer used for announcing the launching of Willy-Esther Foundation Diagnostic Laboratory, August 21, 2017.............. 231

Fig. 8.12: Picture taken during the launching of Willy-Esther Foundation Medical Diagnostic Laboratory on Aug 21, 2017 for use of Awaka Community—a philanthropic act. Left to right are some dignities that attended, Evangelist Peter Chima, Coordinator Awaka Go Forward, HRH Eze Emmanuel Okoro of Emii, Prof. Alex Acholonu, Chief Innocent Ugwuegbulam, Director Avigram Lab, Sister Mary Joy Emereibe of Awaka and lecturer, Alvan Ikeoku College of Education and Mrs. Theresa Wagbara (nee Acholonu) 232

Fig. 8.13: Prof. Alex Acholonu (middle) poses with His Royal Highness (HRH) Eze Okoro (left) and Chief Innocent Ugwuegbulam (right) who attended Launching of the Diagnostic Lab 232

Fig. 8.14: Left to right Rev. Fr. Cornelius Ajaegbu, Awaka Holy Trinity Catholic Parish who prayed, blessed and launched the laboratory, Prof. Alex Acholonu, Sister Mary Joy Emeribe, Mrs. Theresa Wagbara (nee Acholonu) 233

Fig. 8.15: Left to right Mrs. Theresa Wagbara, Bazil Acholonu, Prof. Alex Acholonu and Ugochi Odunze 233

Fig. 8.16: Group picture of some people who attended the Diagnostic Lab. Launching 234

Fig. 8.17: Prof. Acholonu honored by CKC students and their Principal, Dr. Rev. Fr. Charles Okwumuo on one of his visits to the school, his Alma Mater, as a philanthropic donor to CKC 234

Fig. 8.18: Rev. Fr. Valentine Acholonu, the 1st priest of Awaka whom I sponsored his training as a priest. Ordained in July 16, 1994 235

Fig. 8.19: Dr. John Nnadi, young when he came to America. I helped make his coming to the US possible, put him in Howard University, Washington DC and had him live with me for some time before he left to live on his own.. 236

Fig. 8.20a: The newest hostel built at Christ the King College, Onitsha, Anambra, Nigeria. Named after or in honor of Prof. Alex Acholonu for his philanthropic contributions to the College, along with HRH Eze and Prof. Edozien, Cardinal Arinze and Archbishop Valerian Okeke... 237

Fig. 8.20b: Prof. Alex Acholonu and the CKC Principal, Rev. Dr. Fr. Charles Okwumuo (left) with some students. Picture taken during a visit to CKC in 2016.. 237

Fig. 8.21: Prof. Acholonu after courtesy visit to Prof. C. Onwuliri (late), while he was Vice Chancellor, FUTO to which he donated books worth about 10 million naira... 238

Fig. 8.22: Motherless Babies Home in Mount Camel Catholic Church, Emekuku, Owerri North LGA to which donations of babies clothes and money were made on about 3 occasions................ 239

Fig.8.23: Prof. Acholonu visited and made donation of money and babies cloths to the Motherless Babies' home in Uratta, Owerri, 2010... 239

LIST OF RELEVANT CONGRATULATORY MESSAGES AND TRIBUTES

1. Dr. Kenny Acholonu 284
2. HRH Eze Emmanuel Sonde Okoro 285
3. Chief Prof. Augustine O. Esogbue 286
4. Mississippi Academy of Science (MAS) Award, for Distinguished Contribution to Science 288
5. Prof. C.O.E Onwuliri 289
6. Dr. Marinelle Payton 290
7. Prof. Chidi Akujor 291
8. Mr. Nick Udumaga 292
9. Dr. Felix Acholonu and Family 294
10. Dr. Wilfred W. Acholonu, Jr. and Family 295
11. Lolo Mrs. Engr. Leslie Acholonu Okere 296
12. High Chief Kennedy MD and Lolo Engr. Leslie Okere ... 299
13. Atty Esther Eberegbulam Acholonu Streete 300
14. Ms. Kimberly Maxwell 301
15. Mrs. Venessia King 302
16. Ms. Kieurra Sims 303
17. Ms. Sharkiesha Jackson 304
18. Dr. Bettaiya Rajanna, Department of Biological Sciences, ASU 305
19. Dr. Voletta Williams, Chair, Biology Department, ASU .. 306
20. Dr. Babu P. Patlolla, Dean, Arts and Sciences, ASU 307
21. Napoleon Moses, Vice President for Academic Affairs, ASU 309
22. Dr. Samuel L. White Executive Vice President/Provost ... 310
23. Dr. Donzell Lee, Provost and Vice President for Academic Affairs, ASU 313
24. M. Christopher Brown II, 18th President of ASU 315
25. Dr. Alfred Rankins, Jr. 19th President of ASU 317, 318

FOREWORD

It is always good for a person especially a well accomplished person to put in black and white his life experiences for others, for generations to come, to read, learn from it and emulate him or use it as a springboard to launch their own. It is also good to make what he knows and learnt available to others. As Confucius said, "Has God given you knowledge? Give it to others for your own improvement; give it to others for their own betterment".

The autobiography "My Journey through Life" has a befitting title. It truly covers the life of the author from childhood to becoming an octogenarian (80 + years). He appears to have drunk deep the cup of life. It shows that he has gone through life's experiences of various kinds—the good, the bad, and the ugly. He painted a good picture of his life that clearly brings out the ups and downs of life. He showed that he has the requisite experience; the tenacity and technical know how to write the book. He also showed that he is an academician *per excellence,* a seasoned educationist.

He covered much on education; the area where he spent a great part of his professional life. He taught from the time he got his PhD in 1964 to the present time, 2017—a total of 53 yearsmore than half a century! Among other things, he brought out his firsts and key dates in his life as well as his family tree. The book covers 11 varied chapters and spiced up with his views about the Igbos, his race. It has a historical flavor that covers, not only things about himself but also about his town, his place of birth. He nicely sums up his accomplishments under chapter 6 where he dwells on his titles, laurels and professional affiliations.

The author deserves a pat on the back for this lofty accomplishment; for doing what nobody has yet done in his family and town, Awaka. Biographies have been written about some personalities one of which is his late uncle's, (Cyril M Acholonu) (Fig. 2.2), biography. Professor Acholonu's Autobiography is an original first work, a masterpiece that may serve as a reference work for future generations of not just the Acholonu family but others outside his nucleus family. It is well written and deserves emulation. I congratulate the author for a job well done. It is a milestone. It is written for posterity.

He appropriately said that his philosophy of life is, "Take time to work; it is the price of success." He is hard working in the true sense of the words. Another is that "the road to success is always under construction." As we go through life we make necessary adjustments and set new goals. This work is another feather to his cap. This autobiography is recommended for those who plan to write theirs in the future, to scholars of history and to Awaka people and Igbos at large and to mankind as a whole.

Prof. Bart Nnaji, *PHD, FAS, CON*
Former Minister of Mines and Power
Abuja, Nigeria and Robotic Engineer

PREFACE

Autobiography deals or should deal with what a person has done and recorded by himself and not others. The person writes it as he sees it and from his own point of view. As a contrast, a biography deals with the life of a person as seen and recorded by a person or persons other than the person involved. Such being the case, since I am the master of my life and know it better than anyone else, I thought it better to record what I did and know rather than someone doing it for me. After this, I have no objection to someone subsequently writing my biography. This will be a good reference book to use in doing so.

The autobiography was important for, among other things, historical recording of things that happened to me in life and those directly and indirectly related to me. To my knowledge no one in the Acholonu family has written his autobiography before. I however recall that the biography of late Uncle Cyril titled, "The Bridge across Time" was written by Mr. V. C. Nwulu (2004) at the request of his first son, Dr. Kenny U. Acholonu supported by his siblings. Apart from my decision to write my autobiography, some relations have urged me to write something about the Acholonu family before I die, or directly and indirectly made reference to its need. It has taken some years since the decision to write this autobiography was made. But due to circumstances beyond my control, I could not get started. Because of peculiar things that happened in my life while I was growing up, I have always harbored the desire to record what happened to me in the past that made me what I am today. I remember the saying "Those who forget history are doomed to relive it". I have recorded what have happened in my life as factually as possible. What I wrote may be offensive to some. It is always said that the truth is bitter. If some are offensive, they were not meant to be so. If some see any part as a mistake, it is a mistake of the head and not of the heart. I have great regard for everyone. I traveled far and wide; engaged in scientific research, in quest of knowledge and to impart knowledge.

As an academician, I delved into some of these. One in particular is my travel to China as a Visiting Scholar under the Academic Scholar Program to China conducted by the National Association of African American Studies (NAAAS). I was fortunate to be one of those selected to go. I taught at the Huaiyin University located northeast of Shanghai from May 20 to June 5, 2005. My work took me to 51 countries. These are listed in the Appendix.

After what I have gone through in life and what I have learned, I will not forgive myself and my children, and the world will not forgive me, if the knowledge I acquired and the invaluable experiences I got die in me and with me leaving others who have concern for me and about me to guess what I have done and have not done. I want, as one of the earliest in the Acholonu family to acquire his /her education, to leave first foot prints on the sands of time; to make it difficult for my people to forget me and to help generations to come to use it as a springboard to get ahead, to achieve more and possibly more than myself.

There is an expression that says, "Show the way and people will follow" I have read several autobiographies and got fascinated by them and motivated to do same with the belief that what one man can do, another also can. I have browsed through the autobiographies of some famous men like President Bill Clinton, Billy Graham, Edward Kennedy, etc. I remember the words of George Bernard Shaw, "Some people see things as they are and say why? I dream things that never were and say why not." Why not? Why can't I also do what others have done? So I drew my motivation and inspiration from the work of some prominent people.

This book is written in simple form to facilitate comprehension and made picturesque as a belief in the Chinese proverb that says "a picture is worth more than a thousand words". The chapters are chronological as much as possible and logically sequenced. The chapter on the Igbos (Chapter 7) is thrown in as a challenge and to give a base line concept of the Igbo as I see it. It is expected to generate objective reactions and actions that may culminate in what most agree as what is typical about the Igbos; what we can do to better ourselves and work together to improve ourselves and pass this onto generations to come. My family pedigree is included for students of history, for those who believe in "aha m efula" which literally means, let my name not be lost or forgotten, for my children and interested others to know my roots.

To my knowledge, no Awaka man has ventured to put down in black and white the history of Awaka as a town. I have got it started in Chapter 1 and expect others to fill in the blanks and add omissions, if any. I have emulated President Fidel Castro of Cuba and Ignacio Ramonet in the book, "My Life" by concisely recording key dates in my life and my firsts, (appendix) for posterity.

As stated above and as contained in the title, the book logically follows the history of my life, the good, the bad, and the ugly experiences of my life from birth to present. It is written in such a way that people may learn from it, avoid the mistakes I made, emulate the good things I did and pass them on to others. Unlike President Bill Clinton's "My Life", that has numbered chapters only, the chapters in this autobiography have headings that will help readers to know in advance what they are all about and decide to read or skip anyone. Examples were cited where feasible and available. The appendix contains information that are relevant but not so necessary as to constitute a chapter.

I expect this book to become an eye-opener to the Acholonu family, the Awaka people, the Imo people, and Nigeria as a whole. It is expected to be a resource book, a reference book, and an archival book for posterity.

This book is written for the students of history and for those who plan to someday write their autobiography. Because of its historical content, it belongs to the library or desk of every Awaka man, our married daughters and their children as well as academicians, government officials and all and sundry who love reading autobiographies and widening their scope of knowledge. I have recorded what may be new information for many.

Dr. Alex Duarte (1995), author of "Health Alternatives" said: "New information is often controversial. All truth has to pass through three stages of development. First, it is denied, second, it is bitterly opposed, and third, it is accepted as self-evident."

Chief Sir. Prof. Alexander Dozie Wozuzu Acholonu,
PHD, FNSP, FRAES, FAS, OON
Professor of Biology
Alcorn State University
Lorman, MS, U.S.A.

ACKNOWLEDGEMENTS

This book, My Journey through life, is a result of hard work, support, and inputs from diverse people; a collaborative teamwork. It became a reality after several years of nursing the idea of engaging in it. I am glad that it has become a reality. I am most thankful to God for giving me the spunk, the courage, the inspiration, and patience to start and consummate it. My special thanks to Prof. Bart Nnaji, FAS, CON former Minister of Mines and Power of Nigeria who found time to go through the major parts of this work and prepare a foreword for it. I am indebted to the great and cherished editor and advisor whose input in making this work a reality is unparalleled or rather immeasurable, Prof. Chimdi Maduagwu, Professor of English, Lagos University, Lagos, Nigeria. I am grateful to those who reviewed the book or parts of it and put in some technical and information technology embellishments especially, my son-in-law, High Chief Kennedy K. Okere MD and Lolo Engr. Leslie Onyemauchechukwu Okere (my daughter). I found their comments and suggestions extremely helpful. Attorney Ms. Esther Eberegbulam Streete (another daughter), constructed the genealogy (family tree) and for this I am immensely grateful. I am very pleased with the editorial members of the Lagos University Press for the fine job they did and the patience they exercised during its production. I acknowledge the clerical and technical assistances given by my students, Shanterial Moore and Sharkiesha Jackson during the course of preparing this autobiography. They demonstrated interest and exercised admirable patience. I am grateful to Dr. Kadiri A. Babalola, a botanical taxonomist, at the University of Lagos for helping me identify our famous Obu Omumu to species and also Prof. Caroline Umabese, Head of Department of Botany and Dr. Gbenga Adeonipekun of the department for their assistance. I am most grateful to my wife, Lolo Lady Mary Ekeoma Acholonu and our children, Anderson Akopoazu Acholonu, Ms Sandra Akunna

Acholonu, Mrs. Cynthia Onyemaechi Acholonu Grant, Lolo Engr. Mrs Leslie Onyemauchechukwu Okere (nee Acholonu), Attorney Ms. Esther Eberegbulam Streete (nee Acholonu), Mrs. Alexandra Kaonyeuyoaso Fashina (nee Acholonu) and, Alexander Dozie Wozuzu Acholonu Jr., for their moral support and various inputs in making this compendium a reality.

I am very grateful to Dr. Babu Patlolla the Dean of Arts and Sciences and Dr. Donzell Lee, the Provost and Executive Vice President of my University, Alcon State University who took time out of their busy schedule to submit glorifying and inspiring tributes to me. They are a gem to me!

I will be remise if I do not give credit to some others to whom credit is due. While this is my autobiography, I purposely digressed to devote some time to the history of Awaka, my town, since, to my knowledge, no Awaka man, has recorded it in written form before. It has been by oral tradition that is, passed on from one generation to another. I am grateful to several Awaka elders and youths that I consulted to record the much that is contained in this book. Those include Mr. Anthony Ofurum, Mr. Edward Enwere, Mr. Robinson Chukwu, Mr. Vincent Acholonu, Mr. Alphonsus Onybiri, Dr. Theresa Ukpo (nee Cyril Acholonu), Dr. Charles Obichere, and Mr. Leo Egbujor, the son of late Mr. Gabriel Egbujor (popularly known as Gab) from Amuzi, Awaka, a prominent meat seller in my early years.

Chief Sir. Prof. Alex Dozie Wozuzu Acholonu,
PHD, FNSP, FRAES, FAS, OON

Chapter One

Background—Awaka My Home

I was born and bred at the Ancient Town of AWAKA, in Owerri North Local Government Area (LGA), Owerri Senatorial Zone, Imo State (Igbo Heartland), South-Eastern Nigeria. The ancient town of Awaka is part of what is called Alaenyi—the land of elephants. There is a dual interpretation of the name Alaenyi. While the first is as noted, the land of elephants, the other is "the land of friendship". The two approaches are welcomed by the people whose history has been collected and collated from different oral sources by some scholars, even though, I believe that there are a lot more to do by those in the Humanities. The Alaenyi is made up of five clans (towns), namely Ihitta-Ogada, Awaka, Egbu, Naze, and Owerri. These communities are believed to have descended from one tree and as such are siblings. The people accept the order of progeny as follows: Ihitta-Ogada is the first son, Awaka is second, Egbu is the third, Naze is the fourth, and the fifth is Owerre—*Owerre nchi ise* (anglicized as Owerri). Awaka is thus the second most senior. There are three villages, "nchi ato," in Awaka. These are: Ndegbelu, Umuodu and Amuzi. Awaka is flanked by bigger communities of Egbu, Uratta, Emekuku and a relatively smaller town, Ihitta-Ogada. Awaka shares a lot in common with IhittaOgada. For a long time, their market was one, the deity, Ala-Ukwu Awaka is said to be located at Ama Ibeanana, practically in IhittaOgada. Their ceremonies were the same. One may want to believe that since Awaka and Ihitta-Ogada are the smallest of the Alaenyi people, with Egbu, Naze and Owerri endowed with five villages, "nchieise," each, they realized a need to pull together in order to be able to stand before their relatives. They somehow reached an accord to support each other. The inquisitive mind of researchers in oral tradition venture into intricacies of deeper relationships amongst Alaenyi people in general. There may be suggestions that point to the fact that Awaka and Ihitta-Ogada might have been from the same mother while Egbu and Naze were from another mother and the descendants of Owerri are cousins to Egbu. Their father, Ekwem Oha, was persecuted out of Uratta by his wealthier younger brother, Ndum Oha after a major family squabble. Ekwem was welcome to a neutral land by his sister who was, at the time, married to a prominent community leader from Egbu and this introduces a minor complexity in the relationship analysis amongst Alaenyi people. They have all largely remained friends; however, with the large heart of the elephant.

Each community in the larger Alaenyi clan has some peculiarities or what for want of better expression, I may want to term as brand. They have lived, guided by their peculiarities, for a long time. Among other such brand identifications, Awaka people were warriors and still exude war—likeness today. Oral tradition has it that at some point in antiquity, Uratta wanted to annex Ihitta, the closest friend and relation of Awaka. Awaka people fought for Ihitta people, as relations and comrades, to prevent the land from being annexed. In those intertribal war days, when the war cry or slogan "Ekpudo" was sounded and the reply, "mma mma nu" came, it meant fight to a finish; no going back. To symbolize and memorialize this, Awaka Club one members, of which I am one, greet each other with "Ekpudo"; "mma mma nu" with the right palm striking each other. When a meeting is in session and a person comes in, he will raise his hand with the palm open and say "Ekpudo". The rest shall reply with "mma mma nu" (See Fig. 1.1).

There is evidence that some Awaka people had also migrated and settled in other parts of Igbo land, such as in Mbaise where there is Awaka Mbutu, in the now Aboh Mbaise Local Government Area (LGA) and Amuzi, Mbaise. The very clear case is the nearby tale of Umuodu Owerri. Umuodu is one of the five villages in Owerri and also a village in Awaka. It is believed that the two villages are related and as evidence, the two villages did not intermarry for a long time; perhaps until there was a conviction of enough gap to permit marriage. There are insinuations or belief that the present Umuodu Owerri used to be part of Umuodu Awaka. Oral tradition has it that some Awaka people got tired of intertribal wars and engaging in them, the bellicose nature of Awaka people and decided to emigrate from Awaka. I recall that when I was young (about 8 years old) the Awaka Mbutu people came from Mbaise and entertained us with nwalija dance during a Christmas time. After that, our Awaka elders requested them to come back to Awaka. But they said that they would like to stay where they were and still are. The emigrations of some Awaka indigenes may have contributed to Awaka being a comparatively small town.

Awaka people were and are still relatively skillful farmers. They distinguished themselves quiet early in farming and for a long time, have been associated with the production of high quality corn. In days of yore, the palatable corn, which came from the soil of Awaka people was a special species known as "Otulaukwu Awaka." This literally translates as "fat bottomed Awaka corn." It was so called because of the sumptuous corn and bigger lower end of its cob, which naturally permits more grains than could be found in regular species of corn. Otula ukwu species was lavishly endowed with both size and sweetness. Awaka farmers begin sowing of corn quite early, so while other communities would be getting ready to clear the bush and sow their crops, Awaka people already would display their product along the road for prospective buyers. All around Owerri, people would trek, ride and drive down to Awaka to buy Awaka corn. This situation is still going on in Awaka. In fact, it is as if corns were sold all year round in Awaka, and that defeats the seasonal nature of the corn production in Igboland and Nigeria. Awaka people celebrate corn annually. It is however lamentable that the Otula Ukwu Awaka corn is gone and gone forever. It has become extinct!! Apart from the corn, Awaka people cultivate yams, like all other Igbo communities, but sometimes it is not easy to say whether yam is indeed the king of the crops in Awaka because of the emotional relationship between the people and the corn. Neighboring communities tease Awaka people with some folk songs like:

Ufere fema, oka   that is,   When the wind threatens the corn
Awaka ekwema ude   Awaka begins to grumble or tremble

But since after the Nigeria-Biafra war, yam is hardly grown.

I want to indicate that apart from their strong attachment to corn, the people also do extremely well in all other crops. They produce a good vegetable with which they make Ofe-Owerre, their favorite or staple dish—"Ugu". They also produce melon, okra, cocoyam, cassava, just to mention a few. Their interest and prowess in farming was early translated into modern educational attainment and profession in some early accomplished Awaka indigenes who distinguished themselves in practices in agriculture. I recall Mr. John Eme, who used to be the Chief Agricultural Officer for the defunct East Central State (former Imo, Abia, Anambra, Enugu and Ebonyi States). He was a role model for many younger Awaka persons, who used various lower positions in the Ministry of Agriculture and departments under it to enhance the cultivation of corn in Awaka. Today, Awaka's strength in the cultivation, production and consumption of corn still remains an enigma. Even when Awaka women marry into other communities, they still go over there to exude strength in the cultivation of corn. The people attribute their success in other spheres of life, especially in education, to the dexterous efforts in cultivation of corn as implied in this song:

Ogbe achicha ise na oka abuo   that is,   Five loaves of bread and two cobs of corn
ka nde Awaka jiri zuo nde lawyer.   enabled Awaka to train lawyers.

Wherever they are found, Awaka people are tagged corn-eaters and producers. They do not only produce corn, they equally are voracious consumers of corn. Literally, they teach other communities how to cultivate and consume corn. Every Awaka women learns, inadvertently, how to make a variety of dishes from corn. They roast, fry, boil, cook, and make it into porridge, and breakfast food drink, akamu, mkporoshi, usu oka, agidi, moi-moi oka and chim-chim. At special events and on special family and group occasions, visitors and distant family members are treated to creative and innovative culinary arts of corn by Awaka women. Older women, who usually made the porridge, claim to do so with "bare hands," and that means that they do not add any other ingredients, apart from perhaps, salt and pepper to it. Corn porridge in Awaka is not overloaded with present day cooking enhancements, yet it comes out extraordinarily delicious.

Growing up in Awaka was very interesting. My personal experiences remain as fresh as the morning dew because of their memorable nature. As children, we learned a lot from our mothers, fathers and other elders who spent quality time teaching and playing with us. Most of the local learning processes were informal. We learned, at the feet of wise men and women, the creative ones, the funny ones, and the strict disciplinarians. Communalism was the prevailing ideology and practice. Things were more or less done collectively. In the Acholonu family, we lived as one closely knit unit. With the death of Acholonu Nwokoro in 1936, when I was 4 years old, Uncle Alfred Ugwuegbula Acholonu (Fig. 1.2), the first son, became the head of the Acholonu family. Acholonu, my grandfather, had three wives. The first, Nwanyiocha, had six boys; the second, Egbonu, had two boys and three girls; the third, Adamma, had two boys and two girls making a total of fifteen children of ten boys and five girls. My father was the fourth son and from the first wife, Nwanyiocha—my grandmother. We lived together as a unit and in peace. We lived in harmony and did things concerning the Acholonu family as a unit without caring about which mother begot which. We, the children of the direct Acholonu siblings, worked and did things together. As a matter of fact, during the farming season, one day of the week was devoted to working in the farm of our most senior uncle, Alfred Acholonu. Everybody in the whole family had to work for him and he would feed everyone that day. We were bonded together and still are, but not with the same sincerity and closeness as when Uncle Alfred Acholonu was in charge! We, the children, worked together, played together, cleaned our compound and environment every market day (Ekeamma Day) together up to where the big tree, "Obu Omumu", (see Fig. 1.3–1.6) is located and all the way to Ekeamma market and from the front of my father's shop to the road (Owerri–Umuahia Road). We as kids or teenagers, also played lawn tennis there in front of the shop. This shop (Zinc house) was destroyed during the Nigeria-Biafra war of 1967. Some unfair-minded Holy Trinity Catholic Station Council members claimed or rather usurped the area for the church and blocked the front of Willy Wozuzu Acholonu Memorial Mansion (Fig.1.9a&b) a big house, which my father requested that I build for him (in his memory and honor) in place of the shop, before he died. He said to me, "Blessed Alexander, if you like, build the house up to the road. I own the land. My present house is a shack". I carried out his wish. It was the biggest commercial building at Awaka when it was erected in 1978. My late aunt, Mrs. Ugboaku Edomobi, called us (the Acholonu's) "Umu otuji bara ji" (that is, children of one single son (Acholonu) that bore many children; or literarily, one yam that produced many seedlings). Today we are over 400. Those in the USA alone are about 180. The Acholonu family comes from the part of Awaka called Ndegbelu. Ndegbelu is made up of two smaller divisions or villages called Umukwe and Lobo-na-Omioche. I come from the latter. With the suggestion of late Uncle Sir Cyril Manuba Acholonu (Fig. 2.2), when he became the oldest man in our village, the two were combined into LOBOCHE. The Obu to which I referred above, was planted by our elders 91 years ago. The people selected to put it in the soil or plant it after some traditional ceremony, were my uncle, Benjamin Njoku Acholonu (my father's immediate older brother) and a married woman considered to be the best in character and behavior in the village (nwanye obi omma). The woman selected was called Ndomerikwe from Augustine Ekenkwo family, the wife of Etoh. The Obu area was cleaned every market day (Ekeamma day) by all the young boys in the village as stated before. This tree is still flourishing after Uncle Ben died at age 96, 29 years ago (1988). It was planted about 1926 by our elders after they relocated from a place now called "uhu". This is a deciduous tree located on Willy Wozuzu Acholonu street (I newly named it in honor of my father) that sheds its leaves during the dry season starting from about November each year and they come back in full bloom, during the rainy season, starting about March. During this season; it comes back in its full majesty. It is a shady tree. The Loboche village people hold their meetings under it, year in, year out, play under it and hold social gatherings, under it. It has proved to be very useful to the village. It is so shady that it was called "uyo ama" (a house outside). This tree is believed to be of economic value. If a twig is cut, a whitish sticky fluid flows out. This fluid is believed to be used in making rubber or gum. Its Yoruba vernacular name is "Obadan". It impacted my life as we engaged in a lot of childhood plays and other activities under it. Envy, jealousy and mistrust of nowadays, were minimal as successes and failures came under shared responsibilities. Wisdom was impacted through folklores especially, legends, rituals, and myths. We got to know the root of the most unfortunate experience of Awaka people, which we all had to live with. I guess that was a myth, which is generally believed by the child-like minds of the people, because it explained the obvious reality of a big lack in the community. The big gap is lack of a **community river or water.** That, for a long time was the only regrettable dark spot in the proud and ancient town of Awaka. Neighboring communities like Egbu and Emekuku had their community rivers, but Awaka did not have. A particular myth explained that it was an unfortunate narrow miss for Awaka. There is a river called Otamiri, whose source is the present Egbu town (Isiuzo village to be specific), near Awaka. According to the folklore of the people, when this river wanted an abode so that it could bless mankind, Awaka community was approached first, but the approach was a riddle. The river demanded a sacrifice of male and female human beings. Our people could not imagine killing human beings in order to have the luxury of being a source town of a river. They hesitated and the river moved on to Egbu. It was there that the people went to a diviner or fortune teller to seek an answer to the riddle. Egbu people were properly advised on the matter. The interpretation turned out not to be real human beings but metaphor of the need of the river deity. In place of the real human beings, Egbu people were advised by fortune-tellers to produce an ant and "eruru" (larval beetle). On the production of the requirements, the river settled at Egbu and from there, it charted its course ahead, towards Owerri, Nekede, Ihiagwa and other towns. However, it is the same river that nurtured us in Awaka as children, but the difference is that we trekked a long distance to fetch water from the river. We were fascinated by this myth as children, but ever regretting why the river did not settle in our town. Albeit from another angle, we were proud of our ancestors who had very strong principles and would not, for any reason, spill human blood. However, our people did not lose out completely. We could go into the bush and see the trace or the path through which Otamiri passed Awaka. The valley created by its passage is still there and visible to all to date. That is a form of confirmation to the myth of the origin of Otamiri River. Quite a few farmlands benefited from the passage of Otamiri River. Those farmlands, to date, remain very fertile and yield products that are far better than those from other farmlands. This land area is called "Nwa otula ogwugwu".

Many Awaka indigenes are proud of their town. We are regarded as a small community by our neighbors. They call us "akpiri mba." (Small Town). But as small as we are, we are recognized as a wholesome community, a *bona fide Town* ("mba"), and this means a lot to us. It suggests that what bigger communities with 5, 8, 12, or 15 villages can do, we also are capable of doing, if not better; hence, we call ourselves "akpiri mba ejeme ire" (a small but powerful Town). The only minus within our ancient and traditional community is the absence of a stream or river as a direct source of water supply. For this reason, we had to practically rely on Egbu for water supply from Otamiri River. This is the world of children. It never occurred to us, both the Awaka and Egbu children that the running river is a geological occurrence or a gift from God to mankind or a natural occurrence. We just believed that it belonged to or was given to Egbu people. From the scientific or ecological point of view, rivers are known to naturally change their source or course. This usually occurs when the source is disturbed because of a change in its watershed or water basin. It then opens up or surfaces from another lower level or location area. I witnessed this situation when I went to Izimir, Turkey in 1994 to attend the International Congress of Parasitology. We were taken on a sightseeing tour. We visited a place that showed the replica of a harbor. We were informed that the river for which the harbor was constructed shifted its position. It was then miles away from the harbor thereby rendering the harbor unusable. It must be stated that what happened to Awaka, a higher area or terrain than Egbu, may in a distant future (generations to come) happen to Egbu if the ecosystem or watershed is not protected or is disturbed enough through vegetation change—deforestation, flooding, erosion, runoffs, siltation, pollution, excavation, building constructions etc.

Water is a primary necessity for life. It is the driver of life. I call it the *summum bonum* of life (the greatest good). Some traditionalists believe it is the source of life. So, because we share the same source with Egbu people, both of us grew to become best of friends and acquaintances. We intermarried more than any other two communities, at a point in our history. We also quarreled more than any other two communities then. Some children, who went to fetch water, would return with broken calabash and other containers because they probably got into a fight with some Egbu children and the worst that often happened was that Egbu children would break our water calabash and sometimes, deliberately inflict injuries on us.

These issues also defined the relationship between Egbu and some other neighbors. For instance, Naze, another relation of Awaka people was not as favored as Egbu and like Awaka, also depended on Otamiri Egbu for water. So also were some villages of Uratta. One village that stood out in this aspect was Umuoba. A remarkable thing is that the river, inadvertently, became a uniting force for most of the communities that live around it. We got to know one another, individually and as groups. We grew up to become friends; some intermarried and that cooperation made a lot of positive changes within and among us. For reasons such as the ones I have tried to highlight here, we still regard ourselves as one big community. In spite of all our childish ranting and rancor, I believe our bond became stronger as we grew older and at maturity. We understood that nature has a way of creating relationships and building bridges. We are grateful to God for opportunities to unite especially as *Alaenyi group of people*.

Table 1 shows the traditional ruling groups of Awaka Community and their then heads. I belong to kindred 4, Umuacholonu out of 22 Kindreds in Awaka. I was 52 when my constitution drafting committee functioned under His Royal Highness Eze Christopher David Osuagwu. He appointed me chairman of the Committee. At that time, the Acholonu family belonged to the No 5, Umuekenkwo. It appears that 3 more were created when Mr. Sylvester N Egbulaonu became the chairman of Oha Awake with Umuacholonu created, perhaps, by virtue of the fact that they are numerically one of the largest families in Awake, if not the largest. See appendix for part of the constitution as prepared by the then drafting committee which I chaired.

Christianity in Awaka

Awaka is a Christian town with well-established Anglican Church and Catholic Church. See Awaka, the Hub of Catholic Missionaries (Catholic Missionary Stations: Onitsha to Nebuku to Awaka to Ulakwo to Awaka to Emekuku, 1912, for history).

I thank God that I grew up from a Christian family. I feel proud that my late senior uncle, Mr. Alfred U. Acholonu (Fig. 1.2) is one of those given credit for bringing Christianity to Awaka. I want to give some credit to the first effort made to record the history of Christianity at Awaka sponsored by the then Parish Priest, Rev.

Fr. Anukanti (2009-2016). It was a worthwhile effort or venture. I humbly observe that a review of the compendium revealed some errors that need to be corrected and omissions that need to be included, especially with respect to my input in the growth and progress of the church or parish, Holy Trinity Catholic Parish, Awaka (Fig. 1.8a, b &c) One of the outstanding errors is that Rev. Fr. Daniel Walsh "was at Emekuku from 1913 to 1923". I was born in November, 1932 and my younger sister, Mrs. Philomina Osuji and I were baptized by Rev. Fr. Walsh in 1934 as shown in my baptismal certificate (called "big book" in those days) and signed by him. This date needs to be corrected. I am one of those that cut the grass or bush for the first church zinc building before the first mud house was demolished. I participated in the maiden meeting where the discussion for converting the Awaka church substation of Emekuku parish to a full parish was held. I was one of the most vocal members who encouraged the establishment of the parish. There were some concerns as to whether we were financially strong to handle the burden it would cause especially as Ihitta Ogada and Egbu were not interested in joining Awaka to from the parish. I strongly said that we could and encouraged it. I was the first to buy a uniform for all the choir. I was the first to buy musical instruments for the choir (piano) from the time of its inception as a parish, I have continuously made handsome donations to the church. I have been donating N100, 000 every Christmas apart from other donations I make. There are very few who have individually made more donations to the church than myself. I was in the meeting that appointed Godwin Etoh Achodo and some other persons to go to Ikot Ekpeni, Cross River State to go and look at the church there so that we could build our church like the one there that somebody saw. I paid for pews. There was a time that people were told to make donations of one kind or another and that their names would be enshrined on a plaque to be left in the church as a memento. I donated. This plaque was never made as promised by the then church council. I donate clothes to the church poor and needy and distribute calendars and pens to the church congregation every Christmas for many years and still doing it. During the time of Fr. Anselem when the church was running Ekemma Elementary School, (Fig. 8.5) I shipped in books from the USA to start a school library for the students or kids to read. Up till now I donate pens to the kids practically every Christmas. I have renovated the school building several times especially when I have to conduct a medical mission there. I am surprised that no one thought of including my name in the published church history. I am sure that there may be some more whose names were left out that made recognizable inputs in support of the Parish. They need recognition. Books have new editions after every several years (3-5 years). A new edition of the history of the Holy Trinity Catholic Parish of Awaka is long overdue and is hereby strongly recommended.

Security in Awaka

I must say something about security in Awaka community. I am pleased that we have a vigilante group at Awaka. While some of my colleagues living in the USA are afraid to visit their country of birth and go to their respective towns and villages, I visit Nigeria and my town, Awaka, fairly frequently. Several of my colleagues are worried about insecurity in their various towns and villages caused by armed robbery, kidnapping, stealing, family hostilities etc. But I go because, among other things, I have confidence in Awaka vigilante (See Fig. 1.7). They not only do their job well keeping peace and tranquility in Awaka, they give me special coverage any time they know that I am in town! I am proud of them and cherish the good work they are doing in Awaka autonomous community. I do give and will continue to give support to them both morally, technically and financially.

I want to take this opportunity to compliment former Governor Achike Udenwa who, I am told, initiated this group. I extend my compliments to former Governor, Ikedi Ohakem, who continued it throughout his tenure of office and the present Governor, Rochas Okorocha who recognized the group and gave them the impetus to continue the valuable security work they are doing and reducing crime level to a minimum, at least in my town, Awaka. I encourage the Governor to continue to support this good work the vigilante is doing at Awaka and perhaps several other autonomous communities and see that they are paid regularly and as and when due.

Fig. 1.1: Awaka Club One members and some wives, left to right sitting: Herbert Emezi (late), Alex D.W Acholonu, Gibson Nkwo, Henry Opara (late), Simeon Enwere (late), Manace Os`uagwu (Maco) Standing, (Men): John J. Amadi, John Njoku (Ose John), Victor Nwakuna (late), Alphonsus N. Onyebiri

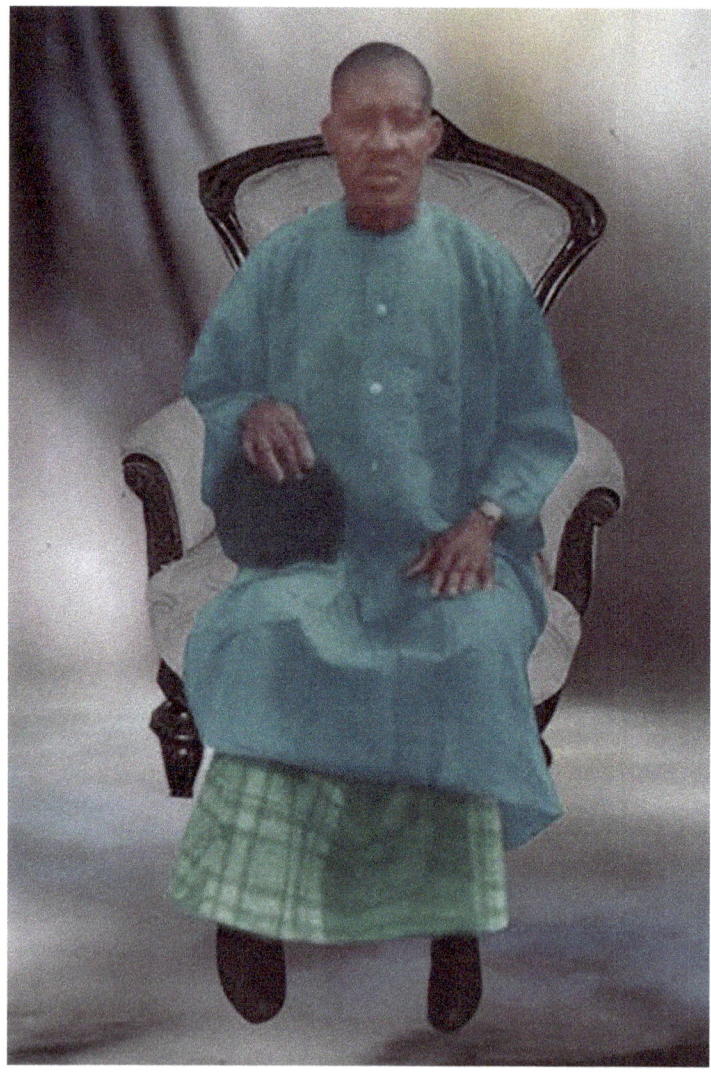

Fig. 1.2: Mr. Alfred U. Acholonu. My most senior uncle a tailor who made clothes for all the priests in the old Emekuku Parish; one of those Awaka people who brought Christianity to Awaka; the man used as banker by many Awaka people because of his impeccable or transparent honesty; the grandfather of Rev. Father Valentine Acholonu, the first Awaka Priest. He died in 1961

Background—Awaka My Home

Fig. 1.3: Obu Omumu (*Ficus vogelii*, Miq.) (Yoruba Name Obadan) in its majesty. It is 91 years old. Picture taken Aug. 2016

Fig. 1.4: Acholonu backing Obu Omumu (*Ficus vogelii*, Miq.) (Yoruba Name: Obadan) in his village, Ndegbelu (91 years old tree)

Fig. 1.5: A dry leave of Obu Omumu (*Ficus vogelii*, Miq.) (Yoruba Name Obadan) in Awaka, a. back of the leaf b. front of the leaf collected directly from the tree (91 years old), on Nov. 21, 2017

Fig. 1.6: A dry leaf of Obu Omumu (*Ficus vogelii*, Miq.) (Yoruba Name Obadan). This shows a bigger sized leaf; collected directly from the tree (91 years old), on Nov. 21, 2017

Fig. 1.7: Awaka Community Vigilante that ensures the peace and security of Awaka, Owerri North LGA people. From the left and standing: Chigbechemba Osuagwu, Florence Ngozi Nnadi, Smart Onwana, Anthony Mbachu, Ikechukwu Nnaemeka, Emmanuel Udeokporo (Coordinator), Donatus Obi, Kelechi Mbata. Squatting on the ground and from left, Christian Nwachukwu, Amaka Ugwuegbulam, Ukachi Ukwuoma

Fig. 1.8a: Holy Trinity Catholic Parish Church, Awaka in its present form and location

Fig. 1.8b: Holy Trinity Catholic Parish Church, Awaka in its present form and location with identification signboard and church (mass) schedules

Fig. 1.8c: Holy Trinity Catholic Church Awaka in its present form and location showing a big crucifix

Background—Awaka My Home

Fig. 1.9a: Willy Wozuzu Acholonu Memorial Mansion, a 3 story building, built in 1978 in honor of my father and in fulfillment of his request before he died in August, 1976. Below, the Parish Church wall blocking it from the front. It was the biggest commercial house in Awaka at the time

Fig. 1.9b: Willy Wozuzu Acholonu Memorial Mansion a 3 story building built in honor of my father and in fulfillment of his request before he died in August, 1976 that I build a big house here in his honor

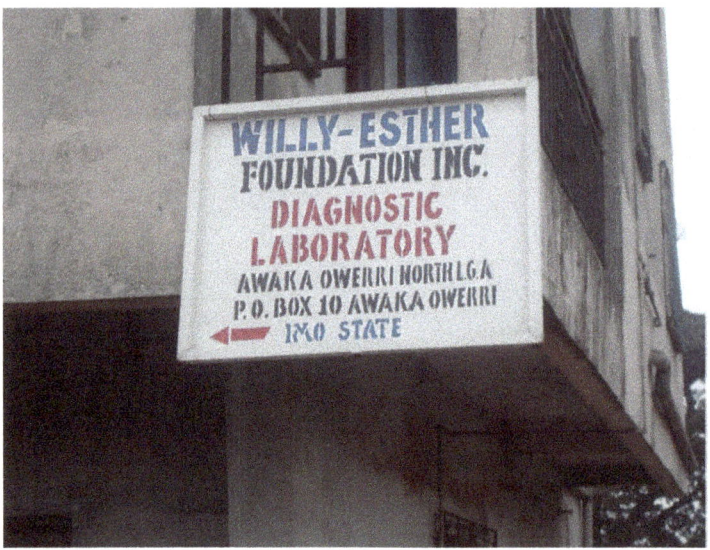

Fig. 1.10: Willy-Esther Foundation Diagnostic Laboratory located on the ground floor of Willy Wozuzu Acholonu Memorial Mansion officially launched on Aug. 21 2017

ANCIENT TOWN OF AWAKA (AUTONOMOUS COMMUNITY)
(OWERRI NORTH LOCAL GOVERNMENT AREA)
KINDRED AND UNIT HEADS OF AWAKA*
(OHA-NA-OKORO-OHA AND OBILOBI)

KINDRED NO. AND NAME	NAME OF KINDRED'S OHA	WHETHER OHA IS ORDAINED	NAME OF KINDRED'S OKORO
	NDEGBELU	**(i) UMUKWE**	
1. Umuoparaku	Sylvester Egbulonu	Ordained	Godwin Egbulonu
2. Umuigbokwe	Kamalu Njoku	Ordained	Bob Onwana
3. Umuchiedo	Brendan Ofurum	Ordained	Donald Ofurum
		(i) LOBO-NA-OMIOCHE	
4. Umuacholonu	Ben Acholonu	Ordained	Dom Acholonu
5. Umuekenkwo	Dennis Ibe	Not Ordained	-
6. Umuekeugo	Seb. Opara	Ordained	Richard Opara
7. Umuokoroada	Joe Udeokporo	Not Ordained	Celestine Emezi
8. Umuekenwuzo	Christian Chukwu	Not Ordained	Sam Chukwu
9. Umunwiche	Simeon Enwere	Not Ordained	Edward Enwere
	B. UMODU	**(i) OGBAKUO-NA-OKORO**	
10. Umuokoro	Fred Nwaneri	Ordained	D. Emeana
11. Umuekegbe	Peter Ugordu	Ordained	Dom. Obichare
12. Umunwagbara Ndukwe	Job Eme	Ordained	John Akahara
		(i) UMUAGWU OGII	
13. Umuodungbafor	Nelson Enwere	Not Ordained	Cyril Ejiogu
14. Umulalenwa	Paul Achonwa	Ordained	Michael Mbata
15. Umuonuekwe	Tom Ukwuaze	Not Ordained	Jeo Ogazi
	C. AMUZI	**(i) UMUEBO-OKEM**	
16. Umuovurunwa	Dan Mbachu	Ordained	Gab. Egbwujor
17. Umuokorolo-boNa-Okoriu-Ukwu	Godson Ikeri	Not Ordained	Alphonsua Onyeneke
18. Umuiwuala	Francis Eke	Not Ordained	John Ezekie
19. Umuofoakuru	Benson Ejiogu	Ordained	Augustine Ejiogu
20. Umuokwonwada	Peter Obichere	Ordained	James Opara
		(i) UMUAGWU OGII	
21. Umuamadi-okorie	Alex Ukwuoma	Not Ordained	Sylvanus Ihenacho
22. Ezhianwuna	Fred Chukwu	Not Ordained	Anoruo

S.N. Egbulonu,
Chairman, Oha Awaka.

*Provided by Mr. Alphonsus Onyebiri

Chapter Two

Early Days of My Life

When I was young, my father (Fig. 2.1, 4.2 & 4.5) was a Court Clerk. The clerks were called "Akilak ode mkpishi," which literally translates as "the writer or officer that writes with pen". It is important to explain this. In those early days of contact with western civilization and literacy, writing was an extraordinary act. Those who could read and write, especially "write," were the closest people to the great white men. Here, in my father's case, the "Ode-mkpishi" is distinguished from other writers because while others, who taught in the elementary schools wrote with chalk on slates (a kind of little chalk-board) or chalkboards, the likes of my father (few indeed) wrote with pen and ink. So "Ode-mkpishi" was even special among writers. For instance, even the teacher was seen by the public as a writer with chalk on the board (that does not mean that the teacher could not write with pen, but I am referring to public opinion here). So my father's distinct position in the society was not in doubt. By virtue of his position as a court clerk, my father was transferred from one place to another in response to the demands of his duty. The court (local) was the highest authority in adjudication of cases, conflict management and resolution as well as dispensation of justice. The court was brought down to the level of the people as much as possible because of the introduction of the Indirect Rule by the British colonial government. The District Officer (DO) was in charge of the courts, which supposedly operated at a district level, but appointment of privies was important, at the town or village levels, for a more effective management of cases.

My father kept records for the local unit of the big colonial set up and by virtue of his profession as a recorder; he captured a number of events and developments. Perhaps, I should state with pride that his profession positively affected both his immediate family and the larger community where he came from. He was one of the very few early symbols of literacy. Being his son and protégé, I consider myself privileged because I had access to him and the documents, or should I say, records that he kept. This is why I can talk, with great confidence, about my birth and other issues, which very many people in my generation would, at best guess at, because they would rely on oral tradition. I am not claiming that I was aware of my birth and especially the birthday, but since records do not tell lies, I know from my father's records that I was born, the second child of my parents in the ancient town of Awaka, in the present day Owerri North, Local Government Area (LGA) on November 30, 1932.

I was born in a local hospital and again, because of the grace of God upon my family, I would say that not too many of my contemporaries had that privilege. I suppose my father already was aware of the risks in childbirth and since he was handy enough to minimize that, he decided that his wife, my mother would have her babies in a proper hospital and not at home like many others. What I cannot state categorically now, is the quality of the hospital. However, being a colonial unit (health), it should have been decent and appropriate. The next point on this, is that my father lived above many of his contemporaries and so would not let my mother and his other wives deliver their babies at home, as the case was at that time. I want to believe that my father was quite conscious of both his status and social roles within the society at his time and as a result of that, he devised special ways of dealing with issues. He needed to set the pace, to show that he had experienced enlightenment and thus, through him, others could aspire towards enlightenment. This is a special attitude of trail blazers. Individuals are capable of raising the standard of communities and societies by injecting into them the positive values they have acquired elsewhere. Right from this early stage, I learnt from him that one needs to share knowledge and new values with one's kith and kin. No doubt, it was part of my inspiration in life to also aspire towards distinction so that I can present myself as an object of emulation to others around me.

Somehow my father knew this and he displayed exceedingly great joy at my birth. Now, this time, I was told and I could see the evidence. To commemorate my birth, my father engaged in an elaborate "Omugwo" (birth celebration). He procured and killed a big cow, the type that was uncommon in my place. There was the local cow, ehi or efi, but the type used during my birth celebration, Omugwo was extraordinary. That took the celebration to the third level of sophistication. Normally, the Omugwo was done with meat that was not classified. In some special cases, a goat was slaughtered when a first son is born and when a first daughter is born and in some rare occasions, a cow, ehi, was killed but in my own case, a foreign cow, which we call 'nnama' (llama), was used. As a proof, the skull of the nnama was persevered and hung in the outhouse, "Obi Umu Acholonu," for posterity. What that explains is that my father additionally wrote my birthday on the skull of the beast as a mark of greatness and for remembrance. I saw the skull and the writing while I was growing up and so did some of my contemporaries. Let me clarify some issues. I know today, Omugwo has become a very popular term in Nigeria. Our colleagues in the Humanities have done a lot of academic research into it, especially those in Performing Arts, Oral Literature and Cultural Arts. They have analyzed and interpreted it from various angles but I know one popular angle (an opinion held by many people at the prosaic level about it) that it is a celebration or a visit by the (older) mother of one (a young mother) who has delivered a baby and the old mother has just came to enjoy the benefit of grandmother-hood. This opinion is in response to the very many celebrated visits of mothers to their daughters abroad, who deliver babies. Though this notion has more or less made Omugwo a national engagement, yet it does not represent the true and complete essence of Omugwo. The truth is that Omugwo is a period of three months after birth, when a woman (who delivered a baby) remains indoors to recuperate. She is barred from every manner of work or labor and is rather taken care of by her mother or those that are close, and around her. During Omugwo, the woman cannot sleep with her husband. She is more or less sacred.

At the end of the season, there is an elaborate celebration. The celebration is observed only by those who can afford to do so. It is not mandatory and there are levels of celebration. One does so according to one's means. It is the celebration that releases the woman to rejoin the socio-economic activities of her community. This is apparently unique among Owerre (Owerri) people in Igboland.

I started school early. This was unlike many other children of my generation. My father was educated and had realized the value of education before I was born, so he took it upon himself to make sure that I and my siblings benefitted from formal education. My early experience in school was exciting but somehow tedious. I had no choice and could not make decisions on issues concerning me and my life, as it is the case with all children. So I had to go from one school to another, from one town to another. I guess it is easy to know why it was so. My father was more or less an itinerant colonial civil servant, and his family had to follow him all along where ever he was sent by government. However, it got to a stage when my father felt that we, his children, were losing time because each time we went to a new station and we had to go to another school, we were sent back to a lower grade, instead of going to a higher grade. It thus appeared as if we were moving backward rather than forward. For instance, I did elementary two in Obudi-Agwa, then my father was transferred to Mbutu-Okohia in Ngor Okpala LGA and when the entire family moved I joined him. I was either going to remain in the last class I was or go back. I was made to remain in the last class. Then after a careful consideration of the situation, my father eventually sent me to Our Lady's School, Emekuku, where my schooling became consistent and I was no longer tossed to and fro, or from class to class and school to school.

Emekuku is a town that is about two miles away from my native ancient town of Awaka. It was and still is a very active town in terms of educational and religious activities. It was an early seat of both religious activities and moral instruction especially for the Catholic Christians. Many people from the town and its neighbors benefitted from the activities of the Catholic missionaries, especially their schools and hospitals. During our childhood days, Emekuku had a relatively big elementary school and later a teacher training college and then a Girls Secondary School. These were to be complemented by another school, Sebastian Academy, a popular High School founded by Dr. John Njoku from Ezeogba, Emekuku and also a Community Secondary School near the main market called Nkwo Emeke founded by Dr. Benedict Njoku who was my standard six (elementary six) teacher and from AzaraOwala, Emekuku. (See Figs. 2.3, 2.10, 4.17, 4.18)

When we registered for school, the system of education was different from what obtains today. I guess that the colonial government had not come up with a single straight forward colonial policy on education. Schools were mainly operated by Missionaries like the Roman Catholic Mission, The Church Missionary Society (Anglican), The Baptist, Methodist etc. although government still had few schools called government schools, for example, Owerri Government School, Umuahia Government School. The mission schools had a tedious system. They had what was called standard one, standard two, and three and so on till it got to standard six. Before this stage however, there was a kind of pre-primary experience, which comprised two stages, namely, Infant one (A-B-C class), and infant two. After that, one is promoted to *sub-one* and it is only after a successful completion of sub-one that one would proceed to standard one. So the primary educational experience was made up of about four sub-sections namely: the Infant stage, Sub stage, Junior Primary, and Senior Primary stages. This system made us stay longer in school than what we have today.

We came to Our Lady's School, Emekuku in the 1940's and met this rather complicated system. When I say we, I mean my elder brother, late Arch. Casmir C.W. Acholonu, and I. I was placed in

Infant Two, which means that I had just begun. I suppose it was a wise decision by my father to let us settle in a place rather than move about like those who experienced nomadic education. So, afterwards, we remained, more or less, more settled at Emekuku. It was so until I got to standard four. My father had two special names by which he occasionally called me: "Blessed Alexander" and Nkwachukwu (that is, God's promise). I was commonly called Alex and Dozie for Dozienze, a name that my grandfather gave me. Dad gave me the reason why he called me Nkwachukwu. He said that while my mother was pregnant of me, he had a vision. He was on a motor cycle and many children cycled around him. He interpreted it as God promising him many children. At some point, after my standard 3 class, my father called me over and said to me: "Blessed Alexander" I want you to go and stay with your Uncle Cyril (Fig. 2.2) so that he may serve as your mentor and help you with your studies. "I want you to go overseas and further your education. Even if it would mean my selling my house at Portharcourt (now capital of Rivers State) to send you overseas, I will do so." He made that promise to me in order to encourage what he apparently saw in me as my academic aptitude and smartness.

I did my Standard Four at St. Joseph's School Ulakwo, Obube where my late uncle, Cyril was the Headmaster and my father wanted him to be my mentor and nurture me. But that school ended at Standard 5, so I did only standard four at Ulakwo, Obube. After I passed standard four, I came back to Emekuku and did standards 5 and 6. While at Emekuku I came across a man, to whom much credit for what I am today can be given.

He was my Standard 6 school teacher named Dr. Benedict C. Njoku (See Fig. 2.3, 2.10, 4.17, 4.18). He taught us much and I learnt a lot from him. I will be forever grateful to him. He was from Emekuku and his wife's name is Josephine presently Dr. Josephine Njoku, a very benevolent loving and accommodating lady. I completed this part of my life experience in 1947. Schooling at *Our Lady's School,* Emekuku presented a unique experience for me although it seemed ordinary. I was going to realize later in life how much that rather long and seemingly twisted encounter was going to affect my life, albeit, positively. It was at this stage of my life that basic Christian and moral principles permeated my personality. Simple elements of catholic catechisms took their roots in me and they would be determining factors of a number of decisions and actions that I would take in later life. At age seven I started attending confessions and receiving communion. I was very religious to the extent that I wanted to become a priest but for my father's objection. At *Our Lady's School,* I engaged in several extra-curricular activities: I was a runner, a chorister, (under Dr. Ben Njoku), a band player, a tennis player, a football (soccer) player, and a dancer.

For many people of my generation, obtaining the standard-six-certificate was a tall order. Once this was achieved, their lives were set and they would enter the world to seek employment. They lived well though; however there was still room for improvement. Others would opt for teaching, teach a little while and then seek admission into the Teacher Training Schools, either became grade three or grade two teachers or go for high elementary teachers training. They were also highly respected, but I was not going to do any of these. I was interested in going to a secondary school so I belonged to the third group that would go to the secondary school and get government civil service work or possibly proceed abroad for Higher Education. So as I was concluding my primary education, I registered for the entrance examination into some prominent secondary schools at the time. I believe that all the secondary schools were highly respected and they were indeed few. However, there were some which were more popular than others or preferred to others by both parents and students. Based, perhaps, on such preferences, I took entrance examinations to St. Patrick's College, Calabar; Government College, Umuahia, and Christ the King College (CKC), Onitsha. So I passed the entrance examinations into St. Patrick's College Calabar and Christ the King College Onitsha and had to make a choice. I chose to go to Christ the King College because my elder brother, late Arch. Casimir Acholonu (Fig. 4.5, 4.41) was there already, and going there I would not be so terribly homesick in college. I was disqualified at the entrance examination into Government College Umuahia because of my height.

CKC (Christ the King College)—a college popularly called *"Primus inter pares"* (i.e. First among equals) (Fig. 2.11-13, 8.14 and 8.17a & b)

> *Harvard of the plains, the Eton on the Niger where academics, sports, and culture comingled....*
>
> *Obaze, 2016*

This statement from Obaze (2016), says it all. I proudly say that CKC, Onitsha is my renowned ***alma mater.*** My experience there started in January 1948 and I was there from 1948-1952 (Class 2 to Class 6). When I completed my normal five years, I sat for, and passed the Cambridge School certificate Examination in grade two. CKC, as Christ the King College is fondly called, left a very strong impression on my formative years. I would say that I am glad I am a former student of that great institution of the Catholic Church. Started in February 1933 by Archbishop Heerey, an Irish clergy, CKC remains one of the best secondary schools in the country and recently ranked 5th best in Africa. The school is very well known in academics, ethics, athletics and other extra and co-curricular activities. It paraded a combination of the high and popular cultures. For instance, in all its seriousness in academics, religious and moral activities, it also excelled in athletics, especially football (soccer). There, I engaged in all it offered.

Living on campus at CKC was not too rough or in any way strange to me, as it was for many young boys who got into secondary school. I was sixteen at the time I entered the school. Although I was relatively young and should naturally feel homesick, that did not happen because my elder brother, Casmir, (Fig. 4.5, 4.39) was already a student at CKC. As if that was not enough, another young fellow that was well known to me, in fact a town's boy (Awaka), Benjamin Chukwueke, was already there also. They were my seniors and thus provided some form of protection for me and made me feel at home there. I also got two friends that made me feel more at home in Onitsha. They were in my class, Mr. Joseph Nwaneri from Obinze, Imo State and Mr. Felix Nze (late) from Naze, Imo State, one year my junior (Fig. 2.8). The motto of CKC was and still remains: *Bonitas* (Goodness), *Disciplina* (Discipline), *Scientia* (Knowledge). The school existed in line with the letters of the motto. We had what was known as "punishment on the spot" for unacceptable behaviors of junior students by the senior ones. Indiscipline, as that was called, included anything that was contrary to the laid down rules and regulations of the school. Acts of indiscipline attracted immediate commensurate punishments. The punishment included manual labor, like cutting grass and washing senior students' clothes on Saturdays and being denied a free day. These tasks were carried out with manual tools, especially the cutlass. Other punishments included flogging, being forced to kneel on the ground for a prolonged period (long enough to feel pain), sometimes with hands raised up, etc. A prefect or senior could punish a junior student as stated above.

I was enthusiastic in academics, endeavored to be good and morally upright. I attended, studied and abided by the canons of the Catholic Church, making sure that I lived by the letters of the catechisms. In addition to all these, I also participated in all kinds of sports. I was the best tennis player for boarders and second best for all students. I was one of the best ballroom dancers and was nicknamed "Sanderson stormy weather." Weekends were usually days for sports and other recreational activities. We all looked forward to them.

CKC is an all-boys secondary school with boarding and day students, located in the heart of Onitsha, a vibrant commercial city in the then Eastern Region of Nigeria, under the colonial rule then. CKC afforded many of us who were privileged to be there various opportunities. Apart from the unique formal instructions in the academic subjects by well trained and qualified tutors, which I cannot stop making reference to, we also had the opportunity to get involved in several co-curricular and extra-curricular activities and I also will never be tired of recalling them. I got exposed to a few life challenging experiences. I recall that in the sporting arena, I was a sportsman, in a sense, a rounded sportsman. But I was excited to learn how to play Tennis and it became my favorite sport. Prior to coming to CKC, I had the privilege of playing tennis in a court set up in front of my father's commercial house (shop). This gave me an advantage over many other students who were going to be playing tennis for the first time. I eventually became the best Tennis player among the boarders in school. We played rounds known as "winner's stand." I became so good in the game that when I entered the Court to play "Winner's Stand," nobody would defeat me. Thus, I was hardly moved from the court. This was because I would beat both my mates and my seniors and thus stayed as long as I wished and only left voluntarily. Sometimes, some overzealous seniors especially the Prefects would request me to leave the court, according to them, to make room for others to play. Sometimes I would voluntarily leave to allow others to play. But most times, we all obeyed the rule of "winner's stand." I represented the College against other great schools like, St. Charles and Dennis Memorial Grammar School (DMGS).

I also played football and hockey, though not as well as tennis. By the second year of my study, I had a dislocation in the hip so I quit playing football and running, and concentrated on hockey and other field events. I was good enough to be in the College Hockey team and we represented the college in all the tournaments it got involved with during our time especially playing against St. Patrick's College, Calabar. During inter-house sports festivals, my house St. Michael's House usually topped the chart of events. A boy called Ezeoke and I were the best recognized in our house. He was the captain while I was the vice-captain.

I was a great dancer and it was through dancing that I got a fun name (or nickname) "Sanderson Stormy Weather." on which I referred above. My contemporaries, in school, gave me that name and I was highly identified with it. I was also a remarkable chorister. I was equally fascinated by photography. Then, as a hobby, I used to take pictures. Pictures were taken, and then developed into what was known as "negative" and later taken into "the darkroom" in our College for further processing before it came out, in black and white. This was commonly known as "washing the picture." My interest in this was great and as the Vice-Captain, I took a picture with my House Master, Mr. Paul Ukaigwe, the House captain, Mr. Ezeoke as referred to above. (See Fig. 2.4)

By far the most important and treasured responsibility I held in school was being the College Librarian. Usually, the design of our secondary school career was such that we were expected to be assigned specific responsibilities when we got to Class Six which was a senior level class, a final year class. It was at this point that I was appointed the College Librarian. I consider that a very special responsibility.

Being the school librarian helped me very much. One important thing it did to me was to introduce me to secluded times of reading. I found that handy when I was preparing for the Cambridge school certificate examination. Then, I would open the library and lock myself there and read for long periods of time unseen. It helped me so much. Since the books were there for me and the willingness to read, also there, I became literally, a bookworm. I was not threatened. Let me say that the competition was quite stiff. When I entered the College, the main business of all around and within the college was to read, so it was all a question of being studious. We were one hundred and twenty admitted as freshman students (Class 2). One was not sure that one would stay in school every year until class six. So only fifty eight of us completed the program; that is, getting up to class six. When one reached the last level (Class 6), and the College felt one would not pass, because the college was competing with King's College, Lagos, Government

College, Umuahia, Queen's College, Lagos, DMGS, Onitsha, St. Patrick's College, Calabar and other great schools, the College would not present the one and others like him as its candidates for the Cambridge School Certificate Examination. Rather, they were made to take the examination as private candidates because since they would not do well, they would negatively affect the image of CKC. The school would not want any disgraceful result to be associated with it. There was a qualifying examination before the main examination, which was designed to weed off likely weak candidates. You will agree with me that it was tough from beginning to finish.

Everything at CKC was structured. We woke up 5 a.m. every morning with a prayer. This was compulsory for everybody. It was after the prayer that we would go and have our bath and after that, we would go to Mass, in the full Catholic tradition. Next to this activity was breakfast; usually at 7 to 7:30am. Following breakfast, we started classes at 8 a.m. The first set of classes would end at about 1:00pm, in time for lunch. Lunch was a time of refreshing. We had opportunity to chat and laugh and ease off the tight daily routine. After lunch, we went for the afternoon rest called siesta, usually for one hour. Though that did not appear to be enough, but we cherished it all the same. Sometimes, we would not feel like having a rest, but we were forced to lie down and take a nap. Following the afternoon nap we would go to study till 4pm and then for evening sports or recreation. After sports, everyone would hit the shower or lavatories for a bath before dinner. Dinner was typically served at about 6:00pm, following which we went for night studies. Night studies lasted from 7:00pm until 9:00pm. We said our night rosary in various dormitories and then went to bed. The next day would begin with a repeat of what had happened the previous day.

The school uniform was White (shirt and shorts). The blazer was a coat with white and blue strips. Sometimes we wore blue ties (seniors only) with the insignia of CKC and trousers. This was the case for all the students from class 5 to class 6. After classes, we were permitted to wear whatever we had and wanted to wear, unlike in other schools where they had prescribed day dress or compound uniform. We were not allowed to leave the school compound at will; however, we had one Saturday in each month that was called Free Day. On those days, students could leave the school in the morning and come back in the evening, not later than 6p.m.

Graduation was very well celebrated. There was a form of events' organization which was known as "Passing-Out", done on a day also known as "Passing-Out Day". On Passing-Out days for the senior students, there was usually a home football game and graduating students would be invited into the football field during the halftime period to greet the school's players and encourage them. CKC was a power house in football (soccer) in the nation at that time. There was a very fierce rivalry in football contests between CKC and Dennis Memorial Grammar School (DMGS) at the time. During most Passing-out events, the senior students could wear anything they wanted to wear. As stated before, I was called "Sanderson Stormy Weather". That was the nickname by which everyone knew me, especially as an athlete and a dancer. On the day that my set "Passed out" we, the finalists went to cheer the football (soccer) players during the half time of the last home game. I wore a velveteen traditional outfit that generated a lot of yelling and acclamation once I entered the field. The air was saturated with loud yells of my nickname: "Sanderson Stormy Weather" as the students greeted me. I was the only one in that kind of attire (Fig. 2.5). Apart from this, I was one of the best dressed students in my set (Fig. 2.6-2.7, 2.9). There were 120 students who were admitted into the first year when we came in but only 58 students made it to graduation as stated earlier. The school was highly competitive. No one was ever quite sure of making it to graduation; so one left nothing to chance. Hard work was inevitable all the way, and it even became more demanding when one approached the examination year and ready to take the

Cambridge School Certificate Examination. The mere thought of a tedious pre examination screening to determine those to write as school's candidates and those to write as private candidates was enough to destabilize anyone. I really worked hard, and so did all the 58 who made it to graduation.

I was among the first set of students to start the Post-Secondary School at CKC, which became more organized later and was known as Higher School Certificate study. We started the course in 1953. It happened that our teachers were Mr. Columbus Obihara (late) from Ulako, Obube, Imo State and Mr. Godfrey Njoku (late) from Umuoba, Uratta, Imo State. Mr. Njoku was the senior teacher. Both of them got scholarships to go to England for further studies. When they left, we did not have enough teachers to continue anymore, so the program was dissolved. After that, I went to Port Harcourt and took what was called the Civil Service Examination. When one finished secondary school in those days, one could take the civil service examination. It was more or less like a qualifying examination which served as a gate way into the civil service work. Candidates who passed this examination were automatically offered employment by government. On employment, government posted the candidate to a government ministry or department. I passed the examination and I was given the option of working for the Ministry of Health or the Treasury. I took the Treasury Ministry and was posted to Enugu, the headquarters or head office. I chose the Treasury Ministry because my elementary class mate and friend, Mr. Anthony Manuba (late) from Azara-Owa Emekeukwu (Fig. 2.9), was already working for the Ministry and was at Enugu. Another person there was my CKC class mate and friend, Anthony Iguh, now a retired Justice. I worked there until I got the opportunity to further my studies in America. I worked there from 1953 to 1954 and eventually left for further studies in the USA in Dec., 1954 after I failed to leave in September 1954 (1st semester) because of insufficiency of funds to travel.

Early Days of My Life

Fig. 2.1: My dad, Court Clerk and Councilor, Wilfred Wozuzu Acholonu in his greener or youthful days, a man to whom I owe a lot! Died in August, 1976

My Journey Through Life

Fig. 2.2: Uncle Cyril Manuba Acholonu (Late). Lived to be 103 Years. Died in 2012

Fig. 2.3: Dr. Ben Njoku (Late), my mentor, my standard six teacher, my benefactor; a distinguished Professor of English and former Vice President of Academic Affairs, Rust College, Holly Springs, Mississippi, USA. Died May 17, 1995

Early Days of My Life

Fig. 2.4: Prof. Acholonu (right) as a sports man at CKC wearing his college blazer. He, another student (Ezeoke) and their house master (Mr. Ukigwe) are holding 3 trophies which they won during intra college sports. They were in St. Michael's House. He was the best tennis player in his set among the boarders

My Journey Through Life

Fig. 2.5: Clothes that I wore during the final year football (soccer) play when we, the graduating seniors, went to cheer the players (CKC team) in 1952

Fig. 2.6: Picture taken as a finalist in Christ the King College, Onitsha, 1952

My Journey Through Life

Fig. 2.7: Alex Acholonu in CKC posing—but not really a smoker

Fig. 2.8: Sitting: Alex Acholonu and Joseph Nwaneri, final year in CKC, and 2 from Owerri in class 5 (following us), 1952. Standing, left to right, Felix Nze and T. Njoku

Fig. 2.9: Acholonu with secondary school friends, 1950. Left to right, Anthony Njoku, Dominic Nwaturuocha, Anthony Manuba, Victor Anyaso and Alex Acholonu

My Journey Through Life

Fig. 2.10: Left to Right: My teacher, mentor, benefactor, Dr. Ben Njoku and me, Alex Acholonu

Fig. 2.11: Picture taken in front of the gate of Christ the King College in 2016. Left to right is Rev. Father Dr. Charles Okwumuo, Principal of CKC, Prof. Acholonu and Some Executive Members of CKC Alumni Association (Old Boys)

Early Days of My Life

Fig. 2.12: Picture taken near the Statue of Archbishop Heery in 2016 who established CKC in 1933

Fig. 2.13: Picture of CKC classroom building in the 40s and 50s while I was there as a student

Chapter Three

Going to America and My American Experience

Before I went to America, I was told that it was a land flowing with milk and honey. This did not mean much to me because I took it literally as a mere statement. But what I looked forward to was the great land of opportunity that America has always been synonymous with. I was eager to explore and experience this situation. It was, as we were told, a place one could work and earn some money while studying in the university. That means that one could pay one's fees and take care of other expenses without depending on home remittances. It was mainly because of this expectation of work and study that I decided against an earlier admission into a Law School in England. England is good and prestigious. It was highly acclaimed by the entire country, Nigeria. But I knew what would happen if I were to go to England. My people at home would have to be sending money to me while in school there and I knew my father and my people would not be able to send me money while undergoing training in England because it was even difficult for them to raise the money I needed for fare to go to America and to study in the first year.

My mind was never at ease working in Enugu. I longed to travel abroad to further my education. Luck came my way one day when I ran into one Professor Hansbury in Lagos. Prof. Hansbury had come to Nigeria from Howard University in Washington, DC. With his help I applied to Howard University and was admitted to study there. I was to start in September of 1954 but I did not quite have the money to proceed.

At that point in time, anybody wanting to go overseas to study had to go through the Government Education Committee. Intending travelers were mandated to make a deposit of Five Hundred Pounds before they were allowed to travel. This would serve as an evidence of serious intention and thus enable the committee to allow the person to travel so that if the person traveled, he would not be a public charge to the country and could be repatriated if need be. I was asked to do so. Unfortunately, my people were able to raise only three hundred Nigerian pounds (£300.00). In addition to this requirement, travelers also were to take full charge of their travel fare. Then, the fare (going by ship), was seventy-five pounds. It was next to impossible to meet up these requirements. I, no doubt, was having a hard time getting the required amount. I was told that if I could get a high up government official or a known rich person to sign an affidavit of support for me, the remaining two hundred pounds could be waived. I wrote Dr. Nnamdi Azikiwe (Zik) (Fig. 3.9) to help me but he courteously declined to help me. I next requested Hon. Raymond Amanze Njoku, the then Minister of Commerce and Industry to do this for me. He was my father's friend and attorney. When he was going to England to study law in the 40s, one of my father's two vehicles was used to see him off. Also his mother, Nne Ada Ejeka, came from my town and village Ndegbelu, Awaka. After some cajoling and fervent begging and bogging, he eventually agreed to it and he did! But for my consistent prayers to God and Minister Njoku's help, I do not think that I would have been able to go to America to further my education. He resided at Ikoyi, Lagos. Then, all Ministers lived in an exclusive area of Ikoyi where the Europeans lived before Nigerian independence. When I left Enugu, my father sent me to go and stay with him while he was Minister of Commerce and Industry and while I worked on my travel to the US. I stayed with him until he requested me to leave. I had to leave to stay with a cousin called Mr. George Mbara from Owerri with whom my father connected me, until my departure to the U.S. Minister Njoku was reluctant to continue to maintain me since I had stayed with him for quite some time struggling to get enough money to travel. It was a difficult trying time, but I am still grateful to him for allowing me to spend the much time I stayed in his residence.

I remember writing to my father and saying that "my life would be the death of me if I fail to go overseas to study." I scared him enough to do something. Even one of my sisters, Mrs. Philomena Osuji (Fig. 4.40), still reminds me of the statement till today and insists that I had threatened to take my own life if I was not enabled to go to America. However, that was not what I meant. I was simply trying to use flowery English. I had come across the expression in a novel I had read and I thought it was a good occasion to use it. So when I wanted to dramatize my desire to go to America and study, I used the statement while writing my father. I did not mean to commit suicide. There was nothing that would have made me kill myself. I was only trying to be clear and emphatic about my ardent desire to leave Nigeria for America for further education. So my father and several of his brothers scrambled to raise the money for me to travel to America.

The deposit requirement of 500 pounds, the fare of 75 pounds and some money to use on my arrival to America, gave my people and myself sleepless nights after they managed to raise 300 Pounds and the 75 Pounds towards the fare. Every effort made to get more money failed. My father, who was no longer working at that time, appeared to have been faced with the promise he had earlier made to me—that he would sell his house in Portharcourt, Rivers State if necessary, in order to finance my education overseas. He was willing to do so but his brothers objected since it would be his only source of income as he did not have pension money. The 300 pounds raised was more or less borrowed money with the collective effort of my people. Bits of money came from several people, but 100 of it came from my uncle, Benjamin Njoku Acholonu (Fig. 3.1) (late) a contractor then who supplied sand to builders at Portharcourt, Rivers State and I was extremely grateful. He was my father's immediate elder brother. What detracted from the credit I give him is the fact that he later demanded the 100 pounds from my father. He said that he gave it as a loan. I had to come up with all the money and give my father to pay him back. I however, recall that one time, when my father was still working, he come back from Port Harcourt and said that the government ordered him to break down his thatched mud house at No 205 Niger Street and erect a zinc building, failing which he would lose the land. My father helped him to erect the zinc building. I expected him to remember that favor and not have my father to pay back the 100 pounds. I am however, still grateful to him because his 100 pounds made it possible for me to go to America. My youngest maternal uncle, Sir Cyril Acholonu (late) (Fig. 2.2), was the one who kept the record of who gave what and who lent what. He was a High Elementary School teacher and I expected him to contribute towards my travel. But up till today, I do not know, for certain, whether he contributed anything or not and if he did, how much. Even so, his son, Dr. Kenny Acholonu, was the first person, outside my nuclear family, that I brought to America after I got there. He is doing quite well at present in Lagos as a successful businessman, managing a company as MD and CEO of Bioorganics Ltd. and has showed gratitude for what I did for him. Another person was Chief Barr. Patrick O. Acholonu, another uncle one year older than I am and with whom I was highly identified right from our childhood days, and my father took care of him after my grandfather (his father) died and requested my father to do so, because he was very young (5years). Like Uncle Cyril (Fig. 2.2), he was a High Elementary School teacher and was paid arrears of salary at the time I was about to travel to America. He refused to contribute towards my travel, much to my great surprise! Irrespective of his refusing to contribute towards my travel to the US for further studies, he was the first I wanted to bring to the US. But my father barred me from doing so. He said that apart from his refusing to contribute towards my travel to the US, apart from showing ingratitude for what he did for him when he was growing up, while he was the headmaster of Our Lady's School, Emekuku his children (i.e. my father's children were being sent home for not paying their school fees on time. I told him to go and reconcile with my father so that I might still bring him to the US. He did not do so. This is the reason why he did not become the first person I brought to the US. But with my Christian heart and love for him as my "childhood brother", playmate and compatriot, when he came back to Nigeria as a licentiate lawyer from England, I harbored him without charge in my house in Lagos while I was teaching at the College of Medicine University of Lagos and while he was in the Nigerian Law School. I also helped him to be admitted into the Law School. In addition, I got his first daughter, Ileen, now Mrs. Ileen Ihedoro, to get admitted into the University of Lagos in my department Medical Microbiology and Parasitology and harbored her till she graduated from the University without any financial assistance from her father. It is unfortunate that as I write this autobiography, he is one of the few in Acholonu family that do not identify with me after all my father and I did for him. This is a useful digression. These were the financial issues that delayed my travel until Dec. 1954 to begin school during the second semester which started in Jan. 1955. It was then that it became possible for me to travel. So the University deferred my admission, at my request to 2nd semester, 1955.

Since we could not come up with the remaining 200 pounds, and the rules in those days allowed that I could search for someone in a position of authority to sign a waiver for me, staying with the Hon. Minister, Barrister Raymond Njoku, and begging him to sign the waiver for me made all the difference. It was a herculean task to get him to do this favor though, but eventually he relented, and for that, I am very grateful. So he became my surety and I got a waiver for the remaining Two Hundred Pounds. That was what actually made it possible, at the last stages, for me to get over to America as stated earlier. For this, I say again that I am immensely grateful to Hon. Raymond Njoku (See Fig. 3.2)

Coming to America dragged along with it many surprises. The initial ones came as early as the physical journey itself. I traveled by sea. The journey was divided into two; the first was a two-week trip from Lagos to Liverpool, United Kingdom. The second phase was also another two-week journey from Liverpool to New York. (See picture of ships used, Fig. 3.3 & 3.4)

So it was that on a sunny day in Lagos, I boarded a ship called M.V. *Aureol* owned by Elder Demister Shipping Line, from Lagos to Liverpool. The journey lasted for two weeks. We disembarked there and boarded another ship named *Saxonia*, Cunard R.M.S Line from Liverpool to New York, which also took another period of two weeks as stated above. God has always given me people to take care of me and I do not know how and why He does it! That time, when we were to board the ship in Lagos, my maternal aunt, late Onyema Onukwugha, put me in the care of a friend, one man who was part of the ship-crew. He was actually a cook on the very ship from Lagos to Liverpool. He took care of me by giving me well spiced meals (with pepper). The regular meals were fashioned to please the British and the Europeans, 'Oyibo' people, so they were not hot enough. That kind of meal made me throw up and the shaky movement of the ship made it worse and made me become seasick. I became alright because of the spicy food and special attention I got from my aunt's friend.

In the cabin, I shared a bunk bed with the late Dr. Nicholas Onyewu from Omolu, Emii in Owerri North LGA. He was an older person, so my father requested him to take care of me. In his case, his village contributed money to send him overseas. He was a High Elementary School Teacher before he left, so he was much more mature than I was. We traveled all the way and arrived in New York together and also proceeded on the same train from New York to Washington, D. C. together.

I found New York amazing! It is therefore, not easy for me to forget the trauma of high sea voyage notwithstanding. But my first experience with New York was a mixture of surprises and excitement. When we arrived at New York, it was snowing. I was experiencing snow for the first time in my life. It was the first indication that I had really come to a different world altogether. There were things falling on my body and the grounds were covered with what looked like white chalk dust, except that it was melting. I asked myself where this could be coming from. For that kind of question I did not really seek any immediate answers. Later, I was to get the answer. I was told that it was snow. I was excited; I never knew what snow meant. I cannot even remember if I had heard of it before. That was part of my first excitement. In the midst of the excitement, a white lady from the US Government helped us get on the train in New York, which took us to Washington, DC. Then, leaving New York by train to Washington DC was another excitement. I was admitted to study Science at Howard University, while Dr. Onyewu was admitted to study Political Science. We both roomed together in Cook Hall at Howard University campus. Eventually we left the dormitory and rented an apartment together in the Washington, DC area. We lived somewhere on Webster Street, NW. and subsequently we went our separate ways.

Howard University

Howard University's history dates back to November 1866. (http://www.howard.edu/Jexplorelhistory.htm). It was an institution, founded to educate African-American clergymen but it soon became a University consisting of the colleges of Liberal Arts and Medicine. The new institution was named after General Oliver

O. Howard, an American Civil War hero who actually founded it. He served as Commissioner for the Freedman's Bureau (a bureau for Blacks). The University charter was eventually ratified by Congress and approved by President Andrew Johnson, who on March 2, 1867, designated Howard University as "a University for the education of youths in the liberal arts and sciences."

In 1926, Dr. Mordecai Wyatt Johnson was appointed Howard's first black president. At that time the University was made up of eight schools and colleges, none of which held national accreditation. The institution's enrollment during this year stood at 1,700 and its budget at $700,000. Thirty four years later, when Johnson retired, the University had "10 schools and colleges, all fully accredited; 6,000 students; a budget of $8 million, the addition of 20 new buildings including an expanded physical plant; and a greatly enlarged faculty that included some of the most prominent black scholars of the day." In 1955, the university reached a milestone by obtaining authority to award earned doctorate degree.

I was happy to be at Howard. As soon as I got there, I knew I had to find a job or more than one job. I deliberately decided that I would not touch the 300 pounds transferred to the Nigerian Consulate office (There was no Embassy as Nigeria was not independent at the time) for me to withdraw and use when needed. Instead, I got a job as a busboy at a restaurant called Virginia Lodge in Alexandria, Virginia (see photograph, Fig. 3.5). I also went to Professor Hansbury (a professor of History) who had helped me to get admitted to Howard to help me get a job. He helped me get a job as a switch board operator at Cook Hall, a dormitory at the University in which I lived. So I had two jobs while going to school fulltime. Subsequently I had several kinds of menial jobs in apartment buildings which included dish washing in restaurants, switch board operator in apartment buildings and construction job (Fig. 3.6). For some time, I stayed on a strict budget of $1.00 a day for breakfast, lunch and dinner. Much of the money I made was sent home to my father to help take care of his three wives and other 24 children, with me as the only one away from home and many children most of whom were unemployed and in school. I also found time to engage in cultural displays singing, drumming and dancing to make people and groups to know more about Nigeria and Africa (Fig. 3.7 & 3.8). This was a display of the dignity of labor in the US which I resolved to embrace for my survival in the US and for keeping my family going.

There were other continental Africans on Howard University campus with us. My former elementary six teacher at Our Lady's School, Emekuku, Dr. Ben Njoku (Figs. 2.3, 2.10, 4.17 & 4.18), had also earlier arrived in the US and was pursuing a doctorate degree at Catholic University in Washington, DC. So we reunited and he took me under his wings again. When we met, it was as if I saw my second father again. He was very kind and fatherly to me and I loved him very much. Incidentally, I did experience overt segregation or discrimination for the first time at the Catholic University area while with him and, about which I wrote an essay at Howard in my English Composition class. The essay was titled "My first experience with discrimination in America," and was sent by my English teacher to a magazine, which surprisingly got it published. The story contained my experience when I went to visit late Dr. Ben Njoku at the Catholic University Campus. He and two white student friends of his took me to a restaurant just outside the University campus. A waiter came to us and said to the white guys with us "I am sorry, "I can serve you but not the other two." And that was it! He just refused to serve us. All of us therefore left. I had not experienced a thing like that until that day, hence I wrote about it in my English Language class.

In addition to the likes of my former teacher at Our Lady's Elementary School, Emekuku, Imo State, there were Africans at Howard while I was there. We had Alexander Ayo Edwards. He was the one that advised me to major in Chemistry. We had Dr. Sofola, who was a medical student and his brother, another Sofola who majored in Social Science and later taught at the University of Ilorin, Kwara State. There was Prof. Essien Udo, who later became the Vice Chancellor of University of Maiduguri, Borno State, Nigeria. There were also Mr. Emeka Nduka, who later became a teacher at one of the secondary schools in Imo State, and late Professor Ogba Okorie who majored in Physics and later, taught at Southern University, Baton Rouge LA with me and next became a professor at the University of the District of Columbia (UDC), where he later died. Another one, and a very good friend of mine, was late Engineer Gregory Okafor, who later worked with the Federal Ministry of Works, (Fig. 3.7 & 3.8) Lagos. My experience with African Americans at Howard was generally pleasant. However, some of them would want to check us out to see if we had tails. They said that they were told that Africans had tails. Many of them were friendly and nice though. I was approached to pledge in the Phi Beta Sigma Fraternity, which I did in 1956. I was convinced by being told that Nnamdi Azikiwe (ZIK) (Fig. 3.9) and Kwame Nkuruma (of Ghana) were members. I had social interactions and went to clubs with them. The Dean of Students at the time was Dr. Ryne, who was extremely helpful to those of us from the African continent. There was a small Catholic Church called Freeman Catholic Church with a Chaplain connected to Howard University to cater for Catholics at the University at First Street N.W, where we went for Mass. I was also one of those that served mass for the chaplain on Sundays. We also had Freeman Club to which I served as Vice-President. There was also the Africa House at First Street N.W where Mr. Goodman, the Director, hired me to work for the African-American Institute, under Mr. Murphy. Dr. Njoku and I worked together at the Africa House on that first St., NW. He was the Executive Secretary of the Pan-Africa Union, which united all continental Africans in the USA and I was the social secretary. There was also a Nigerian Association that often met in New York annually. At that time, there was no World Igbo Congress, or Egbe Omo Oduduwa, or Zumunta, or any of the other ethnic, regional, and parochial organizations that now proliferate in the entire America. We all saw each other and related to one another as Nigerians or Africans.

Rev. Martin Luther King came to Howard to speak at one time while I was a student there. It was the first time I met Rev. King and already, the civil rights movement had started but it was in its cradle. The buses and trains going down South from Washington, DC were still segregated by race as well as the restrooms. In 1956 or 1957 I boarded a Greyhound bus from Washington, DC to visit Dr. Njoku who had gone to Marshall Texas to teach at a college there called Willey College after leaving Catholic University. At some point during the trip the bus stopped and picked up a white guy. The driver ordered me to get up for the white man to sit and told me to go to another seat at the back of the bus. I said, "I did not pay Black money and I am not standing up for him." He could not believe my effrontery. When we got to Monroe, Louisiana (the next bus station), he stopped the bus and called the Police. The Police came and asked me what was going on. I narrated to him what happened and told him and the bus driver that if I was molested I would report it to my Embassy, the Nigerian Embassy. I told them that I would stand up for any elderly person, but I was not going to stand and give up my seat for a man just because he was white and I am Black. I repeated that I did not pay Black money. The Police man left me alone and I went back to my seat. I sat there for the rest of my trip. I apparently did not quite know what risk I took in the encounter. God saved me! Blacks had disappeared for being so unyielding to status-quo at that period. The Police Officer probably acted on the part of caution because of my mention of the Nigerian Embassy. Whatever it was, I was glad to get to Texas in one piece. This incident happened shortly after that of Rosa Parks of **December 1, 1955.** But I did not know about her experience, only later.

I received a Bachelor of Science degree in Chemistry from Howard University in 1958. Then, I was interested in studying medicine. So I applied for a scholarship from the Nigerian government. I was advised to change to Parasitology instead of Medicine; that I might not get the Nigerian scholarship if I put medicine; that I could always switch to medicine after the scholarship was awarded. I did and got the scholarship but when I tried to switch, the embassy official in charge would not let me do so. So I worked on my Master's degree at Prairie View A & M University, Texas and completed it in 1961 in a paramedical field (Parasitology). Since I could not pursue medicine, I decided I would become a "doctor" of something. I told myself that I would not get married until I got my doctorate degree. I got admission at Colorado State University in First Collins, Colorado and finished my Doctorate Degree in May 1964.

My Journey Through Life

Fig. 3.1: Late Mr. Benjamin N. Acholonu, my uncle, the immediate senior brother of my father, the man who contributed 100 pounds towards my travel to the US for further studies in Dec. 1954. He died in 1988 at age 96

Fig. 3.2: Barrister Raymond Njoku (Late), former Minister of Commerce and Industry, Transport and Aviation, 1954-1966. My benefactor who made it possible for me to go to America more than anyone else. He signed a waiver for me

My Journey Through Life

Fig. 3.3: Ship that took me from Lagos to Liverpool – M. V. Aureol Elder Demister Shipping Line, December 1954 (Two weeks journey)

Fig. 3.4: Ship that took me from Liverpool to New York – Saxonia Cunard R.M.S Line, 1954-55 (Two weeks journey)

Virginia Lodge, Restaurant in Alexandria, Virginia
Fig. 3.5: First place I worked in the USA after arrival from Nigeria. I worked as a Busboy removing used plates and cleaning tables in the restaurant

Fig. 3.6: My job as a house construction worker in the US, working to subsidize my cost of education and send money home to dad for support of my family. This is a display of the dignity of labor and the fact that America is a land of opportunity for the strong, mentally and physically. I did two to three jobs at a time while going to school at Howard University to make ends meet; to help my father with three wives and 25 children and no longer working

Fig. 3.7: Prof. Alex Acholonu singing as a musician in an African Band group of which he was the leader, Washington D.C., about 1957. Included is his late friend, Engr. Gregory Okafor to his right

Fig. 3.8 From left to right Agbim, Gregory Okafor, Olatunji and Alex Acholonu singing and entertaining women cosmetologists group in Washington DC in about 1960

Fig. 3.9: Dr. Nnamdi Azikiwe (Zik). Former premier of Eastern Region and 1st President of Nigeria. The person I wrote to help me find funds to go to America for further education but, got a courteous negative response

Fig. 3.10: Picture of Acholonu (left) with Mrs. Flora Azikiwe (Zik's 1st wife) at Howard University in Washington, DC as fellow students

My Journey Through Life

Fig. 3.11: Dr. Mrs. Uche Azikiwe (second wife of Dr. Nnamdi Azikiwe) and Chief Alex Acholonu (right). On the left is my friend, Prof. Anya O. Anya. Picture taken after Zik's Memorial Lecture at Enugu in the 90s. I paid her hotel bill in one of the World Igbo Congress (WIC) Conventions in the US.

Chapter Four

My Family—I am a Husband, Father and Grandfather

Marriage

> Marriage—It's a partnership between two people who decide to take the adventure of life together—sometimes crazy, sometimes routine, lots of times fun, but ALWAYS worth it.
>
> American Greetings, Co. 2017

Parenting

> A full and lifetime job
> Undertaken without lessons
> Tutors, guides or team
> Just the ability to painstakingly navigate
> On hope, prayers and will
> With no one but I
>
> Obaze, 2015

My plan was to get married and as our people say, settle down to a secured family life before or at the age of 30. When I left home for the USA, my father warned me not to marry a white woman or a non-Nigerian. However, on getting to America, things appeared to have changed. The first lady to take interest in me was a white lady. Her name was Joy.

At that time segregation was still very bad and on-going. We fell in love; and she wanted to marry me. She wanted to come to Nigeria and meet my people. I had to let her know my father's warnings about marrying a non-Nigerian. She eventually ended the relationship.

I did make a secret decision about marriage in the midst of all the issues, which was that I would earn a doctorate degree before walking down the aisles. Since I did not get a scholarship to pursue medicine, I decided that I had to get a doctorate in something else, and do it before getting married. I did, in fact, place in one of my diaries a wishful list of the attributes of the woman who would eventually become my wife. I wanted a woman that was good looking, of course, educated, and a woman that gets along with her husband; a woman who would not go East when her husband is going West; someone I could blend with. But unfortunately, by the time I clocked 30, I was still searching. I had not been able to find a Nigerian one.

I had also not been able to go home to Nigeria since I came to America. At the recommendation of my elder brother, late Architect Casmir W. Acholonu (Fig. 4.39), I caused one lady to visit me while I was doing my doctorate degree—studying—at Colorado State University. I hosted her but I did not see in her the things I was looking for in a wife. She was studying Nursing in England when I brought her to America to meet me from England. Moreover, she wanted me to leave America and join her in England. That just did not fit into my idea of marriage—I, packing up and moving to England for her sake. I saw it as a case of the tail-wagging—the-dog relationship. It did not advance beyond the initial visit and the pleasantries therein.

I met an Ethiopian lady named Alganish (Fig. 4.8 & 4.9) while I was still pursuing my doctorate degree. We dated for quite some time. I loved her so much that I decided to forget my father's warning and marry her especially as she was an African. When I finished at Colorado State University and went to Baton Rouge, Louisiana (at Southern University) to teach, I invited her over and actually got engaged to her (see Fig. 4.9). The engagement ritual was done by a Catholic Priest in the presence of my junior brother Engr. Uchenna Acholonu who was living with me and going to school at Southern University and Dr. Nicholas Onyewu with whom I came to America at the same time. I gave her an engagement ring—the first time I gave a woman a ring. My senior brother late Casmir (Fig. 4.39) was not in favor of my marrying her. This, coupled with my father's desire that I marry a Nigerian, precipitated an end to the relationship. She went back to Ethiopia with my engagement ring! As a matter of fact, I named a parasite I discovered and described after her. I called it *Cercaria alganishi* (Trematoda) a parasite from snails.

All the while that I was teaching at Southern University, colleagues and other well-wishers were sending ladies to come and meet me. They thought that I needed to be trapped by at least one person. Some of my friends did a lot to get me out of bachelorhood. I recall quite vividly that as early as when I was coming to America, in fact, in the ship to America, on the first leg of the trip, that is from Lagos to Liverpool, I met a lady by name Victoria Awani from Warri, Edo State. She was heading to England to study nursing. We got somehow attracted to each other and established acquaintanceship. When we got to Liverpool, she travelled to London, England, while I boarded another ship to New York. The relationship was not going to be just a flash in the pan because while we were at our different locations, we still kept in touch by mail until she later informed me that she had gotten a baby by a man in London. I lost interest at that point and we consequently lost touch.

In all these, I knew I was not going to remain single for life, not even for long. This is because there was a strong desire in me to marry and raise a family. So on a more serious note, things started shaping up when in 1966 I went to Nigeria, just before the NigeriaBiafra war started. The sister of my father's second wife, Ezihe, recommended that I go and see a young lady in a village called Umuawuka, Emii. I did and I liked the young lady. I was a little confused, even though I sang a love song to her. I felt that she was too young for me and that I did not think that the marriage would work. But my father called my attention to himself. He reminded me that he could easily have fathered a child of the same age as my mother. In other words, my mother was that much younger than he was too, when he married her. That convinced me. My father was my demi-god who loved and protected me while I was growing up. I could not say "no" to him. I thought of him to be very wise and caring. I nurtured the interest I had already started developing in the young lady, by name, Mary Atukpawu (Fig. 4.5, 4.11-12, 4.14-22, 4.38, 6.2-4, 6.6, 6.8, 6.14 concl. 1 & 2 and wedding pictures). So we started making arrangements to marry, which we almost completed before I left Nigeria for the US again.

There was the required wine carrying to the parents and kindred of the bride and the colorful ceremony of "ipa mmi ukwu" (literally meaning offering the big wine). This formed the climax of the traditional aspects of marriage. In so doing, two families, my family, Acholonu and my bride-to-be's family, Atukpawu would symbolically be joined together as in-laws. Our people say that one's in-laws become one's brothers and sisters. This ceremony was done after my departure to the USA. After all the preliminary activities were carried out, I was ready to travel back to my base in the US. Already, hostilities have mounted in Nigeria. The crises that would result in a three year civil war were apparent and as a result of these developments, my father warned me not to attempt to go back to the US through Lagos because as far as he was concerned, war had started. He advised that I leave through Cameroon. Even though he made sense, given the stories and rumors that were going round, I already had a plane ticket that I was to leave from Lagos Airport, and nowhere else. So I did not have much of a choice but to leave through Lagos. I left home by bus to Lagos with my new wife to work on her visa to come to America and from there, travel back to the US. She and I stayed with my friend, by name Engr. Gregory Okafor (Fig. 3.7 & 3.8) mentioned earlier. On the day that I was to leave for the US, my friend told his driver to take me to the airport from Ikoyi where he lived. When we were close to the airport, an extraction of the Army contingent of the Federal Government stopped us and jumped into our vehicle and decided to take me to their superior with two in front and three at the back with one soldier pointing his gun on my back. The Igbo people that where returning from overseas were singled out and shot once they arrived at the airport of what they had believed was their nation. Federal soldiers were on a rampage and Igbos were the targets. That was what happened. Here I was, and could that also be my fate? My new wife who came to see me off and who was raised partially in the northern part of Nigeria (Kaduna) could hear and understand Hausa language. The soldiers talking in Hausa said that they were taking me to a place where the soldiers were lining up the Igbos and shooting them. They did eventually take me there. When I got to the place, they took me to see their superior officer. As I was brought before the bearded man who was stern and looked like Lucifer himself with overgrown mustache and beard, he ordered me to sit down and started a rapid fire set of questions. I explained that I was an Associate Professor at Southern University in the U.S. He asked for and I showed him my traveling documents and identity card that showed that I was an Associate Professor at Southern University in Baton Rouge, Louisiana, and my passport that showed that I resided in the U.S. The officer softened and explained to me that they were just trying to keep law and order. He said he would let me go and wished me a safe journey back to the US. When I came out alive and released, everyone there including his boys who brought me to him were surprised that he let me leave. From there, I was allowed to go to the airport. I saw it as God saving my life, because many who were brought before this man were shot. I never understood what made him let me go, and I did not hang around to find out. I was so happy when I boarded the plane, and greatly relieved when it took off.

When I returned to the US, I filed immigration papers for my new wife, now Lolo Lady Mary Ekeoma Acholonu, to come as a spouse. She was eventually granted a visa and she joined me, much to my delight. I immediately arranged a formal wedding, which took place on the 27th of March, 1967 in Baton Rouge, Louisiana (See Fig. 4.11-19, Wedding Pictures). The long-held desire to be married and to be a husband was accomplished, even though it took much longer than I had planned. My first child, a son, came nine months after our wedding. He was born on December 31, 1967, to be exact. I named him Anderson Ukachi Acholonu (Fig. 4.5, 4.22, 4.23, 6.4, 6.5, & 8.9). I wanted a son, and as a Biologist, I knew when to sleep with my wife for the greatest chance of a son. It is for whoever that desires a male to know when the egg comes out—a process called ovulation. When this occurs and then, a person sleeps with his partner within 24 hours of that time, the child will most likely be a boy. The reason is that the Y chromosome, which determines the male child, swims faster and dies quicker. So within that window, if fertilization is attained, there is over 90 percent chance of getting a boy. The girls are a lot easier to make. I am a typical Igbo man in the sense that I wanted a son and I was jubilant that the first one was a son ("aham-efula" fulfillment).

I was proud to be a father for the first time! I might have spoilt my first child as a result, because I did just about anything for him including making him to start walking after 8 months of age. The next child was a girl, and she arrived in February 10, 1969. I named her Sandra Akunna (Fig. 4.5, 4.22, 4.24 & 6.4). Subsequently, three more girls came, so I had four girls after the first boy unplanned. It became a concern and a source of some worry because I remembered that Onassis, the shipping tycoon, with all the money he amassed, as a shipping tycoon had only two childrenone boy and one girl. The son died in a plane crash and Onassis never recovered from the loss. He became a vegetable until he died. I suppose that because he had no son left, no one hears much about Onassis anymore. The Onassis family name died. I was concerned that if something happened to my only son, I might suffer Onassis' fate or President Kennedy's fate with his only son dying in a plane crash also. As an Igbo, I believe in "Ahamefula" (May my name never get lost. That is, with reference to genealogy). Who would continue the genealogy of the family when I die? In patrilineal Igbo culture, it is the son that sustains the lineage. That became my concern. So I was eager and anxious to have another son. This is also the situation with President Barrack Obama. It will be great if he and his wife would get another child and that a boy. I agree with Gail, Oprah Winfrey's friend when she said not too long ago that Barrack should get us a boy. With the history he has made, he should not allow his name to be lost.

In 1977, I returned to Nigeria from the US. This was in the real sense of it, a return back home or relocation. I came back with my entire family. While in Nigeria, my wife, unplanned, gave birth to a fifth girl, Alexandra, and subsequently my wife and I seriously tried to get another boy. I kept checking on her ovulation time for a more precise attempt. This happened to the extent that there was this occasion when I made a trip from Lagos to Awaka, my home town. Upon getting to Awaka, I realized that it was my wife's ovulation period, so I thought that I could not afford to be away in Awaka while she was in Lagos. Because of that, I rushed back to Lagos. That was when she conceived and we got a second boy, whom I named Alexander Jr.! Still after that, I was planning a third boy but my wife started having some health challenges. I wanted more boys to ensure continuity in my lineage, so that after me, there would be children from my lineage, who would be left behind to carry my name on. The girls would marry and take on someone's name—though I have been telling my daughters to hyphenate their names at marriage as Acholonu. I tell them their husbands did not educate them—I made them what they are, so they should hyphenate their names as a sign of respect for me because of my efforts in bringing them up and because "Acholonu" is a nationally and internationally known name and could be of benefit to them. Another reason is that several professional married women are now doing so especially women doctors.

I have seven children altogether; five of them were born in America, and two were born in Nigeria after we got back to the country in 1977. The first child we had in Lagos was a girl, but I had thought she would be a boy and bear my name Alexander. However, since she turned out to be a girl, I named her Alexandra (Fig. 4.22, 4.28, 6.4). When the boy arrived after her, I named him Alexander Junior (Fig. 4.22, 4.29, 6.4, 6.5 & 8.9) and he is usually called Junior. My first son at some point had asked me why I named the second son Alexander Junior instead of him who was the first son. I explained that when I was at CKC, I once saw a book called Dictionary of Names in the school's library. I read from the book that the name Alexander came from Anderson and Sanderson. So from that time, I made up my mind that when I start having sons, I would name the first one Anderson, then the second, Sanderson, and the third Alexander to follow the history of the name. The second child came as a girl. I could not name her Sanderson; instead I called her Sandra. Then to the other girls, I gave names according to the stars in the soap opera TV program my wife and I used to watch back then called The Edge of Night. The third child we named Cynthia (Fig. 4.5, 4.22, 4.25, 6.4) after an actress in the Edge of Night. The fourth child, another girl, was named Leslie (Fig. 4.5, 4.22, 4.26, 4.34 & 6.4), also after one of the actresses in the soap opera. The fourth girl (my fifth child) came after my mother pressured me to have more children. I had actually decided to stop at four. But my mother, who I had brought to stay with us from New York where she was staying with my brother, Eng. Uchenna Acholonu at the time, said I should have more children. I had an unusual premonition that the next baby would still be a girl and when the fifth child came and it was another daughter as I had feared, I told my mother that it was all her fault. So, I named the girl after my mother, Esther (Fig. 4.22, 4.27 & 6.4). I also added Eberegbulam to Esther's name. She is the one that is an attorney and a chattered Public Accountant (CPA) now. The fifth daughter as stated above is Alexandra, and the last child, who is a boy, is Alexander Junior.

So my first son was not happy that I did not name him Junior as stated earlier, but there was nothing we could do about it. I explained to him how and why this happened. He felt satisfied. Things did not work out the way I had envisioned it in this direction. So is my journey through life. "Man proposes but God disposes." One cannot always have one's way. It is more of, one wins and sometimes one loses. He has to endure when winning does not come absolutely. But one issue is clear; I never plan to lose and hardly lost. However, if I had known that the sequence of birth would not be what I had planned, I would have named my first son Alexander Junior, because that appears to be the most appropriate thing to do and what is done by many people. But as I said before, I have explained it to him, and he understood. By the way, the Igbo equivalent of junior is *Ogbonna*.

So my marriage did not emerge out of a romantic encounter that blossomed into marriage. It was a marriage by recommendation and arrangement. I have been married for over 50 years. There are two ways to look at marriage. Marriage is not something that is only sensual. Love develops within marriage, and also grows and strengthens as the union matures. Our ancestors told us that character is beauty (Agwa wu mma), not physical appearance. Another similar expression is: The latitude of a man's attitude is his altitude. That is, the worth of a man or woman is determined by his or her character; it is a man's attitude and not his aptitude that determines his altitude or height to which he reaches in life. And there is this notion that our parents, given their experiences, are better assessors of character than we are at the time we start thinking of marriage. For this reason, it is the family (parents in particular) who go out to seek suitable spouses for their children, and quite often the assessment involves the history of the family of the would-be-spouse. There are necessary measures that parents and other elders take whenever there are plans of marriage or more appropriately before the wedding bells. If things are not handled carefully, youngsters can get blinded and infatuated by physical appearances and what can be mistaken to be love. Love does not always develop instantly. That which young people call love may actually be infatuation! If one marries based on infatuation, one may find out that one married a devil incarnate that may destroy one's family and everything in it.

In my case, after having reached age 30 (which was my planned age of marriage) and passed it, going to 35, I pretty much resolved that however marriage comes, let it come. Moreover, two of my younger brothers I brought to the USA had married before me and never cared to let me know. This put me in an awkward position. It is usually untraditional in "Ala Igbo" for the young to marry before their elder brothers and without their consultation or consent. Being conscious of this tradition, I helped to get my elder brother married before me. I contributed the funds used for his marriage; I dared not marry before him even though I was better positioned to do so. So I complied with the tradition of sequence in marriage. However, as luck would have it, it was after I married and had my first child that both of them (the two youngest brothers) began having babies. So my first child happens to be the second grandson of our parents among the boys. The first one, was Joseph from my senior brother, Casimir, and whose mother died after his delivery. Because my two younger brothers married before me, my mother and my father's second wife, Grace, together called my first son "Akopoazu". This means: The wise one married last.

I married someone from home and did that at home, not out of love or an existing relationship. But we developed both love and a good relationship within marriage. If anyone married, like I did, by recommendation, both partners would start off making special efforts to discover each other and appeal to each other within marriage. The marriage tends to get stronger and usually lasts longer. If the marriage starts off with the romance thing, it tends to reach the climax of sexual gratification quickly and early. As a result, the partners find that both of them may begin to lose interest early as well. I speak, of course, as a man and I know that the woman that makes me struggle to get her is often more cherished than the one that gives of herself readily. The sense of value in human nature is that what you suffer to get is often more appreciated than what you get just for the asking. When a woman puts one under pressure as one seeks her, and gives one some hard time, one tends to appreciate her a lot more. That's my take; it may be different for others. So yes, I fell in love with my wife in marriage. And in general terms, when children become involved, they tend to cement the love and relationship, making the entire union stronger.

Incidentally, I have noticed that most of the time, the girls appreciate their fathers more; they take care of them with greater intensity than the boys. The boys do not usually care much about the old man, especially when they go and marry a controlling or domineering wife that does not want anything to do with the family of the man: especially the father-in-law. As I write now, I don't believe I have gone to my first son's house since he got married and spent a night more than once. It is not made any easier that the woman he married is non-Igbo. Wherever love is found is fine. But there is a lot more advantage in marrying someone who shares the same value systems and cultural attributes with a person. Luckily, with the girls, I have no problem. I had reservations about my first son's marriage from the beginning because I wanted him to finish his education before getting married. My warning has come true because after the marriage he has not been able to complete more than an Associate Degree, unlike his siblings with higher and professional degrees. He appears to have more interest in making babies—he has six altogether and aspiring to get the seventh one to catch up with me. Chances are that if my son had married an Igbo woman, I would have spent more time there than I am spending now and he would have completed his first degree. I am not that close to the lady and her parents. Her parents and siblings lived there. Her siblings got their education up to master's level and she, herself, up to PhD level. They practically used my son as their errand boy, took possession of his house and cared less about his own education. In my considered opinion, parents on both sides should not be obligate parasites on a married couple. The couple should be given time to grow, mature and build their future. I humbly feel that my son's wife is 75% responsible for him not getting as high in education as I wanted him and he should have been. He is intelligent; he has my genes and those of his mother. What he needed was an encouraging and supporting wife and not one that imposed obstacles. Obstacles are what you see when you take your eyes off your marital goals. These comments are not and should not be construed as a tribal sentiment. "Behind a successful man there is a supporting wife" (See p 320).

Regarding fatherhood, I consider myself a happy father. I know very well that I am happy. I am happy that I have seven children. I am also happy that I was able to educate them without them impoverishing me and without help from any of my brothers, whom I helped to be what they are today. I find that girls are wonderful so I am equally happy about the girls. They come closer to me and appreciate me more. They show more concern for me. They call to see how I am doing. When I travel, the girls call to make sure I get to wherever I am going safely. The boys do not seem to care as much, which is ironical because I wanted more boys than girls. Generally all the boys do often is to cause headaches and heartaches. My first grandchild is Uzoamaka from my first son, Anderson. She is about 25 years old by now. I was happy to get my first grandchild. My son named her "Uzoamaka" (the road is good). I named her "Chikodinaka" (Chikodi for short). Literally, this means that everything is in God's hand. My first grandson is also from Anderson and I called him Onunukajuo (or Onu for short) (that is, always double check when told something about a person before you act)—a name my mother gave me (Fig. 4.31, 4.32). Next to Anderson's first two children, who are my first grandchildren, are two boys and one girl from my third daughter, Engr. Lolo Leslie Okeke. I called Leslie's first son Omenichekwa (that is, Look before you leap or think before you act) a second name my mother gave me, the second son, Onyekurukeye (that is get your own, be self-reliant). The third, a girl, Ahum onye-hurum (I see those who see me, I care for those who care for me) (Fig. 4.33, 4.34).

I have always been very interested in the education of my children. Of course, that is to be expected, being that I am an educationist. So I should naturally be bothered that my first son has not progressed as others in the educational line. For this reason, I had cause to invite him over so that he could continue going to school. His education was interrupted by his early and premature marriage. I predicted that this was going to be the result of a very early marriage and it happened. However, he came over to Mississippi in order to complete his degree program but was once more distracted by yet another lady, this time an American. I objected to this strongly and even made an appeal to the parents of the lady and tried to create ways of making the youngsters see reason for inappropriate relationship. While all these were on, they had two boys, Aaron and Austin (Fig. 4.30). To hinder their plan for marriage I caused my son's return to his wife in Maryland. It was after he got back with his wife, Gbemi, that they had the boy (Onu) and two more girls, Ugochi and Urenna (Fig. 4.31, 4.32). Altogether he has three boys and three girls. Thus, I have 16 grandchildren, so far. I have six from Anderson (Fig. 4.30-32), three from Leslie (Fig. 4.3334), three from Esther (Fig. 3.35), and Alexandra has four children (three boys and a girl) (Fig. 4.36). I have good relationship with all my grandchildren. Whenever they are in my company, we enjoy each other. Regrettably, because of the frosty nature of my relationship with my first son, I don't get to see his children as often as I would like. I am a proud man, so I do not go to see his children as often as I could. Even when I visit the city where they reside, I prefer to stay in my hotel and have them come and visit me there with their father. My first son is kind to a fault. He is loving and very sociable. He is intelligent. He has what it takes to live a good life, but what he appears to lack is patience required to succeed. Booker T. Washington said: "Success patiently waits for anyone who has the determination and the strength to seize it." I am hoping that my first son that I love dearly, will rise to the occasion and become a late bloomer and take his rightful place in my family both educationally and leadership-wise. I will not stop motivating him until his good becomes better, and his better becomes best. It is never too late to mend.

I am proud that I have 7 children and 16 grandchildren and as happy as a lark. But as my wife and I advance in age, I like to remind them about their responsibilities to us as designed by Providence. I hereby reproduce these words from Ecclesiastes 3: 2-6, 12-14 for their information and for others who do not know:

> "He who fears the Lord, respects his parents.
> The Lord honors the father in his children, and
> upholds the rights of a mother over her sons.
> Whoever respects his father is atoning for his sins.
> He who honors his mother is like
> someone amassing a fortune.
> Whoever respects his father will be
> happy with children of his own;
> He shall be heard on the day when he prays.
> Long life comes to him who honors his father.
> He who sets his mother at ease is
> showing obedience to the Lord.
> My son, support your father in his old age.
> Do not grieve him during his life.
> Even if his mind should fail, show him sympathy.
> Do not despise him in your health and
> strength; for kindness to a father shall
> not be forgotten but will serve
> as reparation for your sins.

With all the above, however, I pray that we do not become a liability to them.

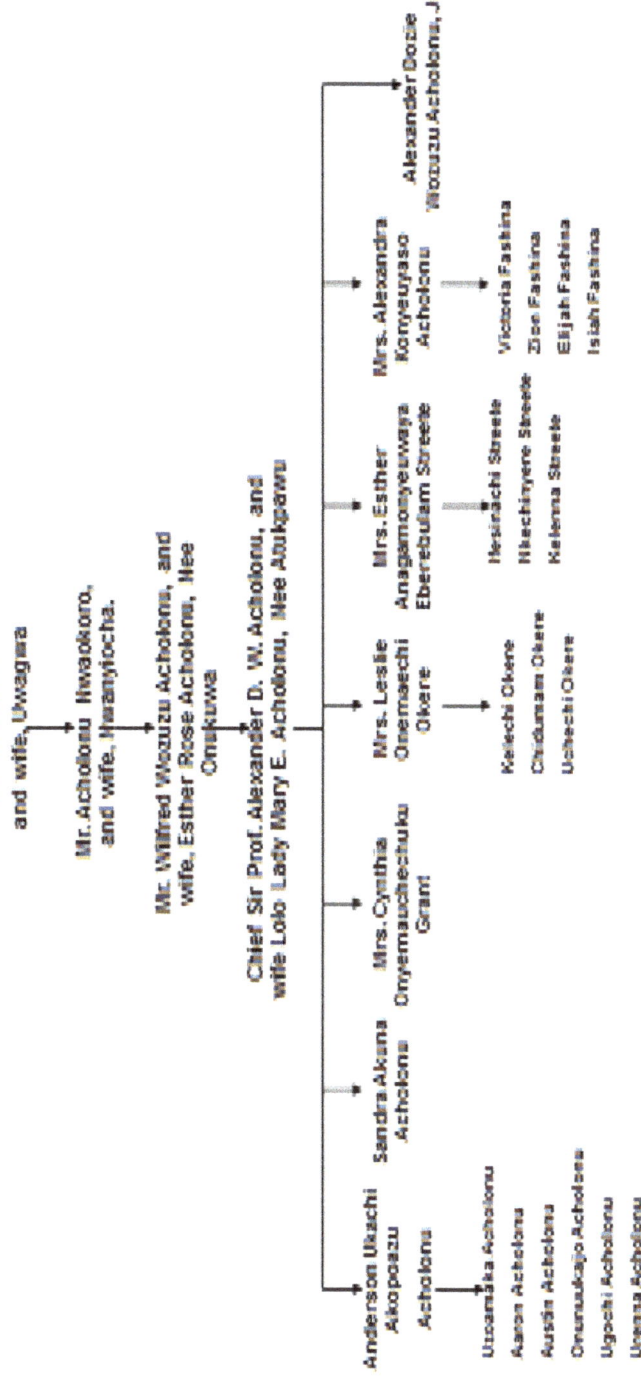

My Journey Through Life

My Father and Mother with their

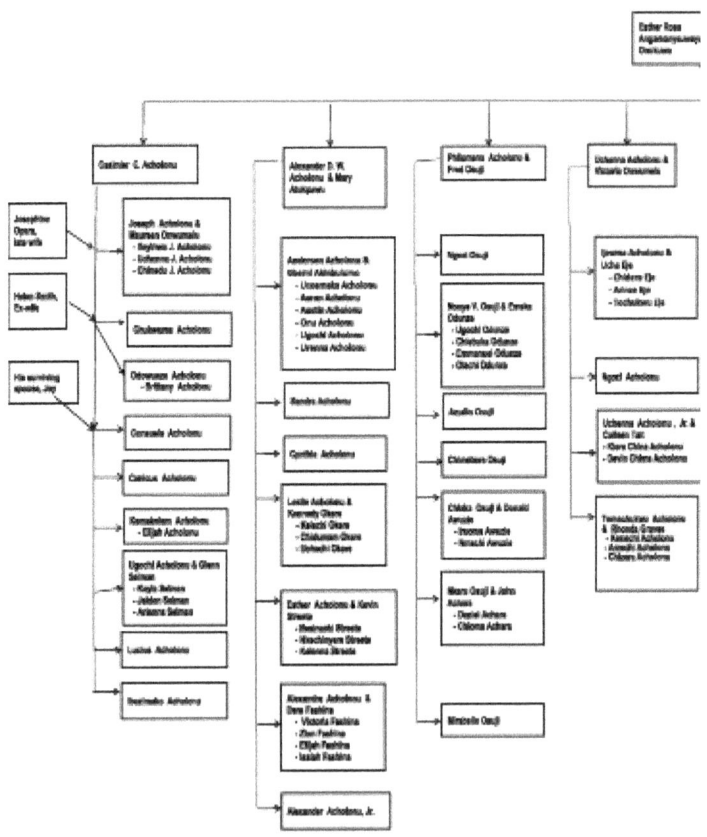

My Family—I am a Husband, Father and Grandfather

1st and 2nd Generations Progenies

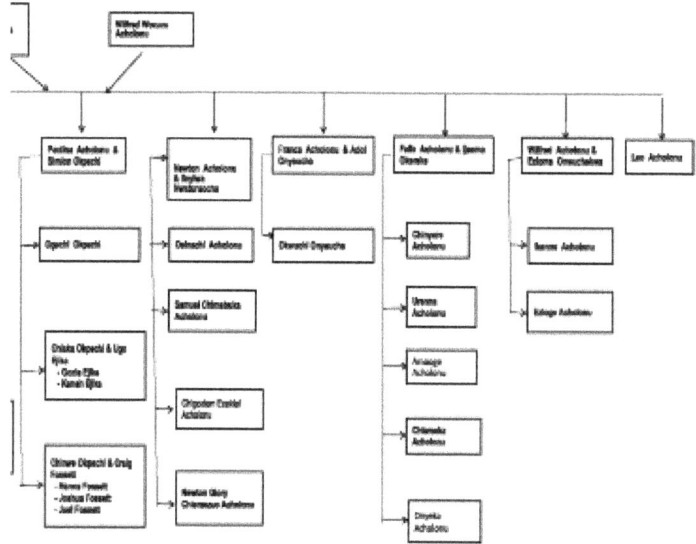

My Journey Through Life

Image of my grandfather Acholonu Nwokoro in 1934. Died in 1936

Mrs. Nwanyiocha Acholonu Nwokoro my grandmother in 1942. Died in 1952

Fig. 4.1: My grandparents, Acholonu Nwokoro and Nwanyiocha

My Family—I am a Husband, Father and Grandfather

Fig. 4.2: My Father, Wilfred Wozuzu and Mother, Esther Rose Acholonu (called "Ekwe-mma" i.e. literally "gong of beauty", by her people because of her exquisite beauty) in their youthful days

Fig. 4.3: My mother and her 12th and last child, Leonard Acholonu

Fig. 4.4: My mother, Esther Rose Acholonu (nee Onukwugha) in her CWO (Catholic Women Organization) uniform. Died Oct. 2000 at age of 92

My Family—I am a Husband, Father and Grandfather

Fig. 4.5: Family Picture with mom and dad: (Middle line left to right) Casimir, Uchenna's Wife, Victoria carrying Uchenna Jr., dad Wilfred W. Acholonu, Esther (first wife), Mary, my wife and baby Leslie, then myself Alexander. (Standing, left to right) Wilfred Jr., Uchenna, Raphael, Newton, Francisca, Joseph, Felix, Oliver (late), Maximian. (Sitting down, left to right) Ngozi, Cynthia, Anderson, Ijeoma, Sandra

These are my dad, Wilfred Acholonu, his first wife, Esther and children in the US by 1975

Fig. 4.6: Young Acholonus coming behind me after my departure for the United States for further education. (Standing left to right) Uchenna, Adolphus (Hitler) (late), Paulina, Francis (late), Jane, Anthony (late), and Sylvester. (Squatting left to right) Caroline, Isabella, Chinyere (late)

My Journey Through Life

Fig. 4.7: Joy, the first lady who wanted me to marry her

Fig. 4.8: My First Fianceé, Alganish, from Ethiopia. I named a parasite after her (*Cercaria alganishi*; Acholonu 1968)

My Family—I am a Husband, Father and Grandfather

Fig. 4.9: My younger brother, Sir Engineer Uchenna Acholonu next to my Financee, Alganish, from left, who lived with me at the time in Baton Rouge, LA. Next to her is Dr. Nicholas Onyewu (late) with whom I shared the same cabin in the ship while coming to America in Dec. 1954. On my right is the Priest who got Alganish and I formally engaged in 1965

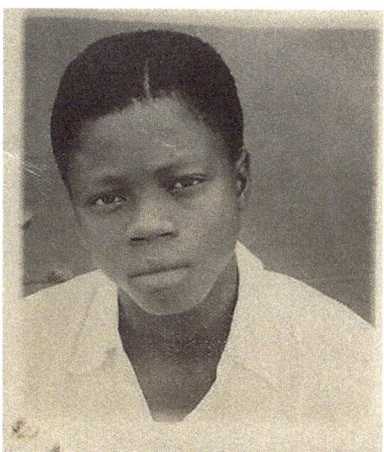

Fig. 4.10: Chief Sir Engineer Uchenna C. Acholonu, my immediate junior brother, next to sister Philomina, when he was very young and who lived with me in Baton Rouge, LA. I brought him to America in 1960

Wedding Pictures (Formal Wedding)

Fig. 4.11: Wedding Picture Mary and Alex Acholonu

My Family—I am a Husband, Father and Grandfather

Fig. 4.12: Wedding Picture Mary and Alex Acholonu. She joined me in Baton Rouge, LA on Jan 16, 1967. We married on March 27, 1967

Fig. 4.13: Wedding Picture Alex Acholonu

Fig. 4.14: Wedding Picture – Mary Acholonu

Fig. 4.15: Wedding Picture Mary Acholonu

My Family—I am a Husband, Father and Grandfather

Fig. 4.16: Wedding Picture—my wife Mary and my sister, Mrs. Paulina Okpechi as one of the bride's maids

Fig. 4.17: Wedding Picture Bride, and groomsmen with Dr. Ben Njoku (left) and my best man, Dr. Moses Nwulia on my right. The others are my Biology Dept. Colleagues

My Journey Through Life

Fig. 4.18: Prof. Acholonu 2nd from left. Dr. Benedict Njoku next to him, Dr. Moses Nwulia, my best man on the left

Fig. 4.19: 2nd from left, Dr. Melvin Clark, the President of Southern University (SU), Baton Rouge L.A. and on the left of Acholonu, Dr. Lewis White, Chair, Dept of Biology, SU

Fig. 4.20: My wife Lolo, Lady Mary E. Acholonu and I in our youthful days shortly after our wedding in 1967

Fig. 4.21: Chief Prof Alex D. W and Lolo Lady. Mary Acholonu. Picture taken after my 70th Birthday, Nov. 30, 2002

Fig. 4.22: Chief Prof Alex, Lolo Lady Mrs. Mary Acholonu and my seven Children. Picture taken after my 70th Birthday, Nov. 30, 2002

My Family—I am a Husband, Father and Grandfather

Fig. 4.23: Anderson Ukachi Akopoazu Acholonu (1st Son)

Fig. 4.24: Sandra Akunna Acholonu (1st Daughter)

Fig. 4.25: Cynthia Onyemaechi Acholonu-Grant (2nd Daughter)

Fig. 4.26: Leslie Onyemauchechukwu Acholonu-Okere (3rd Daughter)

My Journey Through Life

Fig. 4.27: Esther Eberegbulam Acholonu-Streete (4th Daughter)

Fig. 4.28: Alexandra Kaonyeuyoaso Acholonu-Fashina (5th Daughter)

Fig. 4.29: Alexander D. W. Acholonu, Jr. (2nd Son) and last born

Professor Acholonu Grand Children

My Family—I am a Husband, Father and Grandfather

Fig. 4.30: Aaron (left) and Austin (right) (Anderson Acholonu's children)

Fig. 4.31: Urenna, Onu, Ugochi, Amaka (Chikodi) (Anderson Acholonu's children)

Fig. 4.32: Urenna (left), Ugochi (middle), Onu (right) and Amaka (Anderson Acholonu's children)

Fig. 4.33: Kelechi (right), Uchechi (middle), Chidumam (right) (Leslie Okere's Children)

My Family—I am a Husband, Father and Grandfather

Fig. 4.34: High Chief Kennedy Okere MD and Lolo Leslie Okere and their children

Fig. 4.35: Osinachi (left) Kelenna (middle), Nkechinyere (right) (Esther Streete's Children)

My Journey Through Life

Fig. 4.36: (Esther and Kevin Streete's Children)

Fig. 4.37: Esther and Kevin Streete's

Fig. 4.38: Zion (left), Elijah (middle) Victoria (right) and below, Isaiah (Alexandra Fashina's Children)

Fig. 4.39: Prof. Acholonu in his prime of life, 1988

Fig. 4.40: My wife Mary Acholonu on her 50th birthday, April 12, 1999. (Adulthood)

Fig. 4.41: Wedding picture of my senior brother, late Architect Casimir and wife Josephine Acholonu. I brought him to the US in 1961 after the death of his wife at child birth in 1958. He died in May 26, 1991

My Family—I am a Husband, Father and Grandfather

Fig. 4.42: My immediate junior sister, Mrs. Philomina Osuji (1st daughter of my dad) and her husband, Mr. Ferdinand Osuji who wedded at Port Harcourt in 1956. She was nicknamed "Ego-ndu nwaolara iche" (that is, new money that is different) because of her beauty like my mother

Fig. 4.43: The wedding picture of my 2nd Sister Paulina and her husband, Prof. Simeon O. Okpechi who wedded in Baton Rouge LA on July 8, 1967. She joined me in Baton Rouge from Nigeria on Dec. 24, 1964

Fig. 4.44: Mrs. Paulina Okpechi, my second sister next to bother Uchenna who lived with me at Enugu, Nigeria before my departure to US in 1954 and in Baton Rouge, LA before she married in July 1967. I brought her to the US on Dec. 24, 1964

Fig. 4.45: My Third and youngest sister with her wedded husband, Mr. Adolphus Onyeuche who wedded in New York in August 1986 in my presence

My Journey Through Life

Fig. 4.46: My immediate younger brother, Chief Sir Engr. Uchenna Acholonu that I fully sponsored to come to the USA in 1960 and for whom I sacrificed a lot that helped make him what he is today; a brother on whom I demonstrated true love; a brother who on two occasions, publically, called me "the Christopher Columbus of the Acholonu family", and his wife, Lolo Lady Victoria N. Acholonu

My Family—I am a Husband, Father and Grandfather

Fig. 4.47: Dr. Felix Acholonu, a misinformed brother I love so much, a brother I gave the name he bears, Felix; a brother I chose his field of study, medicine, and helped him to get into the medical school; a brother for whom I obtained Nigerian Federal Government Scholarship while in the medical school, among other things. A computer science person turned medical doctor, a man, with God on my side, I helped to make what he is today, and his wife Ijeoma

My Journey Through Life

Fig. 4.48: Dr. Willie W. Acholonu Jr., a brother I love very much, a brother I brought to America in 1974, a brother I nurtured and helped shape his future and has openly and privately shown appreciation for what I did for him, and his wife, Ezioma

Fig. 4.49: Engr. Maximian Nnamdi Acholonu, my junior brother, who lived with me in Washington DC. He was the very first Acholonu son I brought to the US after he finished secondary school at Washington Grammar School, Onitsha where I put him. Fig. A (2nd from left) shows how little he was when I put him in secondary school at Onitsha. Fig. B shows him when he came to the US in September 1959. He is the first son of my father's second wife, Grace, that I brought to the US to demonstrate unity and sincere brotherly love

Fig. 4.50: Late Mr. Adolphus ("Hitler") Acholonu, another junior brother I brought to the US in 1962. He was the first son of my father's 3rd wife, Mezi. He became sick and had to be taken back to Nigeria where he later died

A

B

Fig. 4.51: Dr. Kenny Uzoma Acholonu, President and CEO, Bioorganic Co, Lagos, Nigeria, the first son of Uncle Sir Cyril Acholonu.

a. This is the way he looked when I brought him to the US on March 14, 1965 b. This is the way he looks at present; a scientist; a successful business man

My Journey Through Life

Fig. 4.52: Chief Prof. Alex Acholonu and wife Lolo Mary E. Acholonu with his younger brothers and their wives during his 80th birthday celebration in Vicksburg, MS in Nov. 2012 namely: Felix Acholonu, MD and his wife Ijeoma (left), Wilfred W. Acholonu Jr. Pharm D and wife Ezioma (right)

Chapter Five

Academics and Professional Development

Upon graduation from Colorado State University, I got an appointment to teach at Alcorn State University, Mississippi and this was supposed to start in the summer session of 1964. I accepted the offer and went there. But I later received two other appointments. One was as Chair of the Natural Sciences Department at Atlanta University in Atlanta, GA. It came with big money—$13, 000 per annum at the time. The other was an appointment at Southern University in Baton Rouge to teach for $8, 800 per annum. It happened that there is a brother of mine that I had brought from home and I wanted him to study Engineering. To enter the Engineering School of Howard University, one had to have a certain Grade Point Average which he did not quite have. So for love of my brother, I sacrificed the position in Atlanta, took a job at Southern University, Baton Rouge so as to enable my brother, Uchenna Cletus Acholonu, (Fig. 4.5. 4.6, 4.9, 4.10, 4.46, 6.24) to get into the Engineering School there.

So I left Alcorn State University at the end of the summer session, a smaller institution with no Engineering School and went to Southern University at Baton Rouge which has a School of Engineering and Architecture. It also enabled me to get Casmir, my senior brother, admitted to study Architecture. Casmir worked as a draftsman in Enugu, Nigeria before I brought him over to America, hence I put him in this field. I joined the Biology Department as an Associate Professor and taught General Zoology. I also designed a Parasitology course there because there wasn't any when I got there. My design of the course almost caused a problem between me and another colleague of mine there, who was also a very good friend. His name was Dr. Louis Scott. He got his Ph.D. in Parasitology just as myself but he did not teach it before I arrived. After I designed it, he now wanted to be the one to teach the course. The chairman of the department, Dr. Lewis White (Fig.

4.19) did not handle it well. In any case, I was eventually allowed to teach the course. I also taught Human Anatomy and Physiology and Invertebrate Zoology.

While at Baton Rouge, I got involved heavily in research work. I must have sacrificed (killed) about 150 turtles during my research work on parasites of turtles. My work resulted in the discovery and identification of several parasites that were not known to science at that time. The practice in the Sciences is that whenever a scientist discovers or identifies something new, he has the freedom to name it whatever he or she wishes. So it became my prerogative to do so in my own case and it felt good having to be associated with newness and invention. So I described and named several parasites. One of the students that assisted me in my research was a graduate student, Rev. Sister Mary Joy Haywood (Fig. 5.15.3). We became so close that I paid her a visit in Philadelphia PA from where she came to Southern University. My research and teaching resulted in my getting promoted to the rank of Full Professor in 1968. I stayed at Baton Rouge from 1964 until 1969.

In one of our annual meetings of the American Society of Parasitologists, I met a friend by the name Dr. Ira Jones who was teaching in Puerto Rico. He said that he would recommend me to come and teach at Inter American University (or Inter Americana) in San German, Puerto Rico as he was about to leave and go back to the U.S. He was about to take a teaching position in California. He did and eventually, I was invited to come and teach there. I took the position because I wanted to get experience in tropical Biology before returning to Nigeria. I wanted to get exposed to the Puerto Rican environment because it was like Nigeria in many ways. However, the offer was not a full professorial rank; I was somehow depressed but anxious to leave Southern University. So I took the confidence that I would work hard and get back to full professor level. I worked on sea turtles *(Hawk's bill turtle, Erythmoceles imbricata imbricata)* (Fig. 5.14) as my research there. I went to fishermen and got intestine of sea turtles. I worked long hours and hard examining the intestines and processing the recovered parasites. Just as I expressed confidence and resolve, it did not take long before I was made a full professor. This came after one year of work there. So I again got back my full professional rank and in addition was made the Chairman of the Department of Biology in San Juan campus of the University. I stayed at Inter Americana until 1972 when a position opened up in the Catholic University of Puerto Rico and I had a disagreement with the Dean at Interamerican University. I applied and was hired. I was teaching one day in class when a message came that I had a phone call in the Dean's office. The Dean then and I were very good friends—so much so that I made him the godfather of my second daughter, Cynthia. When I took the call, a man from the State University of New York, SUNO in Oneonta, New York, said that they would like to consider me for the position of Dean of Liberal Studies at their University. I was surprised because it was an unexpected offer. I wondered if it was a joke or a serious business. So I told the caller that if he was serious, he should call me at home. I gave him my home number. I did this for another reason too. In addition to wanting to assure myself that it was real, I also could not speak while the Dean, my friend, was there; because I thought he would not entertain the idea of my trying to leave the University.

Later, I was called at home and asked to come for an interview. I flew to the University and was interviewed by several groups on campus. There, the students, faculty, and administrators, all took turns to meet with me and asked me questions. At one point someone asked that if there became a problem between students and the administration, on whose side would I be? I told him I would be coming in as an administrator and as such would be naturally on the side of the administration. I believe the President loved that answer. When the interview sessions were over and I left, I felt that I would not get the job. My elder brother, Casimir, and my wife thought otherwise. I just thought they were trying their best to be supportive. A week later I got a phone call informing me that I got the job. It was an uplifting news. I was also informed that I would make $25, 000 per annum. That was not in any way comparable to the $10, 000 I was making at the time. Wow! My wife said, "I told you so."

This development resulted in my having to move in 1973 from Puerto Rico back to the USA in a rather triumphant and jubilant way, to become the Dean of Liberal Studies (Arts and Sciences) at SUNO. I was in that position until 1977. Meanwhile, I was also longing to return to Nigeria. To give a matching determination to my urge to return to Nigeria, in 1975, I visited the College of Medicine, University of Lagos (CMUL) and made inquiries about a position there when I went to bring home my parents who stayed with me and my brother, Engineer Uchenna Acholonu (Fig. 4.5. 4.6, 4.9, 4.10, 4.46, 6.24), for about a year. I returned to SUNO, and did not really give serious thought to the inquiry I had made at CMUL. However, soon after the visit, I received a letter from Lagos asking me if I would like to join the faculty at the University's College of Medicine. I looked at it and put it aside. Then another letter came from the same university, this time inviting me to come and join the College. This had been the history of my career; most positions I took came on invitation not by application. I had also inquired about teaching at the Alvan Ikoku College of Education at Owerri. They invited me to take appointment as a Principal Lecturer. They said that they would make me a Dean shortly after but it was senseless to give that consideration, since I would lose my professorship rank.

My father died the following year in 1976. I had written him a letter to inform him that I had received two appointments to teach at CMUL and at Alvan Ikoku College of education, asking him which one he would recommend for me to accept. He never got to read that letter. He died before it could get to him, Meanwhile my brothers and I here in the US decided that we would all relocate to Nigeria and started what we called "operation go home". Since my brother Casmir had got an appointment as an architect with the Imo State Ministry of Works and Housing, and being the first born, (Opara) at the time, it was more fitting for him to be closer to home. So I recommended to him to stay in Owerri while I accept the position at the University of Lagos. That was how I made the decision to join the Faculty of the College of Medicine at the University of Lagos, popularly known as CMUL/LUTH (Lagos University Teaching Hospital) in 1977 after the death of my father.

I started work at CMUL as a Professor. The Head of department I was going to be part of, Department of Medical Microbiology and Parasitology, actually tried to make me come in as a Senior Lecturer, but the Provost of the College of Medicine at the time, Prof. Dosekun, told the head of the Department that it made no sense to bring someone with my background and credentials as a senior lecturer. So they brought me on board as a Full Professor. I later found out that the Provost did not get along with the Head of Department, so he (the Provost) was only glad to enable the Department employ someone who was at par in rank with the Head of Department. This same Head of Department was also the one that had tried to discredit Prof. Njoku Obi, who had discovered the anti-cholera vaccine in the 1970s, Professor Ogumbi. University of Lagos came with its own excitement and challenges. Needless to say that Nigeria is different from the US and it is expected that anyone who relocates must be ready for a total adjustment and even readjustment. So it would be with me. College of Medicine, University of Lagos is a part of the entire University of Lagos, with administrative headquarters at Akoka, Yaba, Lagos, even though it is located in IdiAraba, Surulere. The College is however, semi-autonomous because it has its own 'parochial' administration, headed by the Provost and there is also the College Secretary. Then there are the heads (Chairs) of departments. My department, Medical Microbiology and Parasitology, is one of such departments. Generally, headship of departments is rotational. A substantive head of department has a three year tenure after which another senior member of the department, in fact, the next to the previous, in seniority, takes over. This explains why I had to take over as head of department after the one who sat there completed his term and I was a full Professor. It was extremely difficult for me to serve as a Head of Department because of the hostility I faced from some of my Yoruba Colleagues. Being Igbo, I was not fully regarded as one of them, so they were not happy that I had taken over from a Yoruba Head of Department. I was to catch more hell when I instituted a system of meritocracy in the affairs of the department, which overshadowed ethnic consciousness. This was one of the most uncomfortable positions I had found myself in my long career in academics.

While I was working in the College of Medicine of the University of Lagos, I dedicated my life to academics once more. However, within the period I was there and, in my house one day, a delegation came from Imo State to see me. Actually it was from the government of the State with Chief Sam Mbakwe as the Governor. The delegation informed me that I was going to be appointed the Rector of a new college of technology, the second one in Imo State. I was thus being asked to relocate to Imo State to head it. It was Governor Sam Mbakwe that held the attraction for me. I think he was a good governor so I accepted the offer and asked for a leave of absence from University of Lagos and it was granted. This was in 1983.

I want to make a little digression here. I already started talking about Governor Sam Mbakwe. He was the first governor to think about higher education in Imo State with a measure of seriousness. Well, the politics of the establishment of Imo State University is not my concern but I must say that I was also in the picture. I certainly was not part of any policy that made its establishment a reality but I was among those who advised Mbakwe to establish the Imo State University. When he did, I also aspired and applied to be the Vice Chancellor of the University. The competition for the position of Vice Chancellor, was fierce I suppose, but it eventually came down to between Professor Echeruo and I. Echeruo's brother happened to be a well-known politician and a prominent member of Governor

Mbakwe's party. He was a Senator. Even though my credentials may have been superior, other factors came in to play in the choice of Echeruo as the first Vice Chancellor of Imo State University. He was certainly closer to the political class than I was. Since I did not get the Vice Chancellorship, I asked Governor Mbakwe to let me come home and teach at the university. Mbakwe asked Echeruo to bring me in as a Dean but the new Vice Chancellor apparently saw me as a threat to him at the university. So I did not get an offer even after I personally spoke to him. The same thing happened when the Federal University of Technology came to Owerri. I was recommended for a position there, but the Vice Chancellor, Prof. Gonwalk was also very concerned about the superior credentials I brought and I was not to be considered. This is a major issue with people who have my kind of background and experience. Such people constantly, though inadvertently, pose a threat to others in their profession.

I assumed a position as the Rector of Amaigbo College of Technology in 1983 and was there when the military struck the coup of 1983/84. It was a very unique coup because it coincided with the end of the year. The coup ousted the elected leaders. Governor Sam Mbakwe and his colleagues left governance for the military. Then Brigadier General Ike Nwachukwu was appointed Military Governor of Imo State. I do not know whether to say that the removal of Mbakwe or the appointment of Ike Nwachukwu introduced problems in the educational system in Imo State. The major concern is that Amaigbo College of Technology was proscribed by Ike Nwachukwu. Imo indigenes were deprived the opportunity of an institution of higher learning, which they needed very much. I was not going to be involved in the deep political intrigues which shrouded the proscription of the College. But I understand that Amaigbo people had problems with their neighbors, the Nkwere people. The Nkwere people had links in Ike Nwachukwu's Government and were able to convince him to dissolve Amaigbo College of Technology. When this happened, I left Amaigbo and returned to the University of Lagos, College of Medicine.

Shortly after I returned to the University of Lagos, there was a vacancy for the position of Vice Chancellor at the University. A delegation was sent to me from the university asking if I would be interested in applying. I was convinced that they really did not want an Igbo to become the Vice Chancellor. I remembered what happened to Eni Njoku at the same university. He was driven away from UNILAG when it was obvious he was the most qualified to be Vice Chancellor in the 1960s. I said "no" to the delegation, I told them that I was not interested, and the joy in their faces was palpable. I saw the handwriting on the wall and chose to take a sabbatical leave from UNILAG when I found that I was eligible to do so. This became the beginning of my relocation back to the US.

I left UNILAG for no particular place. I arrived in the US without having received a teaching appointment from any institution at all. However, shortly after I got to the US, I got a teaching job at my *alma mater,* Howard University, in Washington, DC. While I was teaching there during my sabbatical, I was offered a position to teach at the George Washington University, also in Washington, DC. So I was teaching part-time at Howard, part-time at George Washington, and part-time at the University of the District of Columbia (UDC). I feel I should express my gratitude to God because I came back to the US with nothing, and within months I had three teaching positions simultaneously. Howard eventually offered me a permanent teaching position in 1990 while I was on sabbatical leave. I wrote UNILAG to allow me to take the position but the authorities of the University denied my request. The reason given was that my request was contrary to the conditions of a sabbatical leave, part of which is that one on such a leave was required to return to his university of employment and serve for at least, a year before taking any other appointment. Since I am primarily employed by the UNILAG as at that time, I had no choice but to return. I deliberately chose not to violate the

Academics and Professional Development

terms, so I declined the offer of Howard University and returned to UNILAG at the elapse of the sabbatical leave.

After completing the mandatory one year after sabbatical leave in UNILAG, I took another leave, this time a leave of absence and then used it to return to the US. While I was on leave I received an offer to teach at Alcorn State University in Mississippi. I contemplated resigning from UNILAG and taking the Alcorn job. The College Secretary at the time, Mr. Nwabudike, advised me to retire instead, so that I would get my pension. I took his advice. I am glad I did and I am up till now receiving my pension. So, I gave a 6-month notice of retirement to UNILAG and took up the appointment at Alcorn State University. I have been teaching at Alcorn since 1991. It may be apropos to recount how I went to Alcorn State University. While I was in Washington DC/Maryland, I had earlier applied to teach at Alcorn State University but got a negative response from an Acting Chairman of the Department of Biology. I had prayed to God to go and teach there to end my academic career where I started it in the summer of 1964. With the negative response, I forgot all about teaching there with the feeling that God did not answer my prayer. Some months later, one day, I received a phone call like the one I received when I was in Puerto Rico to come and be Dean of Liberal Studies at SUNO. I was told to come for interview for a teaching position there in the Department of Biology. I said that I did not have money to fly down there. I was told to go to the Washington DC airport and pick up my ticket on the day I was requested to come. I did and flew there for interview. A week after I returned, I was sent a letter of appointment as a full Professor. This is how I went and started teaching at Alcorn a second time in October 1991. So God answered my prayer eventually!

I got my highest professional or academic position in 1997 when the Military Administrator of Imo State, Colonel T.K. Zubairu (Fig. 5.10), appointed me the Pro-Chancellor and Chairman of Governing Council of Imo State University. I returned home from the USA for Christmas. A delegation was sent to me to come to the Government house for appointment. I thought that it was for Vice-Chancellor and did not care for that position. The delegation came a second time and said that it was not for Vice-Chancellor. So I went. There, I was offered the position of Pro-Chancellor and Chairman of Governing Council of Imo State University much to my surprised. So I accepted the position (Fig. 5.11-13). I must observe that I continued doing research and publishing irrespective of the academic administrative positions I held. (Fig. 5.5-9) I have been an avid researcher and a willing educationist and have achieved much in this area. They are my forte and I shall continue till I cannot do them anymore. Success is a journey not a destination. There is no resting for us until rest in God (Fig. 5.15).

I am contemplating on retiring at the end of the spring semester of 2018 (May 2018). This will mean my having taught from the summer of 1964 as a freshman PhD at Alcorn State University to spring of 2018 (a period of 54 years). This gives me a sense of great accomplishment, a fulfillment of my goal to end my academic career at the institution where I started it. I have the conviction that God answered my prayer. I have enjoyed my long sojourn at Alcorn State University and all the accolades and recognitions I had while here and the reputation of the university I helped to augment especially being the first professor in the history of the University to get the Mississippi Academy of Sciences (MAS) Award for Distinguished Contribution of Science on February 23, 2012, among others. I loudly sing the Alcorn Ode as I take my exit from this institution in which I put in 27 years of sincere and devoted service.

Academics and Professional Development

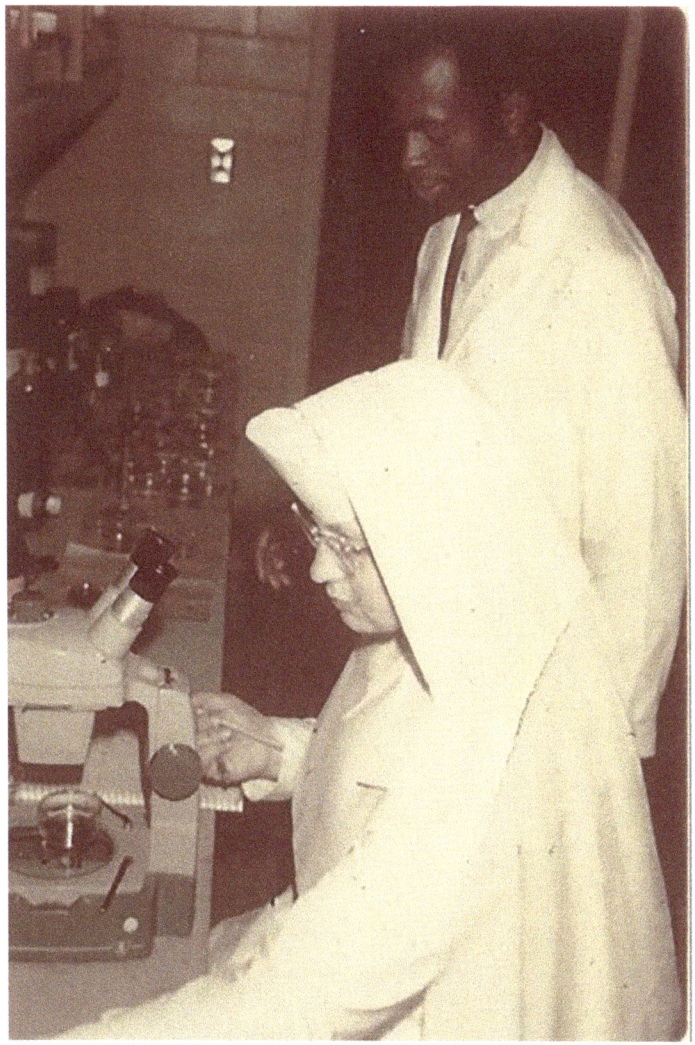

Fig. 5.1: Research with Rev. Sister Mary Joy Haywood from Philadelphia, 1966, a summer program graduate student

My Journey Through Life

Fig. 5.2: Alex Acholonu with Rev. Sister Mary Joy Haywood at a visit to her in Philadelphia

Fig. 5.3: Alex Acholonu's visit to Rev. Sister Mary Joy Haywood and her fellow Sisters in Philadelphia

Academics and Professional Development

Fig. 5.4: Left to Right—Lolo Mary Acholonu, Dr. Clinton Bristow (late), 16th President of Alcorn State University (ASU) and Chief Prof. Alex Acholonu. Picture taken after ASU faculty and staff Xmas party, Dec. 2002. Acholonu as Chief and Professor at ASU and later, President of ASU Faculty Senate

Fig. 5.5: Professor Acholonu lecturing students at Huaiyin University in China. May 20–June 5, 2005

My Journey Through Life

Fig. 5.6: Prof. Acholonu (3rd from right side) in conference with members of the Department of Biology of Huaiyin University in China answering questions from them. May 20–June 5, 2005

Fig. 5.7: Prof. Acholonu and some students from Huaiyin University where he taught and conducted research on water pollution in China. May 20–June 5, 2005

Fig. 5.8: Professor Acholonu doing research with students on the parasites of Cat Fish at Alcorn State University in October 2016

Fig. 5.9: Professor Acholonu on Ecology Education Workshop Field Trip as Director of Ecology Education Program Alcorn State University, summer of 2013

Fig. 5.10: COLONEL T.K. ZUBAIRU, FSS, psc Military Administrator, Imo State The person that appointed Prof Acholonu as the third ProChancellor and Chairman of Counsel, Imo State University

Academics and Professional Development

Fig. 5.11: Prof. Acholonu in academic graduation regalia as Pro-Chancellor of Imo State University and Chairman of Governing Council 1997-1999 appointed by the Military Administrator, Colonel Tanko K. Zubairu. Picture taken after the graduation exercise of 1998

My Journey Through Life

Fig. 5.12: The Vice Chancellor Prof. Thomas Ndubuizu and another Prof. helping Prof. Acholonu to put on his Pro-chancellor Academic Regalia

Academics and Professional Development

Fig. 5.13: Acholonu as Pro-Chancellor and Chairman of Governing Council of Imo State University with Governing Council members including 2nd to my right, Eze Emmanule Njemanze of Owerri (late), next to me by the right, Prof. Ndubuizu, Vice Chancellor, 1997

Fig. 5.14: Found, described and named fourteen new species of parasites (8 from the hawksbill sea turtle) *(Eretmochelys imbricata imbricata)* and six from several species of snails)

My Journey Through Life

Fig. 5.15: Prof. Alex Acholonu doing what he does best working (doing research)

Chapter Six

My Titles, Affiliations and Laurels

Traditional Titles

Over the years, I have received both titles and laurels in diverse forms. I want to revisit them, though in no particular order. I have mentioned or discussed some of my academic involvements of which many have been commended as laudable and I will ever remain grateful to God that whatever I am today, He has made it possible through a sustained favor. He has favored me in my academic career. I have been fortunate to attract the attention of my people and even other people around me. As a result of that, I also have been conferred with three traditional titles, about which I am delighted and excited. Essentially, the first one is Ogbuhoruzo 1 of Amaigbo and Awaka (Fig. 6.1–6.5). The title has an interesting background. I happened to be the first Rector of Amaigbo College of Technology (ACOT), which was established by Imo State Government when Chief Sam Mbakwe was the Executive Governor. Amaigbo is in the Orlu Senatorial zone. It is an ancient town with rich tradition and a handful of industrious citizens. Apparently, they were traditionally traders and farmers with a few who could fish because they have a river, the Nwangele River. I was appointed by the Government as the pioneer Rector of the college and I served until 1984. It is unfortunate that the college did not survive the year 1984 because the civil administration which Governor Sam Mbakwe was a part of was ousted by a military coup d' etat. Brigadier General Ike Nwachukwu was appointed the Military Governor of Imo State. His regime, which was supposed to be military, came with an unimaginable politicking. Virtually all aspects of life were affected. Education was equally a victim of the sad politics.

Amaigbo College of Technology was caught in between. Added to this was a lifelong rivalry between Amaigbo people and their neighbors of Nkwere. Amaigbo people felt that they are the owners of the land and that Nkwere people are migrants that came into the area. It happened that the Nkwere people were more in Government than the Amaigbo people and thus were apparently able to influence the military governor. Whether this was what happened or not, the reality is that the Military Governor came up with the lame excuse that there was no money in the state to continue with the maintenance of this important institution. The College of Technology, Amaigbo became a victim. It was phased out. So, when this was done, I went back to College of Medicine, University of Lagos.

I understand that people go an extra mile in order to get appointed to Government positions like heads of institutions and parastatals but I did not know that, and I did not do anything; I did not also consult anyone nor did I ask for the particular job of the head of the new Polytechnic. I was literally invited by Governor Sam Mbakwe's administration to take up the position as the pioneer Rector of Amaigbo College of Technology. The truth is that a delegation was sent to me in Lagos from Owerri to inform me of the decision of the government as stated above. I accepted and assumed office almost immediately. This was toward the end of the second Republic and that was why the college did not last long.

On getting to Amaigbo, I fell in love with the people. I think this was mutual because they showed me what I perceived as love. The demonstrations of both the people and their royalty, His Royal Highness Eze W.C. Nwosu, the Igbo I of Amaigbo were clear indications of love. I had a short period with them as the Rector of the College of Technology in their place, but the relationship that came out of that short period would be everlasting. So after the closure of the College, and I returned to the College of Medicine University of Lagos, I later got a letter that Eze in counsel and cabinet of the Eze, want to confer on me a traditional (Chieftaincy) title. I was truly surprised, but it was going to be a concrete confirmation of the love that I spoke about, which exists between the people of Amaigbo and myself. I accepted the offer, with gratitude because it is a great honor. I went for it cheerfully and I suppose many of my relations and friends thought that it was not out of place but a great and benefiting recognition.

Such an honor as the one I was going to get, naturally requires an appropriate, or should one say, a befitting title. We cogitated about the title that I would take from the Eze Amaigbo, Igbo of Amaigbo. I wanted the title to be meaningful and to be related to my personal life; my contributions to the world. Charity, they say, begins at home so I started looking inwards to assess myself. I am the first in my family to go to America, and because I did, about a hundred eighty Acholonus are in America today. So I literally opened the gate for them to go to America. Therefore, I wanted a title that would do justice to that history. After considering a few options, we (Eze and I) agreed on a title that will reflect that pioneer status. That is how I got the title of *Ogbuhoruzo 1 of Amaigbo and Awaka* (Fig. 6.1–6.5). As a matter of fact, my brother, Engr. Uchenna C. Acholonu (Fig. 4.5. 4.6, 4.9, 4.10, 4.46, 6.24) at one public occasion, called me the "Christopher Columbus of the Acholonu family." The title literally means "pathfinder." I opened the path to America for the Acholonus. All of the Acholonus in America came through me, directly or indirectly. I had something to do with their coming to America. I opened the gate to America for them.

Amaigbo will continue to be fresh in my memory and the Eze who saw me as worthy of being honored, I will always remember with fondness. I got to know Eze Nwosu, the Igbo of Amaigbo when I was the Rector of Amaigbo College of Technology. We developed a very good relationship and I found out that he was a great football (soccer) player and played with one of my uncles that is about a year older than me—now Chief Barrister Patrick O. Acholonu. Their relationship was close and that also brought us closer. We exchanged visits then, but it was going to be just that until I was told that he wanted to honor me with a chieftaincy title.

Eze Nwosu was a good-natured man. He told me that he was a Policeman, apart from being a great football (soccer) player. His father was the Eze of Amaigbo and as the first son, he ascended the throne of his father after his death. While I was there at Amaigbo, he was kind and friendly and did not restrict me to the College alone. Because of the sense of freedom and cordiality I enjoyed I got involved with few other things in the community. The great Jaja of Opobo was actually born in Amaigbo. I found where King Jaja of Opobo lived and checked it out. Jaja of Opobo was sold to Opobo where he became a King. This is an interesting historical issue and I said this should become a place for tourists to come and visit. I was planning to make it a tourist attraction until Military Governor Ike Nwachukwu came and truncated the whole idea and plan. I do not think anybody has done anything about my interest and the idea to date.

Apart from this idea, it was clear to the Eze and the entire Amaigbo people that I was enthusiastic about making Amaigbo College of Technology one of the best in the country. They knew that I had the experience and the expertise to do so. I had served as the Dean of Liberal Studies (Arts and Science) at the State University of New York. I already initiated a meeting with the Commissioner for Education in Imo State at the time (Prof. Adiele Afikbo) and given him a good plan on how I would run the college and raise money to run the college and work on the Jaja of Opobo project. Then I contacted the President of the State University of New York, Oneonta where I served as Dean and sought his help and he agreed to be of help.

After all the presentations, the commissioner, Prof. Adiele Afikpo, instead of appreciating what I was saying and wanted to do, apparently got jealous perhaps of my plan to make the place succeed or was averse to the colleges success. It clearly looked to me like the government did not want the place to succeed, and so they did not go along with my plans. Ike Nwachukwu, the Military Governor, still came with an excuse of financial constraints and went ahead to close the college. It seems to me that the Amaigbo people appreciated what I did and gave my name as one of the people they wanted the Eze to recognize. This was apart from the fact that the Eze himself knew me well and liked me. There were other people that were pleased with what I was doing. We became personal friends and each time I went home, I found time to go and visit them. There was also Dr. Laz Ihekwoazu, the Medical Director of Federal University of Technology, Owerri from Amaigbo and an ex-student of CKC like me. He was wonderful and kind to me. We got very close to each other after. He was very helpful.

The conferment was a unique event. I do not think there is a blueprint on that awesome traditional event in Igboland. From what I know so far, it varies from place to place and time to time. Sometimes, either the conferring body or the recipient will create the system; in fact both can work together and make the event into what they want. In my own case, I had a bit of preparations before the actual day. I live far from the place where the conferring authorities were, so I had to return. That is, I had to return from the US where I am resident. I also come from a different senatorial zone, and Local Government Area (LGA) from the authorities who were to honor me. As a result of all these, there were needs for me to do some preliminary work. Quite important, in the line of affairs, is the necessity of informing my Umunna, my kith and kin. I went to all the Alaenyi Ezes in Owerri North LGA and told them to join me to receive the honor from Amaigbo. I went to Eze Njemanze of Owerri, Eze Nwankwere of Ihitta Ogada, the Eze of Naze, who was then an interim Eze of Naze, then to Eze Egbukole, Ochoronma of Egbu. All of these are now late. They responded positively to me and we all went *en masse* to Amaigbo. It was a very great day, a day of pump and pageantry!

Before the conferment of the title on me, my curriculum vitae (CV) was presented. People were held spellbound by the content of my CV. Many people from Awaka, men and women, were present. There were intermittent reverberating acclamations from them as my CV was read. They were part of the convoy that escorted me to Amaigbo for chieftaincy conferment. They sang and danced. It was hilarious and impressive, and indeed quite difficult to forget.

Interacting with traditional authorities can be demanding. One must be patient because in some cases, the protocol is long and in other cases there are other challenges. One cannot go to an Eze empty handed. The Owerri people know this and it is covered by their proverb: "ejela agbala aka ahu nwa amuru ohuru eze." Literally, one does not see the first (milk) teeth of a baby empty handed. This means that there are costs attached to acts, actions and interactions. As a matter of fact, some interactions are very expensive. Interacting with Ezes is one of such. Ezes are highly respected traditional institutions and when I went to see them, I did not go empty handed. I took drinks and supported the drinks with money. It is the way such things are done. The palace of the Eze is a dignified place and must be respected. There are always reasons to support paying homage to the Ezes. In my own case, they needed to fuel their vehicles to travel to Amaigbo and to show appreciation as they honored my invitation. So the least I could do was to lend a hand of financial support and appreciation. All the Ezes, but the Naze monarch came and I am still grateful to all of them.

I took a mental note of the proceedings during the occasion. The costumes were impressive. I had to settle those ahead of time. There were other prerequisites that I also fulfilled. I gave a big nnama (llama) and supported that with some money. There were other things, the things I could afford and voluntarily. My costume or regalia conformed to the traditional attire of the chiefs. I was not to wear any other thing apart from my robe until I was conferred with the title (see Fig. 6.1). In fact, the Eze personally adorned me with all the paraphernalia of office after the palace orator (Barr. Ihekwoazu) had read my resume and testimonial of good character to justify the honor.

While the conferment was in session, dance troupes, which accompanied me, were stationed at strategic places outside the main bowl of the palace (Obi Eze) where they entertained the audience. After that main event, we all moved, in a convoy, from Amaigbo to Awaka where a huge entertainment awaited everyone. I was the celebrant and the honored. I was happy to entertain all guests. We used the space at Awaka Holy Trinity Catholic Church compound for the reception and the entertainment went very well. I brought dance troupes that entertained everyone at the place of conferment and at Awaka.

During the title conferment, the Eze of Egbu, late Eze Mitchell Egbukole was selected to speak on behalf of his follow Ezes. By the way, Egbu people don't believe in chieftaincy titles, so he did mention it and talked about himself and Egbu people according me honor in the future. But had he stayed alive for a longer time, he probably would have tried to change that custom of Egbu people—a custom that forbids chieftaincy titles and does not allow anybody from Egbu to become a chief. Maybe in the absence of chieftaincy title, he probably might have recognized me the way they recognize other prominent sons and daughters of theirs and others. He would have also perhaps made effort to change it because traditions can be changed. This first chieftaincy conferment took place on the 24th day of December, 1992 (Fig. 6.1) and was bestowed along with several others one of which was Dr. Ofonagoro of Amaigho a former NTA (Nigeria Television Authority) Chairman.

In 2002, I was privileged to receive another honor of the same magnitude, a second chieftaincy title. It was a follow-up to the first. Its background was quite interesting. After the Ezes from Ala-enyi, my clan, honored my invitation and followed me to Amaigbo to receive the title of Ogbuhoruzo 1 of Amaigbo, (Fig. 6.1–6.5) I made it a point of duty to pay homage to them individually whenever I visited home from the US and it is convenient. I was not going to be tired of expressing my gratitude to them. Many times, I would go home from the US and visit them individually and make presents of drinks and money to them. I was not expecting anything in return; it was just a continued act of appreciation. It was after one such visit to Eze Nwankwere of Ihitta Ogada that he paid me a return visit and said "Prof., I want to consider you as one of the people to be conferred a title during the forth-coming anniversary of my coronation." He said that he, as the Eze of his community, was allowed to select one person to be conferred chieftaincy title and I was the one he wanted to select.

His overture did not appear serious to me at first. On my next trip back home, he made another visit to me and renewed the offer of conferment of title to me. Then seeing the seriousness of the matter, and his sincerity, I accepted the offer and in Dec. 24, 2002, I was conferred with the title and I went through the same process and ceremony just like the first. We went in a convoy to the celebration venue which was in Saint Kyrain's Catholic Church premises. Nicholas Ejiogu of Awaka, read my biography as Fr. Valentine Acholonu who had accepted to read it was unable to come and other things followed: dancing and singing by men, women and children and I was conferred along with several others with the title, 'Ekwueme 1 of Ihitta Ogada and Awaka.' (Fig. 6.5–6.8). We traveled back to Awaka in a convoy and celebrated the conferment at the Holy Trinity Catholic Church, Awaka as we did before.

I must say that I did not choose the title; I got it as an alternative to my desired title, which is "Oka-Omee". It was because the title, Oka-Omee had already been taken that I settled for "Ekwueme". Both titles mean basically the same thing: 'A man of his words; a man who does what he says.' It is a challenge to my personality and I have been trying to live up to this since then and even before. I know that I cannot let empty words come out of my mouth; neither can I make underguarded statements. Any time I open my mouth to make a promise, I try to fulfill it. I will endeavor to do so by the grace of God. It will be noticed that I always attach Awaka to my titles and honors as much as possible. This is because I come from

Awaka in Owerri North LGA. I am a proud son of Awaka and I consider my achievements to belong to Awaka.

For the third Chieftaincy honor, I have to begin by saying that according to my people, whoever that has already dipped his leg into a cold bath will no longer fill the cold that would scare others away from bathing. I have done this once, twice, so doing more will not be scary. When an opportunity came for the third, it came from my in-laws. The title would be given by Eze Emmanuel Sonde Okoro, Omenyi II of Emii, my wife's home. I made the acquaintance of the Eze when I was the Pro-Chancellor and Chairman of Governing Council of Imo State University, Owerri (Fig. 5.11– 5.13). We met during an economic conference in Washington, DC. When we got acquainted with each other, I introduced him to my children because they needed to know the traditional ruler of their mother's home. We seem to have made a connection at that time and the relationship blossomed from there. Whenever I went home I would visit him and when he came over to the U.S, we would connect. So one day I received a letter from Ezein-Council of Emii saying that they had chosen me to be conferred with a title. I said that I had two already and wondered if there was any need to get more. They said yes; that some people have up to five. And then having seen that we have been friends and that the Eze comes from my wife's home and that his mother came from Awaka, I accepted. So this was how that happened.

"Omereoha" was the title the Eze and I chose. This is a title that has no boundaries and brings out the fact that I am a philanthropist. So I was going to say Omereoha of Emii, but the Eze said that Omereoha means that you do and are going to do things for others, including folks that are not from Emii. So, I should not put Emii in the title. I just simply state "Omereoha" and my chieftaincy certificate bears Omereoha only. I must also add that the Eze informed me that Omereoha I of Emii is preoccupied. This name means one who does things for people, irrespective of where they come from and this is what I do and have been doing. Again the process was repeated. During the ceremony we rode in a convoy to the Eze's palace and then to Emii Elementary School premises for the conferment (Fig. 6.9–6.12). It was a celebration of the anniversary of his coronation and a conferment of titles day. After the conferment, I was selected as the one to speak or give vote of thanks on behalf of all the individuals conferred with titles on that day by the Eze. So I picked up the microphone and spoke on behalf of all those conferred with titles and among other things, thanked Eze Okoro and his Emii people for the honor. It was a great occasion and I felt quite honored. After that, there was the usual merriment at Awaka. This time, it took place under the big tree outside the Acholonu Compound called "Obu Omumu" (Fig. 1.3–1.6) to which I already referred, meaning the tree of or a symbol of village procreation or birth, now 91 years old.

The requirements of conferment were, in general terms, similar; however, there were slight variations. For instance, during the conferment of Omereoha on me, I was told that government had introduced some form of tax for chieftaincy title confinements. Each person conferred a title was to pay N40, 000. So I had to make that available to the Eze, in addition to all other community based requirements. Amongst these requirements were also items that I needed to get for myself. For example, there was a cap, a staff, horse whip, a locally made fan that had my title inscribed on it on both sides by local artists (Fig. 6.11), and the neck and wrist wears made of strings of local beads. I want, at this juncture, to say something about the beads and the cap. There is an erroneous opinion that they must be red, hence the idea of 'the red-capped chiefs.' But both the beads and the cap do not have to be red, as I am reliably informed. It is actually the choice of the celebrant. However, what I have observed is that many recipients of chieftaincy honors have inadvertently conformed to the red cap and red beads syndrome. So, it has become more or less like the order of the day.

As I received all these titles (now triple chief, Fig 7.1) and honors, I felt a bit sad about one thing, and that is the absence of the Eze Awaka, Oshimiri Christopher David Osuagwu, Ezikoche I of Awaka who was snatched away from us by the cold hands of death. If he had lived longer, perhaps, Awaka would have been the first community to extend that honor to me. He was impressed with me and made me chairman of the constitution drafting committee of the community. He told me that he was going to confer Chieftaincy title on me. Unfortunately, he died before he could do that. We miss him a lot because he was a great and vibrant man. His death brought about some crisis in Awaka, which may not have occurred if he had signed the constitution which my committee and I prepared (see appendix). The major issue was the problem of the rotational tradition of the Eze stool in Awaka. It was agreed, that the stool would rotate amongst the three villages of Awaka. He was from Umuodu Village and after him, representing Umuodu, by tradition, Ndegbelu Awaka village was to produce the next Eze. I am from Ndegbelu and the Loboche part. We held a lot of deliberations and meetings, and eventually we chose a person by the name of Dr. Patrick Ogbede Nwachukwu, a relation of the Emezi family to take over the Eze-ship. He was a medical doctor who taught at the College of Medicine, University of Nigeria, Enugu Campus. He was the first person to attend Government College, Umuahia from our area on scholarship. He retired from the University of Nigeria as a Reader or Associate Professor. The Emezi family did not want him to be the Eze. They eventually and much later brought out someone else from their family to be the Eze. He was the late Mr. Herbert Emezi. So there was an internal fight that went on and on. This gave the Osuagwu family an opportunity to say that since Ndegbelu, Awaka cannot resolve who would be the choice, they would keep the crown in the Osuagwu family and make it nonrotatory. They went and got some of the Oha people and convinced them to say that there would be no more rotation of the Eze stool. The rest of Ndegbelu said No! Then the crisis deepened. Unfortunately, it has not been completely resolved and is under litigation.

When Col. Tanko Zubiro was the Military Administrator of Imo State and I was serving as Pro-Chancellor and Chairman of Governing Council of Imo State University (Fig. 5.11–5.13), I had close relationship and contact with him. When it was getting close to the time for him to leave as Military Governor, I approached him and asked him not to leave without giving us a legitimate Eze. Akujor Osuagwu was the one from the Osuagwu family who came out for the stool. Mr. Herbert Emezi eventually came out and got a support of a majority of Ndegbelu to be the Eze. Due to so many issues, one of which was the rotational nature of the stool, there was profound disagreement, which ended up in court. Meanwhile, Awaka as a town or autonomous community was losing a lot because of the fact that we had no recognized Eze. This was bugging me a lot. So I appealed to the governor, to find a way to settle the squabble that was fast degenerating into ugly community relationships in Awaka. I opted for Mr. Herbert Emezi (now late) since he happened to come from Ndegbelu, the village whose turn it is to select the next Eze. The Military Governor called the secretary to the State Government, Mr. Uba Osigwe, to bring the file on Awaka. The man did and read through intercom, from the file heavily discrediting Herbert Emezi and projecting Akujor Osuagwu. The governor said that based on the report, he would have no choice but to give recognition and staff of office to Akujor Osuagwu. I had to back down. I did not want the governor to leave office without us having a recognized Eze who would help Awaka people get what is their due from government as other autonomous communities and get the respect it deserves in any gathering. At this stage, I could not tell him not to make an appointment since things did not favor Herbert Emezi. So what I did was to help my Awaka people that I love, to belong. In short, my overriding desire and interest was in having Awaka people get a recognized Eze. This took precedence over personalities. My interest was that we have somebody, so that we would not continue losing political patronage and allocations to autonomous communities because of the vacancy in the Eze's stool. That's how Akujor Osuagwu was given the staff of office. It was after that that some

My Titles, Affiliations and Laurels

aggrieved people went to court. Let me reiterate that Dr. Patrick Nwachukwu was democratically elected by Loboche community. I was the returning officer during the election and Herbert Emezi was not there and was not a contestant at the time. His senior brother Paulinus Emazi was present and did not bring up his name for consideration. But Dr. Nwachukwu was unfairly bypassed because of the fierce resistance of the Emezi family against him. He later died. This, unfortunately, is the genesis of Awaka eze-ship problem. When the late Henry Opara was approached to take it, he was advised by his relation, Richard Opara, not to take it; that if he did, he would die prematurely. Herbert Emezi declared his interest to take it later after he retired from his position as the Librarian at Alvan Ikoku College of Education. Although Akujor Osuagwu is the government recognized Eze, yet some Awaka people still do not recognize him. I am not creating the impression that he does not have support. But what I mean to convey is that there is still a case in court on the matter. However, he has gone ahead to confer chieftaincy titles on people who include people from Ndegbelu and Emezi family (Linus Emezi) and these people still answer chief. Ironically, the late Henry Opara who rejected to take the Eze stool, is one of them.

I also know that the case in court was decided in favor of Ndegbelu Awaka people, but then, the virtual Eze (Akujor Osuagwu) appealed. Even though the appeal is still pending, the present government recognized him. He remains as the Eze of Awaka collecting his salary from government until further action from the appeals court. Well, that I do not have a chieftaincy title from Awaka does not really matter. I already have three chieftaincy titles. However I expected Eze Emmanuel Njemanze (now late) of Owerri Nchi-ise to voluntarily offer to give me a chieftaincy title like his fellow Alaenyi Ezes did but he did not, even though we were very close. Also, Owerri is my maternal home and he knew it so I consider myself a privileged person being that the concept of 'nwa nwa', one born by a married daughter of a community, is very strong in Igbo land. He failed to do what other

Alaenyi Ezes did for me. He later conferred chieftaincy title on my younger brother, Engr. Uchenna Acholonu after informing or consulting with me. Eze Njemanze served under me as a member of the Governing Council of Imo State University while I was the Pro-Chancellor and Chairman of the Governing Council. He and I interacted a lot. I paid homage to him more than the other Alaenyi Ezes that attended my first chieftaincy conferment; and attended Oru Owerri celebrations. I feel very disappointed that he could not do for me what others did; that he did not consider it wise to recognize "nwa nwa" Owerri of my caliber and repute. By the way, I was also reliably informed by my late maternal uncle, Chief Anthony Heukwu-Mere-Owerre Onukwugha, a former Deputy Commissioner of Police, and the former cabinet member of Eze Emmanuel Njemenze's (Fig. 5.13) predecessor, that my maternal grandfather, Onukwugha, was a relation of Njemanze, his grandfather. It was because of his death that Uncle Anthony was named Heukwumere-Owerre. He was born on the day that Osuji Njemanze died as I was informed.

While I hold to high esteem chieftaincy conferment and taking of titles, I naturally will not encourage proliferation of titles in Igbo land. Igbo people are very traditional and very much organized. They have established ways of doing things and where no one remembers how some things were done or where there is a new phenomenon, Igbo people were likely to arrange a study of such with a view to coming up with ways in which to deal with it. In the traditional Igbo system not just anybody is given a title. I believe also that in our contemporary Igbo society, not just anybody can or should get the titles. It may appear as if anybody who is able to put aside a handsome amount of money and make some available to an Eze receives the patronage of the Eze which is expressed in title giving. Titles are usually tied to remarkable achievements and names of such titles indicate the nature of achievement in question. When I got my first chieftaincy title, I was 60 years old. I know I could have worked towards getting it at a younger age but then, what would have been the yardstick for measuring the eligibility for such a profound honor. I consider chieftaincy titles as a great aspect of our socio-cultural development. But I believe it ought to be given at a ripe age and for demonstrated accomplishments. I abhor people between 20 and 35 being given chieftaincy titles. That, I think, is all about money and money alone should not enable a young man get these titles. It should go with age, accomplishments, and character. If 60, which is my ideal age for recognitions is too high, then it could start at about 45. It is said that 40 is the old age of youth and 50 is the youth of old age. A chief should be someone who has advanced in age, accomplished some things, both for his family and community, and acquired some wisdom and respectability.

There is also the impression that traditional rulers, Ezes and Igwes, are partly responsible for inappropriate award of titles, especially to understanding citizens. I cannot comment on this because I am neither a Monarch, that is, Eze, nor one of those who run after them for the purpose of being honored with titles. But what I can say is that if the Monarchs are not noble enough to know who to honor and at what time to do so, then, it is unfortunate. Suffice it to say that if such an insinuation is ever possible, then there is a need to be more careful in selecting who to crown an Eze. So far, in general terms, most of the Ezes I have interacted with are honorable persons. Because I consider them honorable, I think they deserve respect within and outside their areas of domain. Sometime ago, I got involved in a personal assessment of Ezes from Igbo land who supposedly came to America to confer chieftaincy titles on persons on the American soil. Some people condemn that as untraditional but I have a different view. Because I understand the concept and practice of the diaspora, I see nothing wrong with that. If an Eze has a group that has identified themselves as his own people anywhere, no matter how far it is from where he lives, he is still a monarch and it is still legitimate for him to perform his roles as a monarch away from where he lives. So, for this reason, if an Eze comes to America and confers titles on people, he is not out of place. One other thing is, provided that the laws of the place he does the conferment is not against such act. Let me reiterate that the right and power to confer titles are not taken away from him when he leaves his residence. Once he has that right, if there is an impediment to exercising it in his palace, he should be able to do it outside. I do not know how right this is, but I feel it is only logical and it is my considered opinion.

I have heard the argument advanced by some people that the investiture of a chieftaincy is not just a political thing; there is also a spirituality attached to it. For them, it is for this reason that the ceremony is usually done in the Eze's obi, or its vicinity which to them, does not move around with him and based on this, some Ezes have said that it is improper for an Eze to confer titles outside his land. It is an opinion, **not a law** and it makes sense. Mine is also my own opinion. I think we need to understand these issues better. For instance, sometimes, Ezes go in search of those who have demonstrated a measure of strength in character and have made reasonable accomplishments in their lives. They invite such people to their kingdoms to help. There are titles which clearly show these. If this can be, Ezes can also go outside to source such persons and indeed, extend the investitures to their areas of residence. The Queen of England does not give Knighthood outside her domain. But we are not from England and do not have to do what the British do.

Affiliations

Academics have been my life. I belong to it as a body and also to different bodies within it. Although I was not too sure that I was going to end up being a professor because I wanted to study law first, then medicine and become a clinician, yet I should say that I am all the same happy that I am a professor and in paramedical field too. When I got my first degree at Howard University, I was really happy, but it was not celebrated with pump and pageantry like the conferment of my chieftaincy titles. I was more interested at the time in going on to medical school. I had done an assessment of myself by trying to answer a purely personal question:

Now that you have your first degree, what do you know? I felt like I still did not know much. Though outwardly, it felt good to be a college graduate, but I wanted to head on to medical school. So, during my graduation, I took pictures and that was it.

It was the same thing with my Master's degree. As soon as I graduated, I drove all the way to Colorado to begin my doctorate degree studies at Colorado State University in Fort Collins, Colorado. When I finished my PhD in 1964, it was Uchenna, my younger brother, who came to the graduation. He came to witness the occasion and help me pack my things and go with me to Mississippi, where I got my first appointment to teach at Alcorn A and M College as it was called at that time. There was not much fanfare. I was glad I got the degrees, but I did not have many people to celebrate it with me. I worked hard in academics and I should say, that to a reasonable extent, my contributions have also been accorded due recognition. Recognition is important. It is an indication that one has made efforts that are visible. In most cases, for a single effort recognized, there may be about three or more efforts obscured. For me, I have worked individually and in company of my fellow professionals. Let me begin by saying that I belong to many learned organizations. Professional affiliations and memberships are essential for professional growth. They afford interactions, networking, and collaborations that enhance knowledge and progress. A reference to my profile, my curriculum vitae and List of the leadership positions I have held, will show the many professional organizations to which I have been involved from the sunrise of my academic carrier to the looming sunset of it. They include my life memberships. I am presently more active in the following: American Society of Parasitologists (ASP) in which I served as the Chair of the Literature Committee from 1994 to 2001, Helminthological Society of Washington, American Society of Tropical Medicine and Hygiene (ASTMH) in which I serve as President of the Africa Assembly of ASTMH, Mississippi Academy of Sciences in which I served as Chair of Zoology and Entomology Division several times and currently, Chair of the Healthcare Disparity Committee and Renewable and Alternative Energy Society of Nigeria. I am a life member of the Nigeria, Society for Microbiology and became the Editor of the Nigerian Journal of Microbiology from 1982 to 1990. I am a life member of the Science Association of Nigeria, and I served as its Vice President from 1989 to 1990. I was also a member of the Nigerian Association of Medical Scientists. I served as its Vice President in 1989. I am a life member of the Nigerian Society for Parasitology now known as Parasitology and Public Health Society of Nigeria and served as its Vice President from 1979 to 1980 and the President from 1980 to 1981 and Executive Board Member of the World Federation of Parasitologists (2002–2014) (Fig. 6.35).

I was conferred with the Fellowship of the Nigerian Academy of Science (FAS) in 1992, (Fig. 6.19–20) one of the most prestigious academic bodies in both Nigeria and Africa. Being a member of this Learned Academy in Nigeria, says a lot about the academic person. First, it is an indication that one has not only come of age but also has made sizeable contribution to a body of knowledge in a field of study. I was admitted into the fellowship of the Academy at the same time with Late Prof. Olikoye Ransome Kuti and Prof. Jibril Aminu. One interesting thing was that both of them were serving cabinet Ministers of the Federal Government of Nigeria. While Prof. Ransome Kuti was Hon. Minister of Health, Prof. Jibril Aminu was the Hon. Minister of Petroleum Resources. I was the only non-minister in the team. That investiture was one of the most fulfilling events in my academic career. Although it was celebrated like the conferment of Chieftaincy titles, I was emotionally attached to it and will ever cherish it. As a follow-up to it, I have been privileged to give the Nigerian Academy of Science induction Lecture. I have also been recognized at the highest point and admitted into the Hall of Fame of great Nigeria by being awarded the medal of Officer of the Order of the Niger (OON) in 2003. (Fig. 6.54-55)

Religiously and socially, I belong to several organizations and held and still hold positions of leadership in several of them. To name a few, I am a 4th degree Knight of Columbus (Fig. 6.1416). This entitles me to be addressed as "Sir". I was a Member of Council of Elders of World Igbo Congress (WIC), Former Patron of World Owerri People's Congress, (WOPC), current Patron of Imo State Congress of America (ISCA), former Council of Elders, Imo State, Member, Awaka Club One, Member, Igbo Community Association of Mississippi (ICAM), Member, Christ the King College Onitsha, Alumni Association of America (CKC-AAA) and several others.

Laurels

Since I got my doctor of philosophy degree (PhD.) (1964) in the science field, my burning desire has been to become a distinguished scientist. Scientific research has been my forte and my love and this has made me to travel far and wide doing research and widening my scope of knowledge in science. My University (ASU) office has some words of wisdom on the walls to remind me of the direction towards which I am marching or give me a sense of direction and motivate me. They are also there to motivate my students. One of these is "Take time to work; it is the price of success" another is "He who stops being better, stops being good" the third one is the words of Booker T. Washington about success. It says, "Success patiently waits for anyone who has the determination and the strength to seize it." These have been my watch words and have helped me to excel and to get the fulfilling results of awards, accolades, and laurels I have been receiving. As of now, I hardly have space in my office and home to store awards/plaques and certificates received over the years and they are still coming! They are the fruits of my labor—self-propelled labor; labor without prodding. A discussion on my laurels or recognitions is contained in my profile or curriculum vitae under Awards and Honors section. I have been blessed with receiving numerous awards/plaques, recognitions, and honors (Fig. 6.18-55). I will rehash some of the outstanding ones here. They include the following: 2000 Outstanding Intellectuals of the 21st Century (2002), Universal Award of Accomplishments (2002), International Educator of the Year (2003), Top 100 Educators of the Year (2005), and Distinguished Service Award from US Food and Drug Administration (FDA) Advisory Committee (2005). In 1983, I became a Foundation Fellow of the Nigerian Society for Parasitology (FNSP), in 1992, a Fellow of the Nigerian Academy of Science (FAS), the apex or most prestigious in Nigeria. In 2012, I was honored by the Mississippi Academy of Science with the prestigious Distinguished Contribution to Science Award and became the first professor in the history of Alcorn State University to get it. In 2014, I received the fellowship of the Renewable and Alternative Energy Society of Nigeria (FRAES). In February 2016, I was again honored by the Mississippi Academy of Science with a prestigious Contribution to Health Disparity Research Award. In August 2016, I was honored by CKC-AAA for my accomplishments and as an octogenarian member (over 80 years old) (Fig. 6.18) along with Prof. Cyril Enwonwu. I was awarded the Nigerian National Honors medal and Certificate of Officer of the Order of the Niger (OON) in 2003. The latest is the prestigious Imo Diaspora award made to me on Dec. 20, 2016 (Fig. 6.21–6.24).

At the age of 85 years, I still do not feel that it is time to quit; to down my academic and research tools. Continuing research and publishing are still my ardent desires and urging. There is no resting for us until we rest in GOD.

My Titles, Affiliations and Laurels

Fig. 6.1: Prof. Alex Acholonu being inducted as a chief for the first time by HRH Eze Nwosu of Amaigbo in Dec. 24, 1992 with the title Ogbuhoruzo 1 of Amaigbo

Fig. 6.2: Picture after my first Chieftaincy Conferment, as Ogbuhoruzo 1 of Amaigbo Dec. 24, 1992

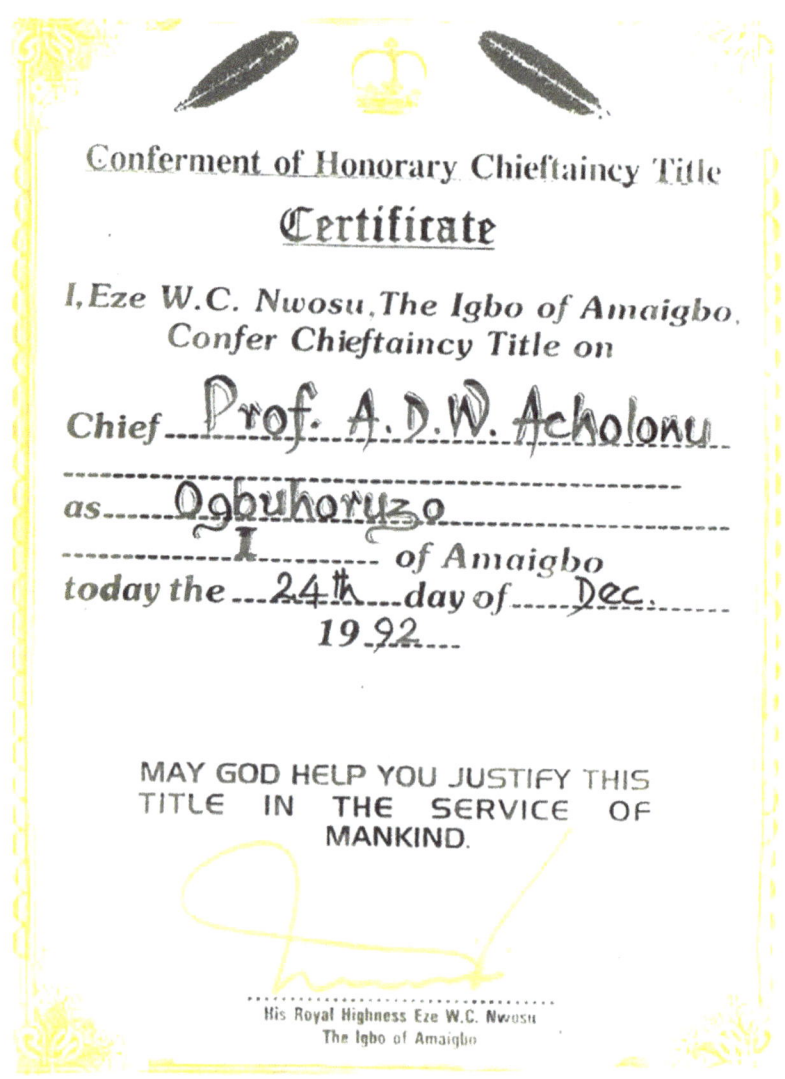

Fig. 6.3: First Chieftaincy Conferment Certificate as Ogbuhoruzo 1 of Amaigbo Dec. 24, 1992

My Titles, Affiliations and Laurels

Fig. 6.4: My Family after my First Chieftaincy title in Dec. 1992

My Journey Through Life

Fig. 6.5: Photo with my wife Lolo Mary E. Acholonu and my two sons Anderson Akopoazu Acholonu and Alexander Dozie Wozuzu Acholonu Jr. after my Induction as Chief Ogbuhoruzo 1 of Amaigbo in Dec. 1992

My Titles, Affiliations and Laurels

Fig. 6.6: My second Chieftaincy Conferment as Ekwueme 1 of Ihitta Ogada Dec. 24, 2002

Fig. 6.7: Second Chieftaincy Conferment Certificate as Ekwueme 1 of Ihitta Ogada Dec. 24, 2002

My Titles, Affiliations and Laurels

Fig. 6.8: Prof. Acholonu in his 2nd Chieftaincy regalia as Ekwueme 1 of Ihitta Ogada with his wife Lolo Mary E. Acholonu on Dec. 24, 2002

Fig. 6.9: Prof. Alex Acholonu's 3rd Chieftaincy Induction Ceremony as Omereoha, March 31, 2007

Fig. 6.10: Prof. Acholonu and his wife, Mary E. Acholonu. Picture taken after his third chieftaincy title as Omereoha March 31, 2007

My Titles, Affiliations and Laurels

Fig. 6.11: 3rd Chieftaincy Title as Omereoha March 31, 2007

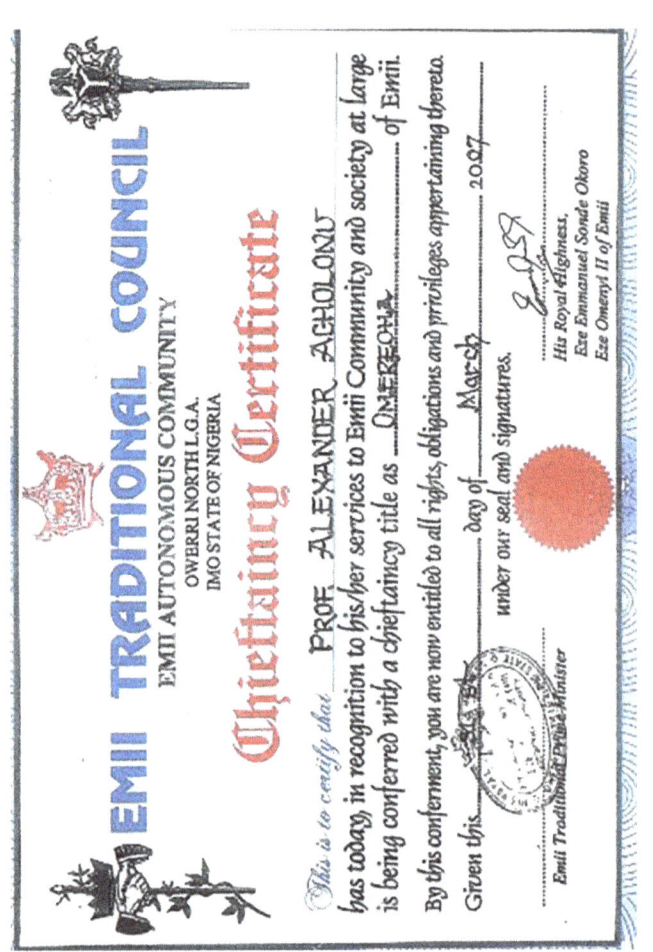

Fig. 6.12: Third Chieftaincy Conferment Certificate as Omereoha March 31, 2007

My Titles, Affiliations and Laurels

Fig. 6.13: Picture of Acholonu showing Chieftaincy red hat; taken after his 70th Birthday in Nov. 30, 2002

Fig. 6.14: Induction as 4th degree Knight of Columbus Prof. Acholonu 3rd from left Feb. 26, 2009

Fig. 6.15: Prof. Alex Acholonu given a religious recognition. Induction as a fourth degree knight of Columbus in 2009. Picture with the grand knight (left)

My Titles, Affiliations and Laurels

Fig. 6.16: Induction as 4th Degree Knight of Columbus, Vicksburg Feb. 26, 2009 (Acholonu row 3 no 4 from left)

Fig. 6.17: My wife and I with 2 Bishops from the Jackson Catholic Diocese, MS who visited our church, St Joseph Catholic Church, in Port Gibson, MS, 1995

Fig. 6.18: Plaque "Distinguished Legend Award" of Recognition from CKC Alumni Association in America, Aug. 6, 2016

My Titles, Affiliations and Laurels

Fig. 6.19: Photo after my Induction as a fellow of the Nigerian Academy of Science (FAS) in 1992

My Journey Through Life

Fig. 6.20: Prof. Acholonu inducted as a Fellow of the Nigerian Academy of Science (FAS), 1992

My Titles, Affiliations and Laurels

Fig. 6.21: Picture of Prof. Acholonu, (right) with Rev. Dr. Clement Amadi (uncle of my son-in-law, married to my daughter, Leslie, High Chief Kennedy Okere, MD) and wife who attended my Imo Diaspora Award Ceremony

Fig. 6.22: Picture of some Imo Diaspora Awardees (left or right) Engr. Marcel Anyanwu, Nze Gibson Chigbu, Chief Ekene Amaefule, Atty Charles Onyerimba, Chief Ngozi A. Duru, Kingsley A Ogu, Chief Prof. Alex Acholonu

Fig. 6.23: (Left to right) Prof. Acholonu, Dr. Austin Orishakwe, Registrar of Gregory University, Uturu and Nze Charles Muruako, Secretary of Imo State Congress of America (ISCA) attendees of Imo Diaspora Award Ceremony Dec. 20, 2016

Fig. 6.24: Eng. Uchenna Acholonu, brother of Prof. Acholonu and Dr. Austin Orishakwe, the person standing on the left is my junior brother Engr. Uchenna Acholonu attendees of Imo Diaspora Award Ceremony, Dec. 20, 2016

My Titles, Affiliations and Laurels

Fig. 6.25: The chairman of the occasion former Pro Chancellor of Imo State University presenting the Diaspora Award to Prof. Alex Acholonu

Fig. 6.26: HRH Eze Emmanuel Okoro shaking Prof. Acholonu after the Imo State Diaspora Award

Fig. 6.27: Picture of Prof. Acholonu 3rd from left with some key position holders in the PPSN which includes Prof. Chinyere Ukaga extreme right, President of PPSN (Parasitology and Public Health Society of Nigeria Sept. 21-24, 2016)

Fig. 6.28: A group picture with some members of PPSN who attended the Abeokuta Annual Meeting

Fig. 6.27-28: Recognition to Prof. Acholonu by members of NPPS as Foundation Fellow (FNSP) of the Society and former President (1980-81)

Fig. 6.29: MAS Distinguished Contribution to Science Award February 23, 2012

Fig. 6.30: MAS Contribution to Health Disparity Research Award February 18-19, 2016

My Titles, Affiliations and Laurels

Fig. 6.31: Prof. Voletta Williams, Chair, Dept. of Biology, Prof. Acholonu and Prof. Babu Patlolla of ASU

Fig. 6.32: Picture taken during the Health Care Disparity ward made to Prof. Acholonu in Feb. 2016 during the Annual Meeting of the Mississippi Academy of Sciences. Left to right are Prof. Babu Patlolla, Dean, School of Arts and Sciences, ASU, Attorney Esther Streete, daughter of Prof. Acholonu, and Prof. Acholonu, the awardee

Fig. 6.33: Picture with the Executive Director of MAS, Dr. Ham. Benghuzzi, after receiving a plaque for "Contribution to Health Disparity Research Award" Feb., 2016

Fig. 6.34: Group Picture, Zoology and Entomology Division of MAS and some ASU students and faculty with Prof. Acholonu (middle) after his Health Care Disparity Award. Picture includes Prof. Julius Ikenga, Vice Chair of Division (left of Prof. Acholonu)

My Titles, Affiliations and Laurels

Fig. 6.35: Executive Board Members of the World Federation of Parasitologists (WFP) 2010-2014. Prof. Acholonu (4th from left front line) was one of those elected to serve as a member of this highest governing body of the WFP, which took place in Melbourne, Australia, 2010

Fig.6.36: Chief Prof. Acholonu receiving award for "Distinguished Contribution to Science" from the Chair of Awards Committee of Mississippi Academy of Science (MSA), Dr. Kenneth Butler, February 2012

My Journey Through Life

Fig. 6.37: Cruise in a boat on the Gulf of Mexico on the way to Ship Island to check damages done by the BP oil spill and damage done by Hurricane Katrina. Accompanying Prof. Acholonu are K-12 Teachers. (Summer Ecology Education Workshop Grant Program) Aug. 23, 2011

Fig. 6.38: Chief Prof. Alex Acholonu and Lolo Mary Acholonu on his 80th birthday with Hon. Mayor Henry Banks and wife (left). He chaired the occasion.

My Titles, Affiliations and Laurels

PROCLAMATION
CHIEF "DR" ALEXANDER D.W. ACHOLONU DAY

WHEREAS, Alexander D.W. Acholonu was born November 30, 1932, to the late Willie and Esther Acholonu in Owerria, Nigeria; and

WHEREAS, Chief Acholonu is the husband of Mary Acholonu and the proud father of Andy, Sandra, Cynthia, Leslie, Esther, Alexandra, and Alexander, Jr.; and

WHEREAS, Chief Acholonu loves some Ose Olugwu "vegetable soup salad", harassing students and telling them that it's All your fault "MY DEAR"; and

WHEREAS, Dr. Acholonu is recognized National and International for his Biological research in his chosen field.

NOW, THEREFORE, be it resolved that the Mayor, Board, and the City of Hazlehurst, Copiah County Mississippi proclaims November 30th 2012 as CHIEF "DR." ALEXANDER D.W. ACHOLONU DAY in Hazlehurst, Mississippi.

Be it further resolved that copies of this proclamation be presented to Chief Acholonu and this proclamation be arhieved as part of the permanent record of Hazlehurst, Mississippi.

Thus resolved this the 23rd Day of November 2012.

Henry C. Banks, Sr. Mayor
City of Hazlehurst

Fig. 6.39: Proclamation: Declaration of Chief "Dr." Alexander D.W. Acholonu Day in Hazlehurst, MS by Hon. Henry Banks, Mayor Hazlehurst, MS on 23rd of November 2002, Prof. Acholonu's 70th Birthday, as a special recognition for his accomplishments

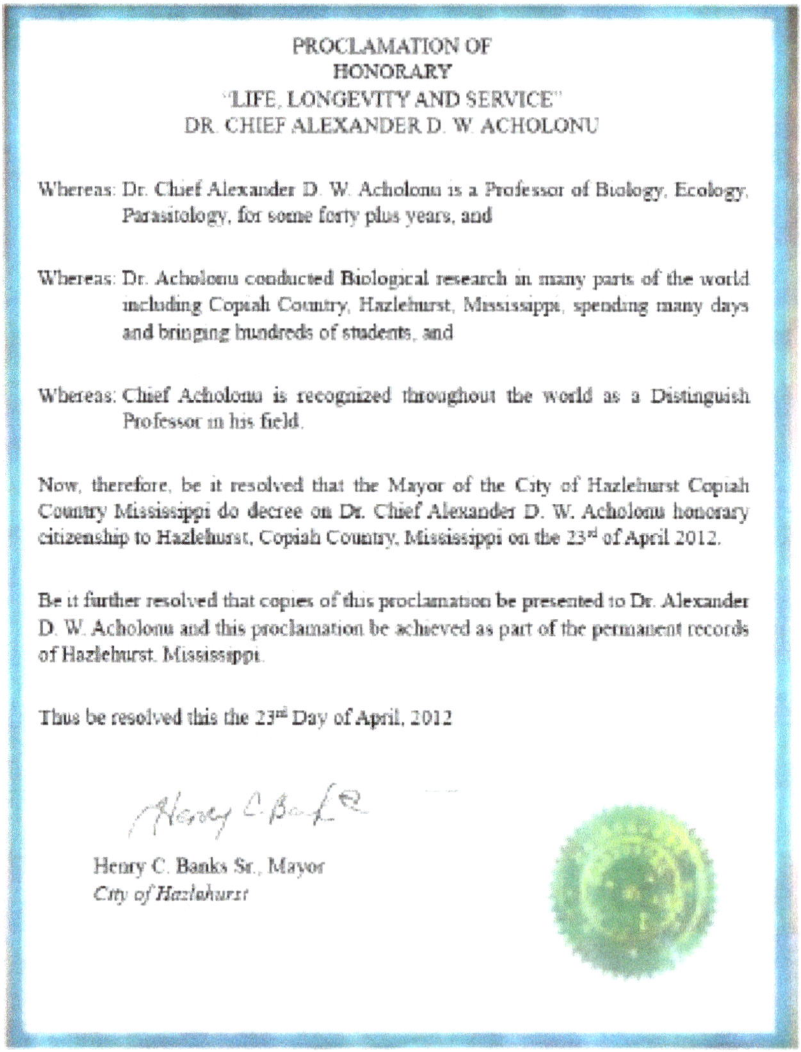

> **PROCLAMATION OF HONORARY**
> **"LIFE, LONGEVITY AND SERVICE"**
> **DR. CHIEF ALEXANDER D. W. ACHOLONU**
>
> Whereas: Dr. Chief Alexander D. W. Acholonu is a Professor of Biology, Ecology, Parasitology, for some forty plus years, and
>
> Whereas: Dr. Acholonu conducted Biological research in many parts of the world including Copiah Country, Hazlehurst, Mississippi, spending many days and bringing hundreds of students, and
>
> Whereas: Chief Acholonu is recognized throughout the world as a Distinguish Professor in his field.
>
> Now, therefore, be it resolved that the Mayor of the City of Hazlehurst Copiah Country Mississippi do decree on Dr. Chief Alexander D. W. Acholonu honorary citizenship to Hazlehurst, Copiah Country, Mississippi on the 23rd of April 2012.
>
> Be it further resolved that copies of this proclamation be presented to Dr. Alexander D. W. Acholonu and this proclamation be achieved as part of the permanent records of Hazlehurst, Mississippi.
>
> Thus be resolved this the 23rd Day of April, 2012
>
> *Henry C. Banks*
> Henry C. Banks Sr., Mayor
> *City of Hazlehurst*

Fig. 6.40: Acholonu given honorary citizenship to Hazlehurst, Copiah Country, Mississippi on the 23rd of April 2012 Earth Day Celebration at Alcorn State University by Mayor, Hon. Honorable Henry C. Banks Sr. for his achievements

Proclamation
Of
"EARTH DAY"
Hazlehurst

WHEREAS: Earth day is an annual event, celebrated on April 22 World Wide, to demonstrate support for environmental protection; and

WHEREAS: John McConnell proposed a day to honor the Earth at a conference is San Francisco in 1969; and

WHEREAS: Senator Gaylord Nelson made it official in the United States in 1970; and

WHEREAS: Chief "Dr." Alexander D. W. Acholonu continues that celebration and traction until today. The City of Hazlehurst join with him and the Alcorn State University Family to celebrate, promote, and show appreciation for our environment

IN TESTIMONY WHEREOF, I have given under my hand and the seal of the City of Hazlehurst, Mississippi the 23rd Day of April 2013.

Henry C. Banks
Henry C. Banks Sr., Mayor
City of Hazlehurst

Fig. 6.41: Recognition for Prof. Alex Acholonu for conduction of Earth Day Celebration at Alcorn State University for many years

My Journey Through Life

Fig. 6.42: Mayor Henry Banks giving city key to Hazlehurst City, MS to Prof. Acholonu April 23 2012

Fig. 6.43: Mayor Henry Banks giving a proclamation to Alex Acholonu in recognition of his accomplishments April 23 2012

My Titles, Affiliations and Laurels

Fig. 6.44: Chief Acholonu holding key to Hazlehurst City, given to him by Hon. Mayor, Henry Banks, April 2012 (Symbol of rare honor making him Honorary Citizen of the City) on Earth Day Celebration at Alcorn State University

Fig. 6.45: Picture of Prof. Acholonu with Hon. Darryl Grennell, Former member of the Dept. of Biology, ASU, former President of Adams Country Board of supervisors and now Mayor of Natchez, MS. Benefactor of Prof. Acholonu. He gave Prof. Acholonu a prominent recognition as President of Board of Supervisors when he received his distinguished contribution to science award in Feb. 2012. Picture taken during his retirement ceremony from ASU. Dec. 2016

RESOLUTION

WHEREAS, Doctor Alex D.W. Acholonu received the prestigious 2012 Outstanding Contribution to Science Award from the Mississippi Academy of Sciences on February 23, 2012; and

WHEREAS, Doctor Alex D.W. Acholonu has a long and distinguished career with numerous contributions to science through research and education. Dr. Acholonu was awarded a BS from Howard University, a MS from Prairie View A&M University, a PhD from Colorado State University. Dr. Acholonu is a member of the Sigma Xi Research Honor Society and the Beta Beta Beta Biological Honor Society and his honors include: Outstanding Intellectuals of the twenty-first century, A Great Mind of the twenty-first century, and the Universal Award of Accomplishment. Dr. Acholonu holds the honor of being an Officer of the Order of the Niger which was bestowed unto him by the President of Nigeria; and

WHEREAS, Doctor Alex D.W. Acholonu became the first professor to receive the award in the 141 year history of Alcorn State University, an institution that is vital to the education, health, and general welfare of the citizens of Adams County;

NOW THEREFORE, BE IT RESOLVED by the Board of Supervisors of Adams County, Mississippi, that our warmest and heartfelt thanks be extended to Doctor Alex D.W. Acholonu for his dedication in education and science that earned him the Mississippi Academy of Sciences 2012 Outstanding Contribution to Science Award;

BE IT FURTHER RESOLVED that this resolution be entered on the permanent minutes of the Adams County Board of Supervisors and a copy be delivered to Doctor Alex D.W. Acholonu as an expression of our appreciation and recognition of achievement.

SO RESOLVED, this the 16th day of April, 2012.

ADAMS COUNTY BOARD OF SUPERVISORS

Darryl V. Grennell, President

Mike Lazarus, Vice-President

David Carter, Supervisor District 2

Angela Hutchins, Supervisor District 3

Calvin Butler, Supervisor District 5

ATTEST:

Thomas J. O'Beirne, Clerk

Fig. 6.46: Resolution honoring Prof. Acholonu for his award from MAS for distinguished contribution to Science by Hon. Darryl V. Grennell President, Adams County Board of Supervisors on 16th April 2012 and currently Mayor of Natchez

Fig. 6.47: "Alexander DW Acholonu, PH.D., FAS, OON is recognized and honored for contributions made to the education of our nation's youth and is hereby acknowledged for excellence as a distinguished educator in WHO'S WHO among America's Teachers" (see above)

My Titles, Affiliations and Laurels

Fig. 6.48: Prof. Alex Acholonu with Mr. Agbaso Udeokporo ("Ababanna"), the famous top Awaka vocalist, who in his several records, recognized me for my accomplishments. Among other names, he called me "an international educationist by nature" Picture taken on May 2016 after Medical Mission at Awaka

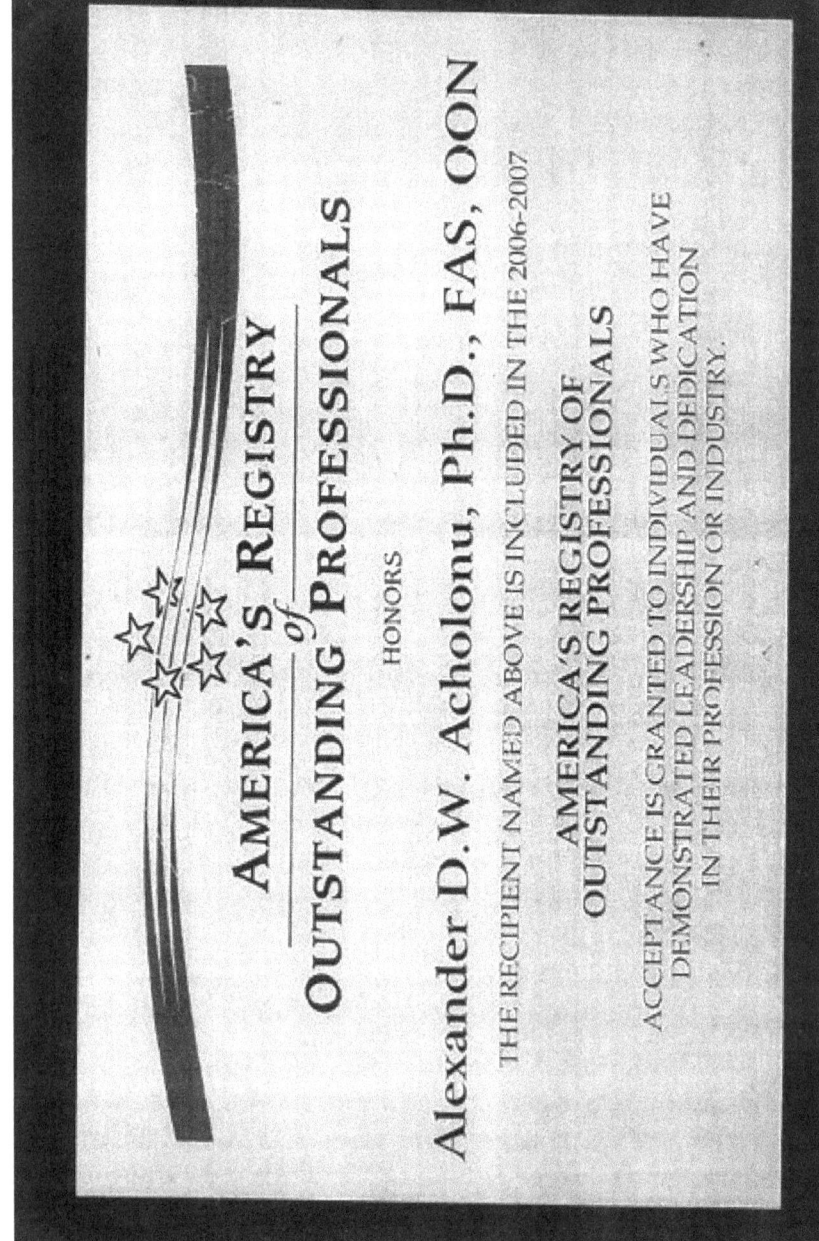

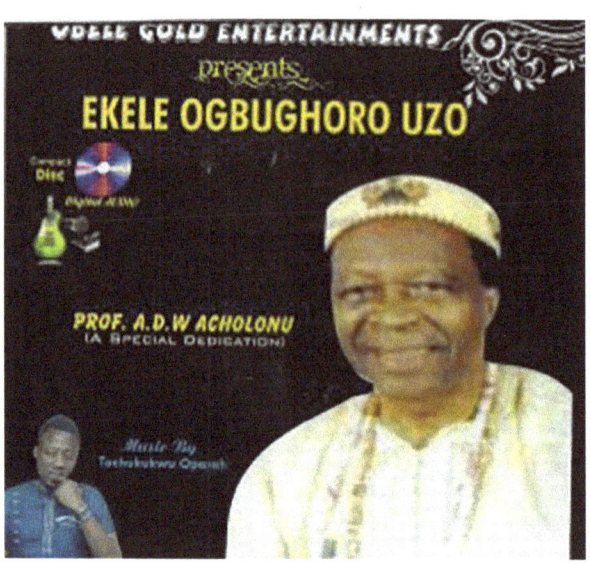

Fig. 6.49: Chief Prof. Acholonu special dedication disk (front) by Mr. Tochukwu Oparah 2017

My Titles, Affiliations and Laurels

Fig. 6.50: Chief Prof Acholonu special dedication disk (back) by Mr. Tochukwu Oparah Special recognition of Chief Prof. Alex Acholonu by a Young and Rising Vocalist, Mr. Tochukwu Oparah from Awaka, 2017

Fig. 6.51: Recognition by the Editorial Board of Advances in Science and Technology Journal

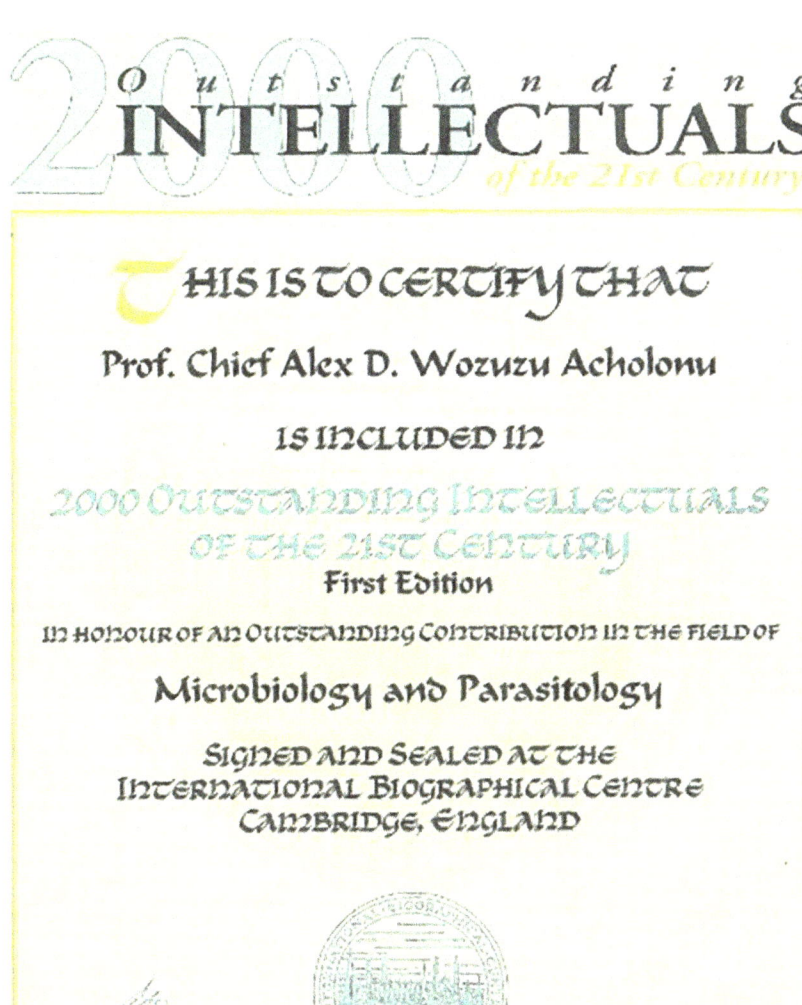

Fig. 6.52: Prof. Acholonu recognized as one of the 2000 Intellectuals of the 21st century, May 2002

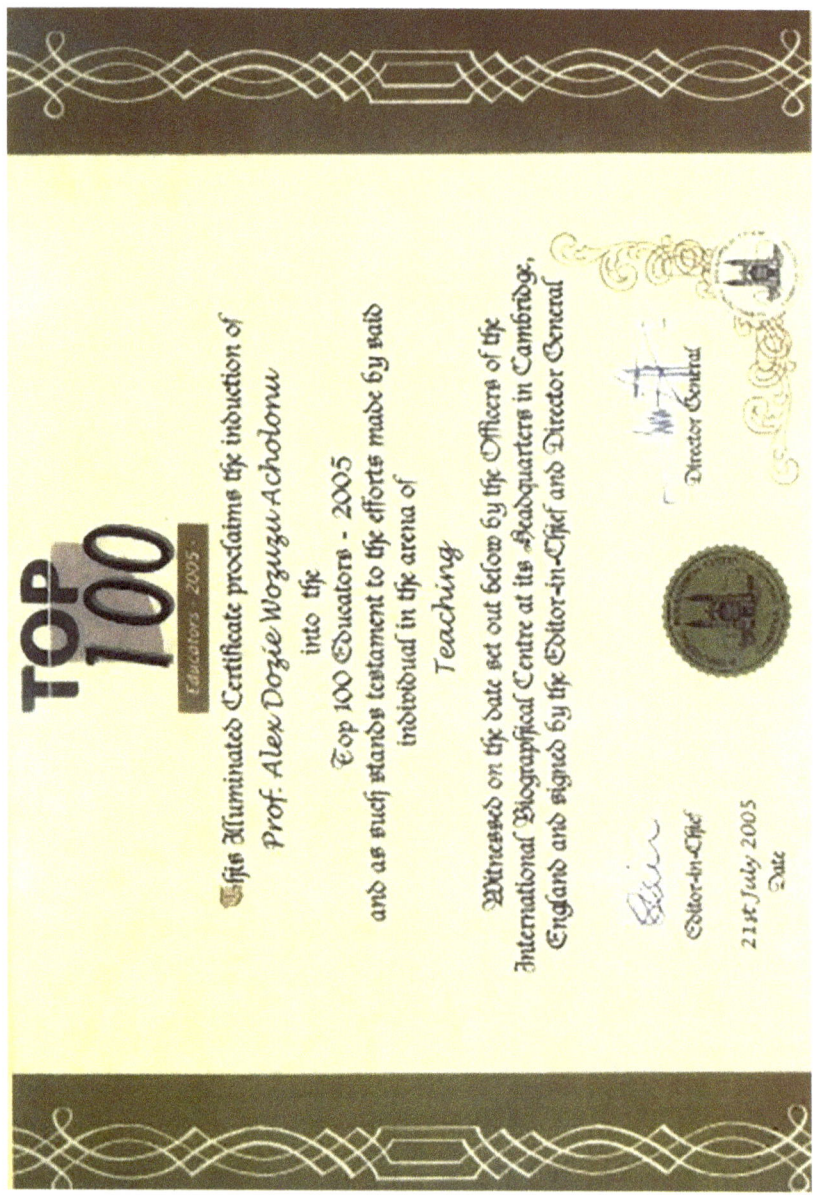

Fig. 6.53: Prof. Acholonu recognized as one of Top 100 educators of the year 2005

My Titles, Affiliations and Laurels

Fig. 6.54: OON (Officer of the Order of Niger) Certificate 10 December, 2003

My Journey Through Life

Fig. 6.55: Prof. Acholonu being congratulated by the then President, Chief Olusegun Obasanjo of Nigeria after he was conferred a high award of OON (Officer of the Order of Niger) due to his academic and social accomplishments, 10 December, 2003

Chapter Seven

The Igbos and Their Neighbors (My Views)

The Igbo people attempted to secede from Nigeria and that resulted in a thirty month war. People call it the Nigerian civil war but there are some who insist that it is Nigeria-Biafra war. Everybody knows that the old Eastern region declared herself to be the independent state of Biafra and put in place an admirable structure under the leadership of the then military governor of Eastern region, Col. Chukwuemeka Odimegwu Ojukwu. He later became the people's General and Head of State of the Republic of Biafra. I was not in the country at that time. I was in the United States of America so I cannot give firsthand information on the events in the defunct Biafra. Be that as it may, I and many others outside the country were drawn into the crisis either by conviction or by sympathy. I think I belong more to those who fall into both categories.

I recall my own little share of the danger and ill-treatment. This was in the early days of the hostilities. I came home to finalize arrangements for my marriage. I had done what I needed to do and was on my way back to the United States through Lagos. Everywhere was tense but I had to go back to my base. Please see chapter 4 for this episode. When I think of this incident, I realize how kind God has been to me. God has deliberately kept me for the work He wants me to do and I am grateful to Him.

Over here in the United States, we were not happy about what we heard about our people during the war. We had no choice but to help in ways considered decent and appropriate. We were asked to make financial commitments. We were encouraged to borrow money if we did not have enough and for the first time in the history of my life, I borrowed one thousand dollars and gave for the execution of the war. They said the Government would pay the money back to us. Till today, I never got paid back. So that was some of the ways I helped in the war even though I regret the war especially how it ended.

I want to clarify few things here. I did not have problems with the secession of the east, at the time it did, giving the way news about the maltreatment of easterners came to us in the USA. I think it was proper to do so. I consider that decision and the subsequent action an act of defense. There could have been alternatives, though, but we just have to consider the relatively best option. No Igbo person was happy with the treatment meted out to Igbo people. Stories of the unusual and inhuman treatment filled the air waves and pages of the newspapers. They called it pogrom, but we know it was genocide. It is unfortunate that justice has not yet been done but I want to join those who have accepted that bygone be bygone. From another angle, I am glad today that we have one country, Nigeria. I don't know if Biafra could have survived as a country given what I have come to learn about the nature of the average Igbo man. Our culture is "PHD"—Pull him down. I don't know why we Igbos generally cannot get along with our brothers and sisters. Every time, wherever we are today, we hardly can be in peace. We always agree to disagree. We have not learnt how to come together. We have not learnt from our past mistakes. The Igbo man is highly competitive but there is also a high degree of unhealthy rivalry among them. The Igbo man gets into dirty rivalry, jealousy and envy especially towards his fellow Igbo man. Those of us who have been privileged or through the grace of God have grown to become elders, have been talking about this. We have maintained that it is very disappointing. Even here in America, each time we have a meeting, we hardly get along very well. You find in several Igbo organizations, one person is suing another person in the law court as a result of one form of disagreement or another especially with reference to money. So one can only imagine a country made up of a people with this kind of attitude and temperament.

In addition, it would not have been an easy split for the entire Nigerians. My imagination projects that if the East had successfully seceded with the majority being Igbo, then the other major and minor ethnicities within it would have equally agitated for same. After all, every group is entitled to self-determination. If this is the case, then we would have had several pockets of countries within what remains today as a strong virile and large country. Perhaps, it could have been a terrible thing if we had a country in which the Rivers people are breaking away and the Cross River people also because of lack of trust and the spirit of self-determination or self-rule. So God has worked wonders by seeing to it that we are a country today and I like us to be a country—Nigeria, not Biafra, Benin, Portharcourt, Calabar, etc. although people are still pushing for Biafra. I believe it is an exercise in futility. The Igbo should spend time to learn how to get along. We have not learnt that yet.

The other non-Igbo components of the Biafran movement would not have been comfortable in an Igbo dominated Biafra because they would have that deep sense of minority that the Igbo people are 'lording' it over them. It is the problem of the 'minority.' It will always be there; the minority against the majority. Discrimination and feelings of inadequacy will always be there no matter what we do. They would still feel that they are not being adequately taken care of; that all the great things in the country are going to the majority and not to the minority. That is the problem we have in the world. It is a global problem and can hardly be solved. This is not just in Nigeria; but also in America, in Russia, in Brazil, and many other countries of the world.

I have been involved with the World Igbo Congress (WIC) since it was founded in 1994. I have attended virtually all the conventions of the group, starting with the Chicago convention, because I am appreciative of what it means to have the Igbo organized again. I have pleasant memories of the old Igbo Union that provided a lot of support and direction for the Igbo before the Nigeria-Biafra war. It was great to see that after the war, and in faraway America, the Igbo could organize themselves and begin to act again like the nation it is. At some point I was appointed a member of the Council of Elders of WIC. It therefore sickens me that someone or a group of people could sow the seed of discord and disunity in the World Igbo Congress. It is also not palatable that as a last resort, WIC had to go to court, after several prominent Igbo leaders tried to settle the problems within, in order to restore order. The Igbo is an argumentative lot and everyone thinks he/she knows better, which is why the problems have lasted long and ended up in court. I do not believe in fancies and emotions; I believe in facts. I am trained as a scientist to believe in and respect facts, not sentiments. The fact is that the Joe Eto's group is a breakaway group. They know that the tail does not wag the dog. Dr. Joe Okeke appears to be the mastermind of the whole thing on the Joe Eto adventure. Based on what I know, Engr. Eto has no locus standing in what he did. From now till kingdom come, the Eto group should not be the legitimate WIC. I am hoping and praying that we can settle the problem and put this behind us for the good of the Igbos in diaspora.

I don't know why the Igbo people cannot find peace; there is so much disagreement amongst them and for that, they hardly can come together. They are yet to learn from past mistakes. The Igbo man's unhealthy rivalry with another Igbo man is very disappointing. It is popularly said that "the enemy of the Igbo man is the Igbo man". Even here in America, each time there is a meeting of the Igbos, there is likely to be a breakdown of law and order. You find in several Igbo organizations, one person is suing another person in the court of Law or the Igbo organization to which he belongs. Perhaps, it could have been a terrible thing if we had a country of our own where all these things are happening. Then to worsen matters as stated before, Rivers people would become disgruntled and soon be asking to break away; and the Cross River people do not trust us and would also feel like seceding. So God has worked wonders by seeing to it that we are a country today and I like us to continue being a country—Nigeria and not Biafra. For those pushing for Biafra, it is an exercise in futility. We would have more to lose than to gain. The Igbo should spend time to learn how to get along and how to sanely and insistently push for their needs.

I have to really reemphasize that I have related well with the panIgbo group. I am a member of The World Igbo Congress and rose to become a Member of the Council of Elders. I also served as a member of Council of Elders of Imo State representing WIC during Gov. Ohakim's regime or tenure of office. For years and years, we have had problems, leadership problems; with leaders and sets of leaders warring against each other. When the present Chairman was fighting tooth and nail to take over the mantle of leadership against the will of many people; we, as Council of Elders, tried to solve the problem and we did everything possible to bring about peace. There was a litigation that went on for some time which divided the Council into two. A group supported one faction while another group of which I was a member including Chief Egwuonwu former chairman of WIC supported the incumbent. This caused a lot of problems. As a matter of fact a day came when I decided not to be involved with The World Igbo Congress as long as the present chairman, Joe Etoh, is there. It is just a *locus classicus* of all I have been trying to say—that the Igbo people agree to disagree. In practically every organization of Igbo people in the USA, there is hardly any where there is no leadership tussle or financial squabble or problem. There are several litigations as I make these comments now, in several Igbo organizations, including WIC. Why? One hardly finds this happening among the Yorubas I suppose. It hardly happens among the Hausas. If it does, it may not be as frequently as it occurs among the Igbos. I think that it is mainly among the Igbos. Why do we agree to disagree? Why do we engage in PHD—Pull him Down syndrome? Why do we hardly show respect to our leaders? Why do we always accentuate the negative rather than the positive? Could it be because we appear to be republican in nature? If one does what is good as a leader, people should give him credit for it rather than look for what is bad about it! Good leaders shy away from coming to lead because our people are difficult. A person once said that God created us of two kinds—those to lead and those to be led. One should do soul searching and find where one belongs. Does one have the skill and the capability to lead? This is a big question we must continuously ask ourselves. Should people who lack leadership qualities want to come out and lead just for recognition? It is the truth that we have had people smuggling themselves into leadership positions when they know they do not have the qualities of leadership in them. They just want the name or they want it as a stepping stone to government positions. The problem of the Igbo is that we are rivals of one another. We mistrust ourselves; we are, in the main, querulous.

However, all these do not mean that there is total loss of hope for the Igbo people. The Igbo nation can move forward because they are a very strong, intelligent, creative, and resilient people. But a lot needs to be done. As it is, my advice, as I said before, is that we have to start learning how to commune with one another; start learning how to work together. We have to stop being egocentric or anthropocentric. We should learn to comport ourselves well and center our interests on all of us rather than on our individual selves; learn how to admit a mistake when it is made. We become too doggedly about issues even when we commit errors; we continue to argue even when we know that we are wrong and this is what Dale Carnegie referred to as *The Feeling of Importance in Individuals* in his book on: How to win Friends and Influence People. We do not know how to eat the humble pie, that is, how to say "I am sorry" even when we know that we are wrong. We should humble ourselves. When one is wrong, one should be able to say "I am sorry." Americans do not find it difficult to say I am wrong; I am sorry. It is a short cut to unnecessary arguments. Struggling to convince people that one is right when one is wrong may not make sense most times; it is not good and this is what is breaking us apart. President Lincoln said: "When you are wrong, ten angles swearing that you are right will make no difference." As long as this continues, this feeling of self-importance, seeing oneself as not wanting to be let down; as long as we have this in us, we will never be able to work together. Leadership position among the Igbo is extremely tedious. There is hardly any Igbo man that holds and completes a leadership position and others reach out to him and say 'Great; job well done.' But when he dies, they may then start talking about the good things he did. The Igbos tend to be insatiable people, hard to please!

There are three kinds of people in the world, namely, the uninformed, the misinformed, and the well-informed. The Igbos tend to belong to the second group—the misinformed. They often times judge people and act or ostracize them based on hearsay, gossip, or bias. Even so, Igbo nation has produced wellinformed people with impeccable character; people who made things happen rather than sit and watch things happen or wonder about what happened. We have witnessed people with great leadership qualities. We have prominent Igbo sons and daughters who have demonstrated strength of character, charisma, sense of direction and focus and were opulent. I have had interesting encounters with Igbo persons and groups. Some have been quite pleasant and others naturally have been unpleasant. First let me begin from Awaka, my home of origin. While I was growing up, the 3 people that stood out in Awaka that I would call Giants amongst the Lilliputians were, John Emezi who happened to be an interpreter, David Osuagwu, who happened to be Inspector of Police and my father, Wilfred Wozuzu Acholonu, (Fig. 2.1, 4.2, 4.5) who happened to be a court clerk and the first in Awaka to own two vehicles at a time in the 40s—a car and a commercial vehicle. If you come to Awaka and ask Who's who—these were seen as people of worth, who earned a good place, fame or height in the society. These three were the ones that stood out at the time. Incidentally, Mr. John Emezi happened to be the godfather of my father. The next person to remember is Mr. Ben Opara. He was a Railway Pay Master. Another is a man nicknamed Corporal Tombo from the Onyeneke family. He was a police man, tall and huge. He got his nickname because he used to drink palm wine a lot. Next is my senior uncle, Alfred Ugwuegbula Acholonu, the first son of Acholonu. He was a prominent tailor, the tailor of all the Reverend Fathers in the old Emekuku Parish. Additionally he was one of those who brought the Catholic Church to Awaka. He was also the "Bank" of Awaka people. He was so reputed as an impeccable honest Christian that people from all over Awaka town gave him money to keep for them. The next and last person I remember is Mr. Fred Chukwu. He was a well-known petition writer.

Beyond these, as I kept growing up, the person that I can see is Mr. Stephen Nnadi, who was my father's god-child and the famous catechist at Mount Camel Catholic Church, Emekuku and Saint Paul's Catholic Church, Owerri. The next person is Mr. Paul Chukwueke. He was a good High Elementary teacher. Also, he and his wife, Rachael, were wonderful people. He was the first person to get matriculation at Awaka. He was the person my father sent my elder brother, Casmir, to live with. Socially, he and his wife made us happy when we were growing up. They had a grammar-phone which we usually listened to and had fun with each time we visited them. They were sociable, loving, and kind people. He taught at Holy Ghost College, Owerri.

Awaka happens to be a small town of three villages and whenever anybody visited Awaka, in my greener days the families that he was likely to find outstanding were the Acholonu family, the Emezi family, the Opara family, the Nnadi family, the Chukwueke family and the Njoku family in Ndegbelu village; the Osuagwu family, Eme family, Nwaneri family and Osuji family in Umuodu and in Amuzi village, the George Eke family, the Ejiogu family, the Onyeneke family, the Anuforo family, and the Fred Chukwu family. There may be others but these are the ones that I remember and that stand out in my boyish eye and humble opinion.

Apart from the encounters and contacts I have had at the local level in Awaka, my home, there are other great Igbo people who have made strong impact on me, and the general life of all Igbo people and others in the country. While some of the encounters are negative, several of them have been positive.

Some of them are dead, though, but a number of them are still alive. Let me start by remembering Dr. Nnamdi Azikiwe, yes, Zik of Africa (Fig. 3.9). This man did a lot for the Igbo man and should never be forgotten. Zik was the person that gave much stature to the Igbo. I would not say that I have had very personal experiences with him. I never really encountered him but I felt him like any other Nigerian and especially Igbo persons. However, I had good rapport with his first wife, Flora, when both of us were students at Howard University in Washington DC in the 50s (Fig. 3.10). I also met his second wife, Mrs. Dr. Uche Azikwe (Fig. 3.11). I took a picture with her and my friend. Prof. Anya O. Anya during the Zik's Memorial Lecture at Enugu in the 90s. She also came to one of our WIC Conventions in the US and I took care of her hotel bill. When I was trying to go to the US for further studies, and looking for money, there was hardly any place I did not go to find money and no person I hesitated to contact for money. I wrote Zik a letter requesting him to help me get money to go to the US as stated before. He replied my letter and I believe that I still have that reply somewhere. Though, his reply was a polite negative, yet that did not tarnish my interest and admiration for him. That was my main encounter with him. He was and still remains a great man to me.

The second republic governor of Imo State, Governor Sam Mbakwe is another man of stature from Igbo land. I liked him in a way, though I have some reservations about him. He, among other things, established factories in Imo State (e.g. Shoe Factory, Owerri where I served as a Governing Board Member). The famous Concord Hotel was established during his tenure as Governor. When I came home to Nigeria from the US, I really worked hard along with some others, to get him to start Imo State University. Those of us in the University of Lagos formed a committee that urged Governor Mbakwe to start a university in Imo State. I still remember one Professor Anyanwu (late) who was made the

Chairman of the University Establishment Committee. He was an Obowu indigene. But let me reiterate that I was also to be the first Vice Chancellor of Imo State University because as at the time I applied for the position along with others, I consider myself as the most experienced academic administrator and the most qualified candidate for the position. Before I came back to Nigeria from the US, I had served as Professor and Head of Department at Inter American University of Puerto Rico and Dean of Liberal Studies (Arts and Sciences) in the State University of New York, Oneonta and hardly any of the candidates had held the two administrative positions or matched my research accomplishments. I may be one of the first Igbo persons to hold that kind of position in the US, at the time and in a predominantly white institution. So what I claim about my superiority to others who put in application with me is without prejudice because I was reliably informed by a member of the Vice Chancellor Selection Committee that I was found most qualified. I got to know this later. He said that I had better record than Prof. Echeruo but Echeruo's father's influence and that of his brother who was a Senator, played into the choice. Perhaps if my father who was a well-known Court Clerk and a Councilor was alive, I would have got that position. Even when Governor Mbakwe referred me to Prof. Echeruo to take me to be one of the Deans and I went to Echeruo and talked to him, he did not want me to serve. So I continued to stay at the University of Lagos. When another Prof. Anyanwu from Obowu, became the Secretary to the State Government, I was given the position of Rector of Amaigbo College of Technology. I started it as stated earlier. It is my considered opinion that Governor Mbakwe did not appoint the first Vice Chancellor (VC) of Imo State University on the basis of merit. It may be part of the reasons why I, without applying, was invited to start the Amaigbo College of Technology and be its first Rector.

Governor Mbakwe was succeeded by the then Brigadier Ike Nwachukwu who became the military governor after the successful military coup of January 1, 1984. Brigadier Ike Nwachukwu removed me from office and shut down the school. He was not that good. He cannot be compared with Sam Mbakwe. He was sectional and served with bias. I am sorry to say that. But it is my honest opinion. One of the awful things he did was to move Imo State University to Uturu nearer his home where it had terrible erosion problem, among others. When he was campaigning to become the President of the Country, and came to us in the US to attend The World Igbo Congress annual convention and address us, I confronted him. I looked at him straight in the face and said to him, "I was the Rector of Amaigbo College of Technology which you closed. If you become President of Nigeria would you do something like that again? He felt embarrassed. He also shut down or rather sold the several industries that Governor Mbakwe started and today we hardly have any industries in Imo State. The Imo State University in Uturu, now Abia State University, has been having erosion problems among others. When I was a member of the Governing Council of Imo State University, during the tenure of Governor Amadi Ikweche, erosion problem was one of the problems that occupied our attention.

Next is Late Hon. Raymond Amanze Njoku (Fig. 3.2). He was a Minister of the Federal Republic of Nigeria before and during the first Republic. But for him, people like me would not have had the opportunity to travel abroad for further studies. So he made it possible for me to go to the US as stated before (Chapter 3) and I will forever be grateful to him although before I travelled, and apparently out of pressure from his wife, he wrote me a letter to pack out of his house. This did not overshadow my gratitude to him. He signed the waiver for me that made the Federal Education Committee to approve my travel to the US to further my education.

The late Mr. Nathan Ejiogu (Fig. 7.3), Dr. Kema Chikwe's father, and Chief Chinyere Asika, was a fantastic man. He was Chief Inspector of Education for Eastern Region and later became the Chairman of the Civil Service Commission, Eastern Region. When I was going to school at CKC, Onisha, he gave me money on one occasion to travel home to Owerri when my father's transport money for me did not arrive in time. He also gave me 5 pounds when I was about to leave for the US. He was my father's bosom friend. Mr. and Mrs. Eunice Nuga (nee Onukwugha, my maternal aunt), Mr. Dennis Agukwu and his wife, Agnes (nee Acholonu), Mr. Raymond Onukwugha, my maternal cousin, Mr. Cyril Ugwuliri, my father's great friend, from Umuawuka, Emii, all gave me money when I was preparing to go to America for further studies. These are all Igbo people who were magnanimous, who determined to help in advancing the cause of Igbo people through education. They did not belong to the Pull Him Down group (PHD). They are examples of Igbos who had the milk of human kindness in their breasts; examples of how Igbo people ought to relate with each other; to be their brothers' keepers, to build bridges of affection, succor and success rather than destroy them.

Another person I must devote time to talk about is late Dr. Benedict Chiaka Njoku. He was an exemplary Igbo man; a man that needs to be emulated. I made reference to him in chapter 2—Early Days of my Life (Fig. 2.3, 2.10 4.17–4.18). He was the Academic Dean of Rust College, Holly Springs, MS and rose to become the Executive Vice President of the College. He, by teaching me in Elementary Six at Our Lady's School, Emekuku, gave me the educational foundation that catapulted me to being a Ph.D. degree holder. Providence brought him and I together again when I ran into him shortly after I arrived in the US, to be more specific, in Washington DC. He took me like a son and was extremely helpful to me. He was a great Igbo man, a benevolent man, a philanthropist and a distinguished academician. He helped not only myself but many of his sanguinary relations, Emekuku people, Owerri people and Nigerians at large. He helped to admit many of them into Rust College and got scholarship for many of them. He touched the lives of many Nigerians. To crown it all, he established a Secondary School in his home town, Azaraowala, Emekuku, a School now called Emekuku Comprehensive School, to help his people (Fig. 7.4 a & b). He, by all means, deserves a posthumous award not only for his academic accomplishments as a distinguished scholar but for his great philanthropy—for what he did disinterestedly for Igbo people both at home and in the US before his death! I, through this medium, propose the naming of the secondary school he single-handedly established, after him as a memento or something connecting him with the school.

I must not fail to mention some of my contemporaries and colleagues whom I feel impacted my life in one way or another, and furthered the cause of the Igbos. They are Prof. Bart Nnaji, FAS, CON, the former Minister of Mines and Power, a benefactor of Awaka people, his in-laws that love him. He is married to one of the best daughters of Awaka, Mrs. Agatha Chinyere Nnaji (nee Chukwueke) an amiable, charismatic and unassuming lady. He, among other things, provided a transformer to my Awaka people that enabled them to have light while he was the minister of Mines and Power. We have had long contact with each other and to crown it all, he ably chaired the celebration of my 80th birthday in Dec. 2012 which took place at Imo State University.

Prof. Anya O. Anya, FAS, OFR, (Fig. 3.11) is the former ProChancellor of the Federal University of Agriculture, Umudike, Abia State. He has been my longtime friend and colleague. When I was the Head of Department of Medical Microbiology and Parasitology at the College of Medicine, University of Lagos, he acted as my External Examiner. I also reciprocated and acted as the External Examiner for one of his PhD candidates. We have kept touch with each other since then. He also gave my 80th birthday Lecture.

Another is Chief Prof. Augustine O. Esogbue, FAS, NNOM, Emeritus Professor at Georgia Institute of Technology (p. 286). He has been my bosom friend for a long time. We have interacted in several organizations and above all, he attended my 80th birthday celebration and read my citation. He wrote an impressive and highly cherished tribute about me. He also attended the wedding of one of my daughters, Alexandra, in Atlanta GA. He is involved in many organizations including ones that involve Igbos. He chaired one National Diaspora Day during president Obasanjo's tenure of office.

The next one is Prof. Chidi Akujor, FRAES, FAS, (Fig. 8.4) a relatively young professor with a bright future. He was the Vice Chancellor of Imo State University for a short period. He and I have been interacting from the time I was Pro-Chancellor of Imo State University till the present time. He is the current President of the Renewable and Alternative Energy Society of Nigeria and has been engaging in many activities concerning Igbos. He is the one that organized the celebration of my 80th birthday in Nigeria after I celebrated it in the USA. He has chaired the WillyEsther Foundation Inc. Free Medical Mission of which I am the Founder and President, several times. He is the Managing Editor of Advances in Science and Technology Journal while I am the Editor-in-Chief and he is a Professor of Astrophysics at the Federal University of Technology, Owerri.

Another is Prof. Peter Okorie, a hydrologist at IMSU. He and I have been collaborating in research for many years and have published several papers together. He also attended some of my free medical missions and several functions I organized or that involved me. He is currently the Dean, Faculty of Science at IMSU and Director, IMSU Consultancy Services. Last but not the least is Mr. Anthony Omeni Njoku J.D. (Fig. 2.9) (popularly known as Agbara-agbara), author of "Owerre man is not an Owere man" (Njoku 1995). I wrote the forward for this philosophical book. He hails from Ihitta Ogada, Owerri North LGA. He was the principal of Sebastian Academy Emekuku and the Education Secretary Owerri Municipal, Imo State. He is my age mate and boyhood friend. We have continued to be friends from elementary school till this time of writing this autobiography. He has attended all the free medical missions I have held. At one time he was the acting

Chairman of the opening ceremony until the Chairman came. We have been mutual friends in the real sense of the word and we have been acting and interacting with each other. He is also my name sake with one of my Igbo names given me by my mother being, Omeni-chekwa.

All these deserve the recognition I am giving them. They have individually accomplished more than I have space to indicate here and influenced my life.

I like to close this chapter by reproducing a passage from Oseloka Obaze's "Regarscent Past: A Collection of Poems" (2015) which I consider apropos. It has the title: "An Ode to My Igbo Origin":

I am that which I am Not of choice
But of God's infinite wisdom
And to wit, my color, language and culture
My entire being.

I am that which I am
No apologies served
Even though a change I may elect
But whence to, and for what purpose
Must I mutate from that which is preordained?
So be it then, my antecedents, my origin
I am that which I am
Onye Igbo Chukwu kelu
A true-son-of-the-soil, left and right
The burdens of my origin like my negritude
I must endure, and its joys and grace cherish
For all said and done, for good or bad
I am proud, that I am that which I am
I am an Igbo Man.

While I have said all that I said; while I have recorded my views, positive and negative, I mean no harm. I have no malice against any one. I am an Igbo man; I am proud to be Igbo. If there is reincarnation, I pray that I come back as an Igbo. But let us resolve to accentuate the positive and change the negative for the better. Let us resolve to turn over a new leaf: to eschew our loathsome characteristics. Let us bring out the best in us and purge ourselves of the bad. We can change! "There is nothing so certain as the certainty of change". It is as sure as the day follows the night.

Let us learn to show appreciation for what is done for us rather than claim to be self-made and hide what is done for us. No man is an island; a tree cannot make a forest. It is a give-and-take world at any level or stage of life and any relationship (father and children, brother and brother, sister and sister, brother and sister, friend and friend etc.) Life is not a one way traffic. It is a mutual relationship. A person said: "Love unpaid, ends in disgust."

In Igbo language we say: Ole onye ele ya ni, olu hiri ya ahiri.

Literally it means: A person who looks at another person that does not care to look back at him, ends up developing a strained, stiff, or crooked neck.

The famous Awaka vocalist, Agbaso Udeokporo ("Ababanna") said:

> "Akari kwo akaipa, akaipa akwo akari, ha na abu adi ucha"

In English, this means: Right hand washes left hand; left hand washes right hand and both of them become clean. How so true! This is the game of life; the way to get along with little or no friction.

The Igbos and Their Neighbors (My Views)

Fig. 7.1: Chief Sir Prof A D W, Acholonu poses as a triple chief with the following titles Ekwueme, Omereoha and Ogbuhoruzo

Fig. 7.2: Prof. Alex Acholonu receives World Igbo Congress (WIC) Chairman's Community Service Award. He was also a member of the WIC Council of Elders and Imo State Council of Elders under former Gov. Ohakim, representing WIC

The Igbos and Their Neighbors (My Views)

Fig. 7.3: Late Mr. Nathan Ejiogu former Chairman, Civil Service Commission, Eastern Region, Nigeria. He gave me five pounds after my father and I visited him before my travel to US for further studies

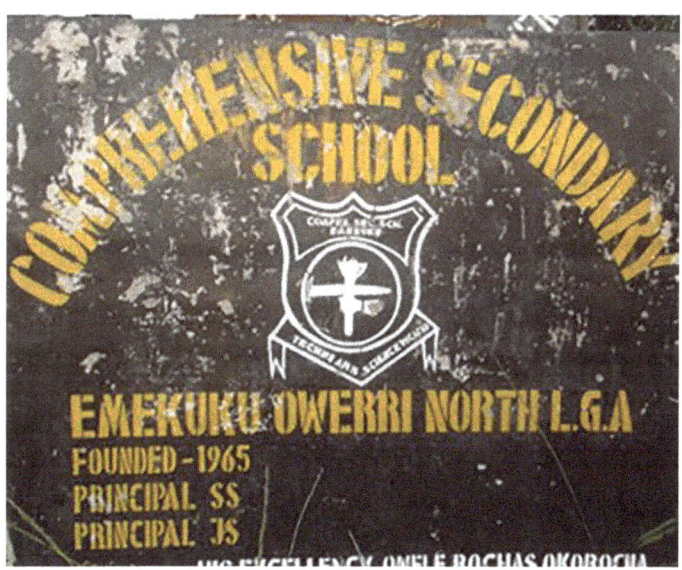

Fig. 7.4a: Secondary school founded in 1965 by Dr. Benedict Chiaka Njoku of Azaraowala, Emekuku, Owerri North, LGA, my mentor. He deserves a special recognition for this achievement and others

Fig. 7.4b: Classroom building of Secondary school founded in 1965 by Dr. Benedict Chiaka Njoku of Azaraowala, Emekuku, Owerri North, LGA, my mentor, former Vice President for Academic Affairs, Rust College, Holly Springs, MS, USA

Chapter Eight

Philanthropy

> "Those who bring sunshine to the lives of others cannot keep it from themselves."

My father prepared me for what I am today. I believe that I am more or less like his dream. He had high hopes in me and created great expectations for me, in myself. First, he enabled me to go overseas for my university education at a time it was quite difficult to do so. I will therefore, never be tired of acknowledging him. Through his kind-hearted and benevolent or philanthropic nature, he was very helpful to his siblings especially Uncles Cyril and Eugene. He practically fathered his very junior brother now Chief Barrister Patrick Acholonu as requested by his father as well as his nephew, Sebastian (Uncle Jonathan's first son) that he helped to train in school after I brought him back to Awaka from his maternal home (Uratta) where he fled to when he was not getting along with his father. I personally requested my father to take over and help him and he obliged! He gave freely of what he had to many within his family and outside. His help to Uncle Cyril was acknowledged is his biography "The Bridge Across Time…" (Nwulu, 2014). Here is an excerpt from it: "Consequently, he ever remains grateful to his brother, Wilfred Wozuzu Acholonu, who as a court clerk in the 30s had considerable wealth to ensure his younger brother, Manubaa went to school since he showed so much promise." He gave name and prominence to the Acholonu family or did so more than anyone else. So my father showed the way and I followed it. He was generous and showed me how to be philanthropic. As soon as I found my feet as a student in the United States, I quickly drew up a blue print for what I would do to impact lives in my home, my town, Awaka and country, Nigeria. Like they say, charity begins at home and drawing upon this common cliché', I began from my very or immediate family and compound, then extended to the larger Acholonu family. My father had three wives that were still in the compound. My first goal was to enable the first sons of the other two wives of my father to come to the US. I figured that if I accomplished that, each of them would, in turn, help their immediate siblings to come over to the US. This would form my first assignment. The next, which is also like the first will be to go a little further, still within the Acholonu family and get one child of my father's brothers to come to the US for further education; that is, get one child, each from all of my uncles, to cross over, so that every household in the Acholonu compound would have someone in the US or overseas.

The implementation of my plan of action was exciting and straight. I started with bringing my brother, Maximian Nnamdi Acholonu, the first son of my father's second wife to demonstrate unity. Maxie eventually, became a well-established civil engineer, a field I choose for him and that is what he is today and retired from the Ministry of Works and Housing, Imo State. Next I brought my immediate junior brother, Chief Uchenna Cletus Acholonu, a successful Engineer that worked for the New York Transit Authority and now retired. He currently lives in Augusta, Florida. The next person I brought was my immediate elder brother, Casimir Chukwuma Acholonu to come over and join us in the US. Casmir, at my urging studied Architecture and returned later to work for Imo State government in Nigeria in the Ministry of Works and Housing like Engr. Maxie Acholonu. He is now late. I also tried to enable the first son of my uncle, Benjamin Njoku Acholonu, the immediate senior brother of my father, to become a beneficiary of my plan for the Acholonu family. This uncle of mine, contributed 100 pounds out of the total amount of money needed to be raised before I could go to the US. Unfortunately, this first son by name Francis Chukwuemeka Acholonu now late, was not up and doing and resourceful enough to make it. So I tried his second son, Lewis (Dokie). Everything was going on well with the second son until it was discovered that he had health problem. So, his coming to America failed for health reasons. Then I also tried to bring the first son of Uncle Sylvanus Anukam by name

Sylvester Acholonu, but it did not work out because of some legal issues he had. I next brought the first son of my fathers' third wife by name Adolphus Acholonu, (nicknamed Hitler) (Fig. 4.50). He became mentally sick and had to be sent back home where he later died. Next, two sons of my father's third wife were brought over with input from my brother, Uchenna. They were Charles Jemandoma Acholonu and Benjamin Acholonu. So, all of my father's 17 boys from his 3 wives eventually went to the US with the exception of one, who was not well enough to go (Jude Adim, now late). Subsequently several others came. All 6 male children of my father's 2nd wife came over, with the help of Maxie and the only daughter (Isabella) went to London with her husband. All of my mother's 7 sons and two daughters, Mrs Paulina Okpechi and Mrs. Francisca Onyeuche came over. The first daughter, Mrs. Philomena Osuji stayed at home with her husband but eventually came and she is now in the US. So, of the 25 children of my father, 22 came to the US or overseas. I want to say that there are now about 180 Acholonus in the US, and all of them trace their being here directly or indirectly to me. As I have stated before, this is why my first chieftaincy title is Ogbuhoruzo 1 of Amaigbo and Awaka. It was given to me by the Eze of Amaigbo in recognition of my being the one that opened the gate to the US for the Acholonu family and several in Awaka and elsewhere in Nigeria.

It is also exhilarating that at this point in time, my goal for the Acholonu family has been practically accomplished. There is only one uncle (Damian Ofor Acholonu) now late out of ten of my uncles or direct sons of Acholonu that has not had a child oversees or abroad! I expected his immediate elder brother, Barr. Patrick Acholonu that went to England to get him over. But he failed to do so and his children were too young then. This is a clear indication of the fact that I am not selfish or discriminatory but rather philanthropic and broad minded and that I staunchly believe in unity. I also helped some maternal relations to come overseas or to America. They include Chidi Onukwugha, the first son of Raymond Onukwuagha who gave me 5 pounds before my travel to the US and Jude Onukwugha the son of Uncle Francis Onukwugha. Next to the Acholonus and my maternal relations would be my immediate kindred and Town, Awaka. I have always been alert to my responsibilities as a citizen and as one who has had the privilege of early education and exposure. I made it possible for Dr. John Nnadi (now late) (Fig. 8.16) to come to the US, cared for him, and helped him get admission to Howard University in Washington DC along with brother Maxie (Fig. 4.49). I also helped Adolphus Offrum to come to the US. In addition, I made it possible for Professor Boniface Obichere to come to the U.S. I brought my in-laws son (my wife's senior brother), Alexander Atukpawu to the US and helped his first daughter, Christiana (Mrs. Ajoku) to come also to the US. I also gave some assistance to their relation, Mr. Nick Udumaga to come to the US (Page 264) One particular issue that has bothered us, as a people (Awaka people) over time, is good source of water. As noted before, our neighbors, the Egbu people have natural flowing river called Otamiri River, and Awaka people have none. When I became aware of the fact that modernity can be of immense help to us in the direction of providing solution to our age old problem of water supply, I quickly explored the options available and that resulted in my establishing a bore hole to enable Acholonu family and Awaka people to get water from the depths of the Earth, groundwater (bore hole). I made this available to all and sundry without charge.

I have confessed that God has been my keeper and helper. He has been extremely kind to me in many ways; in fact, in ways I am unable to articulate. For that and other reasons, I made up my mind to be relevant in the work of God. I have donated generously to the Holy Trinity Catholic Church in Awaka (Fig. 1.8a-c) and have been doing it continuously annually. Among other things, I was the first to buy uniform for the choir (choristers), to buy a piano for them, to pay for some church pews. I need not say that I am equally responsive to education, probably because that is my constituency. I have made some handsome input to Ekeama Elementary School at Awaka. I periodically make donations of pens to all the school children and their teachers. I one time shipped books to the school. I am also in the healthcare sector and for that I should be felt in matters concerning health. I renovated some of the classrooms, especially when I use them for Medical Missions for Awaka community (Fig. 8.1-10) and environs, another philanthropic activity. In my Awaka community, I have tried to do several things. I have seen to the location of a medical clinic in my house at Awaka to help people get treatment and not necessarily run to Emekuku or Owerri. This provides an opportunity for Awaka people to have a resident medical doctor to whom people can go for emergencies and health care.

Generally, I have shown interest in a number of sundry issues. For instance, I have established a business center at Awaka under the auspices of Willy-Esther Foundation, an NGO (non-governmental organization), so that the people can be served at their doorsteps, rather than go for a long distances to Owerri town for treatment of matters that require documentation such as typesetting, photocopying, scanning etc. They can now have those things done right there at Awaka, thus saving them the cost and risk of travelling to Owerri and back. I also recently established a diagnostic laboratory (Aug. 21, 2017) to help Awaka Community and others (Fig. 8.1-16).

I established the Willy-Esther Foundation Inc. to continue the good work of my father, Court clerk and Counsellor Wilfred W. Acholonu, who was a philanthropist and my mother, Esther Rose Acholonu, a kind-hearted women freely giving of what she had. The Foundation was incorporated in 2001 in the US. I also registered it in Nigeria. The objective is to help the poor and needy all over the world, with particular focus on Nigeria and the US. The Foundation is involved in a number of projects carefully designed to be of benefit to commonly needy people. Currently, it is handling, in association with Awaka Club One (Fig. 1.1), the construction of a Health Center or Civic Center in the community as part of my interventions. Awaka Club One is an elite group of

Awaka men and their wives, of which I am a member. Every year or time I travel to Nigeria, I take clothes from the US, donated by my students, and give them away at home in Awaka where they are needed.

The Foundation, as part of its agenda, awards scholarships to deserving students at the elementary, secondary, and tertiary school levels based on availability of funds. Further I have made several donations to CKC, my *alma mater*, (Fig. 8.17, 8.20a & b) as a result of which I have been accorded several recognitions. For instance, I renovated the Physics Building two times and my name is written on the outside wall of the building in recognition of what I did. Also, one of the newest hostels is named after me along with some prominent personalities (Fig. 8.20a). Under the auspices of Willy-Esther Foundation financial donations and baby clothes are given to motherless babies homes (Fig. 8.22-23).

After the Nigeria–Biafra war, I resolved to modernize Awaka, my Town to be part of its growth and development, to site any commercial venture there and nowhere else. Apart from my house (residence), I have three commercial properties there that would fetch a lot more money if built in Abuja, Lagos, Port Harcourt, etc.

When I was Pro-Chancellor of the Imo State University (1997 to 1999), I saw a practically empty library. That was quite disturbing. So I made plans to improve the condition. My intervention was remarkable. I sent about 4 shipments of 40 feet containers of books from the US that were used to bring the library up to par with those of similar institutions, and even more that helped the University to get accreditation in several of its academic programs. I also shipped books to FUTO (Fig. 8.21). I conduct free medical missions to help with health disparity problems in Awaka and its environs (Fig 8.1-10). I sponsored the training and ordination as a priest of Rev. Fr. Valentine Acholonu (Fig. 8.18), the son of Mr. Lawrence Acholonu (late) and grandson of my most senior Uncle, Mr. Alfred Ugwuegbula Acholonu (Fig. 1.2) who was one of the four people that brought Christianity to Awaka. (As I was informed by Mr. Edward Enwere and Alphonsus Onybiri. The others are Mr. Phillip Enwere, Mr. Jacob Opara and Mr. Francis Ofurum. I pay school fees for some Acholonu family members' children in secondary schools and universities some occasionally and some continuously, as well as other external relations and non-relations under the auspices of Willy-Esther Foundation (WEF) Inc. I have helped many poor and needy people in Awaka, Owerri North LGA, Imo State, and Nigeria as a whole and I will continue to do so as long as I live and can help.

Fig. 8.1: Free Medical Mission at Awaka by WEF in collaboration with Awaka Go Forward, NGO May 2016

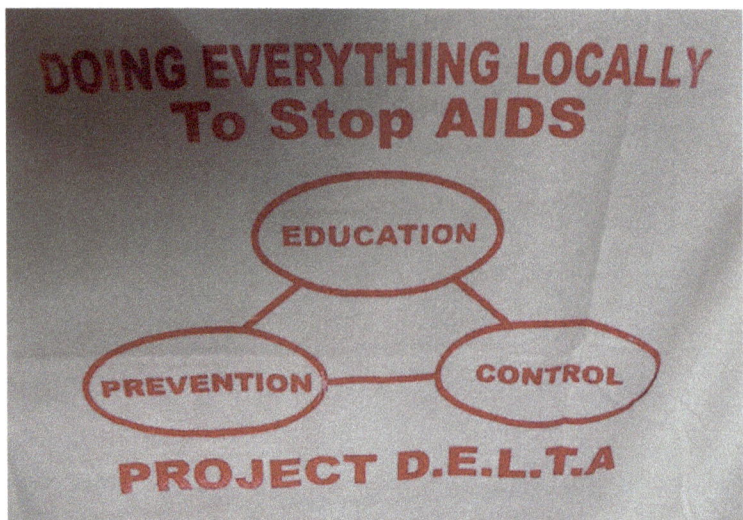

Fig. 8.2: Medical mission and Willy Esther medical mission slogan D.E.L.T.A (Doing Everything Locally to Stop Aids)

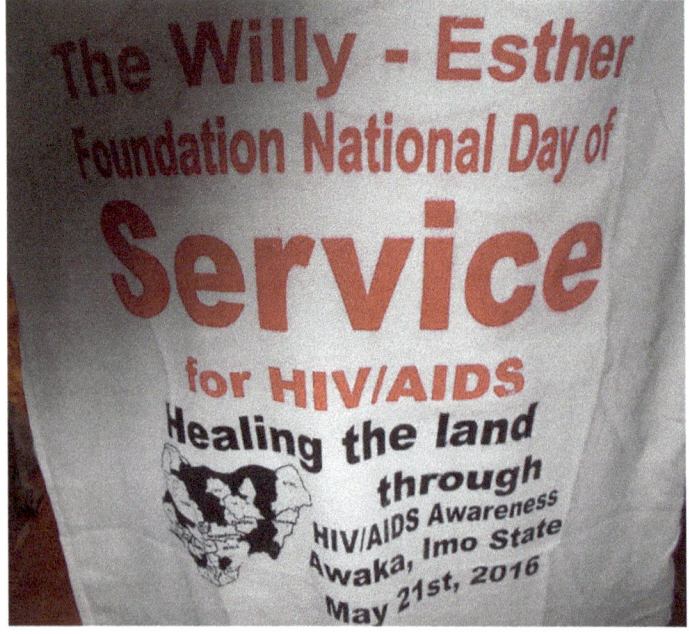

Philanthropy

Fig. 8.3: Prof. Alex Acholonu with HRH Eze Emmanual Sonde Okoro of Emii (left) and Pascal Nnadi, Chief Justice of Imo State going to cut the ribbon and declare the Medical Mission of May 2016 open

Fig. 8.4: Prof. Alex Acholonu with the individuals who officiated during the May 2016 Willy-Esther Foundation Medical Mission

Fig. 8.5: Prof. Alex Acholonu with Prof. Chidi Akujor of Federal Univ. of Technology (left), who chaired several of Willy-Esther Foundation Free Medical Missions opening ceremonies including the one of May 2016 and HRH Eze Godwin Merenini (right) of Umudibia, Nekde who attended the 2016 Medical Mission

Fig. 8.6: Anthony Omeni Njoku DJ (my bosom friend) and Prof. Alex Acholonu

Philanthropy

Fig. 8.7: Prof. Alex Acholonu with Mr. Nwakolobi of Ihitta Ogada. At age 91, he was the oldest man that came to the May 2016 Willy-Esther Foundation Medical Mission held at the Ekeamma Elementary School Awaka Building behind Prof. Acholonu and Mr. Nwakolobi

Fig. 8.8: Prof. Acholonu (3rd from left) and his brother Dr. Wilfred Acholonu Jr. (4th from left) and student laboratory scientists from IMSU that officiated during the Medical Mission of 2010

Fig. 8.9: Prof. Acholonu flanked at both sides by his sons—Anderson Acholonu (right) and Alex Acholonu (JNR) (left) who worked with him during the Medical Mission of 2010. In the background is the Ekeamma Elementary School, venue of the Medical Mission

Fig. 8.10: Prof. Acholonu showing Laboratory Technology students from Imo State University how to test blood sugar in patients

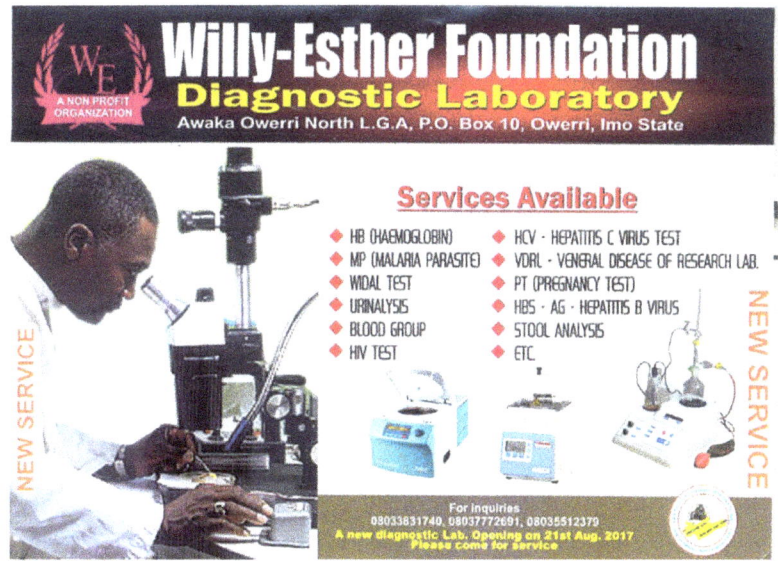

Fig. 8.11: Flyer used for announcing the launching of Willy-Esther Foundation Diagnostic Laboratory, August 21, 2017

Fig. 8.12: Picture taken during the launching of Willy-Esther Foundation Medical Diagnostic Laboratory on Aug 21, 2017 for use of Awaka Community—a philanthropic act. Left to right are some dignities that attended, Evangelist Peter Chima, Coordinator Awaka Go Forward, HRH Eze Emmanuel Okoro of Emii, Prof. Alex Acholonu, Chief Innocent Ugwuegbulam, Director Avigram Lab, Sister Mary Joy Emereibe of Awaka and lecturer, Alvan Ikeoku College of Education and Mrs. Theresa Wagbara (nee Acholonu)

Fig. 8.13: Prof. Alex Acholonu (middle) poses with His Royal Highness (HRH) Eze Okoro (left) and Chief Innocent Ugwuegbulam (right) who attended Launching of the Diagnostic Lab

Philanthropy

Fig. 8.14: Left to right Rev. Fr. Cornelius Ajaegbu, Awaka Holy Trinity Catholic Parish who prayed, blessed and launched the laboratory, Prof. Alex Acholonu, Sister Mary Joy Emeribe, Mrs. Theresa Wagbara (nee Acholonu)

Fig. 8.15: Left to right Mrs. Theresa Wagbara, Bazil Acholonu, Prof. Alex Acholonu and Ugochi Odunze

Fig. 8.16: Group picture of some people who attended the Diagnostic Lab. Launching

Fig. 8.17: Prof. Acholonu honored by CKC students and their Principal, Dr. Rev. Fr. Charles Okwumuo on one of his visits to the school, his *Alma Mater*, as a philanthropic donor to CKC

Fig. 8.18: Rev. Fr. Valentine Acholonu, the 1st priest of Awaka whom I sponsored his training as a priest. Ordained in July 16, 1994

"This is one thing I ask of the Lord, for this I long to live in the house of the Lord, all the days of my life, to savor the sweetness of the Lord, to behold his temple".

Fig. 8.19: Dr. John Nnadi, young when he came to America. I helped make his coming to the US possible, put him in Howard University, Washington DC and had him live with me for some time before he left to live on his own

Philanthropy

Fig. 8.20a: The newest hostel built at Christ the King College, Onitsha, Anambra, Nigeria. Named after or in honor of Prof. Alex Acholonu for his philanthropic contributions to the College, along with HRH Eze and Prof. Edozien, Cardinal Arinze and Archbishop Valerian Okeke

Fig. 8.20b: Prof. Alex Acholonu and the CKC Principal, Rev. Dr. Fr. Charles Okwumuo (left) with some students. Picture taken during a visit to CKC in 2016

My Journey Through Life

Fig. 8.21: Prof. Acholonu after courtesy visit to Prof. C. Onwuliri (late), while he was Vice Chancellor, FUTO to which he donated books worth about 10 million naira

Philanthropy

Fig. 8.22: Motherless Babies Home in Mount Camel Catholic Church, Emekuku, Owerri North LGA to which donations of babies clothes and money were made on about 3 occasions

Professor Acholonu as a Philanthropist

Fig.8.23: Prof. Acholonu visited and made donation of money and babies cloths to the Motherless Babies' home in Uratta, Owerri, 2010

Chapter Nine

Some Key Dates in My Life (1932–2017)

This Chapter contains what I consider the outstanding events in my journey through life. While some of the information here may already be in some of the previous chapters, this is an effort to crystalize them for ease of reference. They constitute the good, the bad and the ugly. It clearly depicts what life is all about. Life is like a roller coaster. Sometimes we are up; sometimes we are down. Sometimes we have good fortune; sometimes we have bad fortune or misfortune. Sometimes the worst of things happen to us; sometimes the best of things happen to us. *C'est la vie* (i.e. that is life). It is a life of struggle and contention. We should however, expect the best while prepared for the worst. As Jessie Jackson said, we must 'keep hope alive' until we take our exit from this world.

Nov. 30, 1932	I was born at Ndegbelu Awaka, Owerri North L.G.A., Imo State
Dec. 1947	Got Standard Six (Elementary Six) School Certificate.
Jan. 1948	Entered Christ the King College, Onitsha, Anambra State.
1952	Got Cambridge School Certificate. Grade II
Jan. 1955	Entered Howard University, Washington DC
1956	I experienced my first discrimination in the US in a restaurant near the Catholic University of America when in the company of late Dr. Benedict Njoku, my former standard six teacher, my mentor and benefactor and his two white friends. The man in the restaurant (waiter) said that he would serve the white men but not both of us

1957	I was miraculously saved from drowning in a lake in Virginia where I went with two white friends to muse and have fun.
1957	I experienced my second discrimination when I was travelling in a Gray Hound Bus to Marshall, Texas to visit Dr. Ben Njoku. We stopped at a bus stop next to Monroe, LA. The bus driver told me to get up from my seat and let a white man that entered sit while I go to the back of the bus. I refused and said that I did not pay black money
May 1958	Got B. S degree in Chemistry from Howard University.
May 1961	Got MS degree in Parasitology from Prairie View A & M University
May 1964	Got PhD degree in Parasitology (under Zoology) as Federal Government of Nigeria Scholar.
May 1964	Taught at Alcorn State University (summer session)
May 1964-1969	Taught at Southern University, Baton Rouge, LA
Mar. 1967	I got married in Baton Rouge, Louisiana. This marks a remarkable change of status from being a bachelor for 35 years to being a married man.
Dec. 1967	I became a father with the birth of my first child and son, Anderson Ukachi Akopoazu Acholonu, another remarkable and welcome change of status.
Feb. 1968.	I got my first daughter, Sandra Akunna Acholonu also in Baton Rouge, LA. That I got both sexes so early as children, was remarkable and fulfilling.
Sep. 1968.	Became full Professor at Southern University
1969–1972	Taught at Inter American University of Puerto Rico.
1972–1973	Taught at Catholic University of Puerto Rico Ponce, Puerto Rico.

Some Key Dates in My Life (1932–2017)

1973–1977	Worked at State University of New York, College at Oneonta as Dean of Liberal Studies (Dean of Arts and Science)
Feb. 1976.	My father died after he stayed with us in the U.S for 1 year
1982 (about January)	6 assassins, apparently hired by my blood relations from the Acholonu Family, were sent to kill me. Not finding me home (thanks to Almighty God), they shot my wife in the thigh region, took all her goods and expensive Jewelry and left. As luck and God would have it, she survived the bullet wound.
1983	One of my 17 brothers, whom I had helped to come to America for further studies, from my father's third wife, after apparently making juju with his cohorts, told me straight in my face, the day I was to die. Thanks to God. The day came but I did not die. His (or their) juju failed!
1983–1984	Worked at College of Technology Amaigbo, Imo State, Nigeria as First Rector. (Now called School of Health Studies)
May 1985	I got my second son and last child, number 7. This was a fulfillment of my dreams and desires. I named him Alexander Dozie Wozuzu Acholonu, Junior
Feb. 1988–Jun. 1988	Worked at Howard University, Washington D.C. as Adjunct Professor
1977–1991	Taught at College of Medicine, University of Lagos, Nigeria; Head of Medical Microbiology and Parasitology (1979-1982)
Oct. 1987–Jun. 1988	Worked at University of the District of Columbia Washington DC, as Adjunct Professor/Research Associate, during my sabbatical leave from University of Lagos; completed the big house my dad requested, and named it after him, "Willy Wozuzu Acholonu Memorial Mansion"

1991–Present	Taught at Alcorn State University, Lorman, MS
1999–2004	I was elected President of Alcorn State University's Faculty Senate and served for the maximum of 6 years (that is, 2 terms)
1991	I voluntarily retired from College of Medicine, University of Lagos and came back to the USA mainly to see that my children get a good quality education
1992	I got my first Chieftaincy title as Ogbuhoruzo I of Amaigbo
July 16, 1994	Ordination of Rev. Fr. Valentine Acholonu, 1st Awaka Priest whose Priest-hood training I sponsored (see Fig. 8.15)
2001	I established the Willy-Esther Foundation, Inc., a philanthropic nonprofit organization, in honor of my father and mother and to help the poor and the needy
Nov. 2002	I celebrated My First Major Birthday in the US, My 70th Birthday in Vicksburg, MS there was also a proclamation: **Declaration of "Chief Dr. Alexander D. W. Acholonu Day: in Hazlehurst, MS by Hon Mayor Henry Banks** as a special recognition for my accomplishment
Dec. 24, 2002	I was Conferred My 2nd Chieftaincy Title As Ekwueme 1of Ihitta Ogada
2005	I travelled to China, selected as a visiting scholar to teach in a university for 2 weeks. I also did water quality research while there that resulted in a publication.
Mar. 31, 2007	I got my 3rd Chieftaincy title as Omereoha
Feb. 2012.	I received a prestigious award for distinguished contribution to Science from the Mississippi Academy of Science and became the first in the history of Alcorn State University which started in 1871 to receive this award.April 23, 2012 I was given a key to Hazlehurst city and made a citizen

Some Key Dates in My Life (1932–2017)

Jun. 2012	of Hazlehurst by Hon. Mayor Henry Banks (see picture pg. 166-167) Proclamation of honorary "Life, Longevity, and Service" Mr. Derryl Grennell, the President of the Board of Supervisors in Natchez, MS (and now the Mayor), and his Board Members gave me a special reception and honored me with a PROCLAMATION IN RECOGNITION OF THE PRESTIGIOUS AWARD/PLAQUE I RECEIVED FROM THE MISSISSIPPI ACADEMY OF SCIENCE IN FEBRUARY, 2012.
Nov. 23, 2012	I celebrated in a special way, my 80th birthday in Vicksburg, MS and in Nigeria in December The Mayor of Hazlehurst, Hon. Henry Banks who chaired my 80th birthday celebration.
Feb. 2016.	I received another prestigious award/ plaque from the Mississippi Academy of Science for my contributions to Health Disparity Research
Aug. 2016	CKC-AAA (Christ the King College Alumni Association of America) honored me with an award/plaque as a well accomplished member and an octogenarian (80 years old)
Dec. 20, 2016	I received the Prestigious Imo Diaspora Award For professional accomplishments and excellence
Aug. 21. 2017	I formally established Willy-Esther Foundation Diagnostic Lab. in Awaka, my home town, Imo State, Nigeria.

Chapter Ten

Profile and Curriculum vitae of Chief Sir Professor Alexander Dozie Wozuzu Acholonu, PHD, FNSP, FRAES, FAS, OON

I have known Professor Acholonu for several years. His resume speaks volumes about him. His worth as one of the most accomplished and distinguished academicians in our Country, Nigeria, are indisputable. He has continued to be productive even at the age of 85 years. Among other things, he is still excelling in the academic world both nationally and internationally. He is a man that deserves emulation. I am proud to paint below a vivid picture of his profile to prove beyond shadow of doubt his unalloyed qualifications.

Education

Chief, Sir Professor Alexander Dozie Wozuzu Acholonu was born at Awaka in Owerri North Local Government Area (LGA), Imo Sate, Nigeria, on November 30, 1932. He was the second son of Court Clerk and Counsellor Wilfred Wozuzu Acholonu and Mrs. Esther Rose Acholonu, both late, but now the oldest of the living children. He got his Standard (elementary) six certificate in 1947 at Our Lady's School, Emekuku now known as Fr. Croonan Primary School, Emekuku, Owerri, Imo State and his Cambridge School Certificate at Christ the King College, Onitsha, Anambra State, in 1952. He got his B. S degree at Howard University in Washington D.C. in 1958, M.S. at Prairie View A& M University, Texas, 1961, Ph. D. at Colorado State University, Fort Collins, Colorado in 1964 and Continuing Education Certificate in Public Health and Tropical Medicine, at Tulane University, Louisiana in 1994.

Academic Administrative Experiences

Prof. Acholonu is an academician *per excellence*. He is a man who has held practically all administrative positions in academia.

He was Professor and Chairman, Department of Biology, Inter American University of Puerto Rico, 1970-1972 and Professor and Head of Department of Medical Microbiology and Parasitology of the College of Medicine, University of Lagos (CMUL) and Consultant at Lagos University Teaching Hospital (LUTH), 19771991. He was Dean of Liberal Studies (Arts and Sciences) at the State University of New York, Oneonta, New York, 1973-77, the Rector of the former Amaigbo College of Technology (now School of Health Sciences), Imo State, 1983-1984, a Member of the Governing Council of Imo State University, 1981-83 and the Pro-Chancellor and Chairman of Governing Council of Imo State University, 1997-99.

Professional Accomplishments and Recognitions

He is a seasoned and renowned educator and a scholar who has published one book, two booklets, four book chapters and over 100 scientific articles, and presented numerous papers to various scientific organizations (over 50). He has excelled in his field of expertise and has won many national and international recognitions and accolades. He is cited in the American Men of Science, Men of Achievement, International Who's Who of Intellectuals, Who's Who in America, and Who's Who in Nigeria. In 2002, he was cited as **one of 2000 Outstanding Intellectuals of the 21st Century,** and as **one of the Great Minds of the 21st Century** by the International Biographical Center, Cambridge, England. In the same year, he received a Universal Award of Accomplishments in Microbiology and Parasitology from the American Biographical Institute, International Educator of the Year 2003, One of the Top 100 Educators of the year 2005 and Who's Who Among America's Teachers, 2005, America's Registry of Outstanding Professionals,

2006-2007, listed in the **Global Directory of Who's Who, 2007**, Vicksburg's Prominent 400, Mississippi 2006. He is a recipient of the Nigerian National Honors award Medal of **Officer of the Order of the Niger (OON), 2003,** a Life Achievement Award in Microbiology and Parasitology, 2004 by the Nigerian Academy of Science. He is a Fellow of the Nigerian Society for Parasitology (FNSP) and a Fellow of the Nigerian Academy of Science (FAS), the highest honor given to a scientist in Nigeria. He was the Editor of the Nigerian Journal of Microbiology, 1982-90, and President of the Nigerian Society for Parasitology, 1980-81. He was an Executive Board Member of the World Federation of Parasitologists 1998-2002; 2002-2006, and re-elected in 2010-2014, and a member of Council from 1998–2014. He was the Chairman of the Division of Zoology and Entomology of the Mississippi Academy of Sciences, 2002–2004, Vice Chairman and a Board Member, 1998-2002, Vice Chairman, 2006–2009, and re-elected chairman 2010–11; Chairman, Healthcare Disparity Committee, 2012-present re-elected Chairman of Zoology and Entomology Mississippi Academic of Science, 2017. He served as President of the Faculty Senate of Alcorn State University in Mississippi from 1999–2004.

He is currently the Editor-in-Chief of Advances in Science and Technology, an international journal (2007 to present) and Editor-in-Chief, Community Voice Action Magazine, 2016 to present.

Prof. Acholonu is an intellectual giant whose research and quest for knowledge have taken him to many parts of the U.S. and the world. He was one of those selected to participate in the 2005 Academic Scholars Program in China as a visiting Scholar to teach at Huaiyin Teachers University from May 20 to June 5, 2005. He has supervised the research of many under-graduate and graduate students (B.S, M.S, and Ph. D.). He has been doing good things on both sides of the Atlantic Ocean and getting recognitions. In 2002, he was appointed a Member of the Food Advisory Committee (FAC) of the U.S. Food and Drug Administration (FDA) to serve in this capacity from 2002 to 2005, because of his expertise in Microbiology and Parasitology—a rare and prestigious appointment, and received a Distinguished Service Award in 2005 from FDA. He served as Chairman of Review Panel, US Department of Agriculture, 2016.

One of his most outstanding research accomplishments is his discovery, naming and description of 14 new species of parasites.

Service to Nigeria

Prof. Acholonu has rendered service to Nigeria in many ways. He was a member of the National Expert Committee for the Control of Sexually Transmitted Diseases (STDs), 1990-92 (He was in charge of the eastern region of Nigeria); Member of the Committee for the Control of Malaria, 1982-86; and Member of the Governing Board of Nigerian Institute for Trypanosomiasis Research, Kaduna and Chairman of the Research Program Committee, 1981-1983. He established a prize for the best Medical student in Parasitology at the College of Medicine, University of Lagos, a prize at the Federal Polytechnic Nekede, Imo State for the best student in Architecture in honor of his late brother Arch. Casime C. Acholonu and a prize at Imo State University for the best student in the Biological Sciences. He donated five hundred thousand Naira (₦500,000) for annual lectureship in honor of his late father at Imo State University in 1998; delivered four (4) shipments of books to Imo State University worth over ten million Naira (₦10,000,000) each, one shipment of books and educational materials to the Federal University of Technology, Owerri worth ten million Naira (₦10,000,000) and one shipment of books and educational materials to Federal polytechnic, Nekede, Imo State, and Christ the King College, Onitsha, Anambra worth 55 million Naira. He made a donation of ten thousand naira (₦10,000) to the Red Cross Motherless Babies Home in Owerri, Imo State in January, 2002, twenty thousand naira (₦20,000) in January 2007 and twenty five thousand naira (₦25,000) in January 2008 and a big sack of used and new baby clothes. He awarded scholarship to a young man to study Engineering at FUTO through the WillyEsther Foundation of which he is the Founder/President and CEO. The young man graduated in 2010. In 2004, he made a donation of ₦726,000.00 (seven hundred and twenty-six thousand naira) to his *alma mater*, Christ the King College, Onitsha for the rehabilitation of the Physics Laboratory. He sank a borehole for the Acholonu family and Awaka community to provide them with much needed potable water and donated ₦50,000 naira to the Awaka Club 1 in 2003 and another one of ₦350,000 (three hundred and fifty thousand naira) in 2004 for the construction of a civic center that will serve, among other functions, as a center for HIV/AIDS education and support services. This project is expected to continue. He has been instrumental in the education of many Nigerians both his relations and others-sponsoring and helping them to go to America to acquire knowledge for the betterment of his community, local government, state and Nigeria at large. Because of his national and international accomplishments and services to his community and Nigeria, Prof. Acholonu was in December 24, 1992, conferred a chieftaincy title with the name: **Ogbuhoruzo 1 of Amaigbo and Awaka** (that is, the one who opened the gateway to America for his people). On the 24th of December, 2002, a traditional ruler, His Royal Highness, Eze Godwin Nwankwere of Ihitta Ogada, Imo State, now late, conferred on him another chieftaincy title as a further recognition of his accomplishments and good deeds and gave him the title of **Ekwueme 1 of Ihitta Ogada and Awaka.** In March 2007, His Royal Highness, Eze Emmanuel Sonde Okoro of Emii conferred on him a third title as **Omereoha** because of his accomplishments and philanthropic activities.

Very much interested in continuing to help his people, in 2008, **The Willy-Esther Foundation, of which Professor Acholonu is the president and founder, collaborated with Horizon International Medical Missions, Inc. (HIMM) to carry out a medical mission in Awaka, Owerri North Local Government**

Area. It was a very successful medical mission and was very much appreciated by the people and the Government of Imo State which showed support of the mission. Since then he has conducted three more, namely 2010, 2014, and 2016 and has decided to conduct more medical missions in the future as funds become available because of popular demand and his love for his people— Awaka people.

Social Organizations

Prof. Acholonu belongs to several religious and social organizations. He is a 4th degree Knight (Knight of Columbus), which gave him the title of "Sir" which he uses rarely. He is a member of Phi Beta Sigma Fraternity, Owerri Progressive Union in the U. S. since 2006, Christ the King College, Onitsha, Alumni Association in America (CKC-AAA), a group that gave him Exceptional Service Award in 2006 and honored him with another prestigious and legend award in August, 2016, a member of Center Point, and Awaka Club one etc. He was a member of the Council of Elders of the World Igbo Congress and Imo State Council of Elders; a member of Imo State Congress of America in which he serves as a patron, etc.

The Acholonu Family

Today, the Acholonu family members in America number up to 180 and he is directly and indirectly responsible for their living in the United States and flourishing. Their professions practically cover all walks of life. There are medical doctors, attorneys (lawyers), pharmacists, engineers, scientists (Biochemists, Microbiologists, etc.), computer scientists, clinical laboratory scientists, accountants/CPA, Book keeping and finance experts, Public Health experts, Nurses, etc. Many are in universities that include the Ivy League schools like Harvard and Stanford.

Prof. Acholonu is a hard-working indefatigable man. He said that his motto is: "Take time to work. It is the price of success." He further said that the road to success is always under construction. At age 84, he looks unbelievably strong and professionally agile.

Professor Acholonu has seven children-two sons and five daughters and 16 grandchildren. He is married to Lolo Lady Mary Ekeoma Acholonu, (nee Atukpawu of Umuawuka, Emii) a former Vice-Principal at Herbert Macaulay Grammar School in Lagos, Nigeria and a former High School teacher in the U.S. with M.S degree in Education Administration.

Professor Acholonu has other national and international accomplishments too many to mention here. He is a man who has made monumental contributions in education, research, and in service to his community, his state, Nigeria and America alike.

He is a man of many parts, a benevolent man, and a well-known philanthropist hence, the title bestowed on him on March 31, 2007 as **Omereoha** (meaning one who does or helps people in general) by His Royal Highness, Eze Emmanuel Sonde Okoro, Omenyi II of Emii, who in his infinite wisdom decided to give him a further recognition for his achievements and contributions "to the development of humanity and communities" by conferring on him a third Chieftaincy title as stated before.

Chief, Sir, Professor Alex Dozie Wozuzu Acholonu deserves the honors bestowed on him. The Federal Government of Nigeria and Imo State should not hesitate to add more feathers to his cap by giving him more recognitions.

High Chief Kennedy K. Okere, MD
Aka ji Ogwu 1 of Owerri West, Imo State
Founder and President
Horizon International Medical Missions

Curriculum Vitae of Chief Prof. Alex D. W. Acholonu

ALEXANDER D.W. ACHOLONU
DEPARTMENT OF BIOLOGICAL SCIENCES
ALCORN STATE UNIVERSITY
1000 ASU DRIVE #843
ALCORN STATE, MS 39096
(601) 877-6236
FAX (601) 877-2328
E-mail chiefacholonu@alcorn.edu
chiefacholonu@yahoo.com
cheifacholonua@gmail.com

EDUCATION:

B.S., Howard University, Washington, D.C., 1958
M.S., Prairie View A&M University, Texas, 1961
Ph.D., Colorado State University, Colorado, 1964
Continuing Education Certificate, Tulane University, School of Public Health & Tropical Medicine & Hygiene, Louisiana, 1994

PROFESSIONAL EXPERIENCE:
Teaching and Administrative Positions

1991Present	ALCORN STATE UNIVERSITY, Alcorn State, Mississippi Professor, Department of Biological Sciences
19982004	MISSISSIPPI STATE UNIVERSITY Mississippi State, Mississippi Adjunct Professor, College of Veterinary Medicine
1977-1991	COLLEGE OF MEDICINE UNIVERSITY OF LAGOS, Lagos, Nigeria

	Professor, Department of Medical Microbiology and Parasitology Head of Department (1979-1982) Head, Medical Parasitology Unit (1988-1991)
1977-1991	LAGOS UNIVERSITY TEACHING HOSPITAL Lagos Nigeria Consultant, Medical Microbiology and Parasitology
Feb 1988-June 1988	HOWARD UNIVERSITY Washington, D.C. Adjunct Professor, Department of Zoology
Oct. 1987June 1988	UNIVERSITY OF THE DISTRICT OF COLUMBIA; Washington, D.C. Adjunct Professor, Research Associate School of Life Sciences
1983-1984	COLLEGE OF TECHNOLOGY (Now school of Health Sciences) Amaigbo, Imo State, Nigeria Rector (President)
1973-1977	STATE UNIVERSITY OF NEW YORK, COLLEGE AT ONEONTA Oneonta, New York Dean of Liberal Studies (Dean of Arts and Sciences)
1972-1973	CATHOLIC UNIVERSITY OF PUERTO RICO Ponce, Puerto Rico Professor, Department of Biology Chairman, Research and Development Committee

1970-1972   INTER AMERICAN UNIVERSITY OF PUERTO RICO
San Juan Campus, Puerto Rico Professor and Chairman, Department of Biology

1969-1970   INTER AMERICAN UNIVERSITY OF PUERTO RICO
San German Campus,
Puerto Rico Associate Professor

1964-1969   SOUTHERN UNIVERSITY
Baton Rouge, Louisiana Associate Professor (1964-67),
Professor (1968-69),
Department of Biology

1964 (summer)   Alcorn State University,
Associate Professor

MEMBERSHIP IN SOCIETIES

Honor Societies
Sigma XI Research Honor Society
Southern University Chapter, (*President, 1968-69)
Beta Biological Honor Society

Professional Societies

Nigerian Association of Medical Scientists (Life Member); *VicePresident, 1989
Science Association of Nigeria (Life Member): *Vice President, 1989-90
Nigerian Society of Microbiology; *Editor, Nigerian Journal of Microbiology, 1982-90
Nigerian Society for Parasitology (Life Member) now Parasitology and Public Health Society of Nigeria (PPHSN)
*President 1980-81; *Vice-President 1979-80

African Union against Venereal Diseases and Treponematosis (AUVDT), *Vice President, 1987-1991.
Fellow of the Royal Society of Tropical Medicine and Hygiene, 1970-1985
Society of Protozoologists
American Society of Parasitologists: *Chairman, Literature Committee, 1994-2001
Helminthological Society of Washington
American Society of Tropical Medicine and Hygiene
President Africa Assembly of ASTMH
American Association of Veterinary Parasitologists (Newsletter Editorial Board Member)
Mississippi Academy of Sciences (Life Member) *(Zoology, and Entomology Division: Vice Chair 1999-2001, Chair, 2002 to 2005, 2016–present and Board Member, 1998-Present): Chair, Health Care Disparity Committee 2016-present.
Faculty Senate, Alcorn State University, 1998-2004; 2007-2016 President 1999-2004.
University Faculty Senate Association of Mississippi Institutions of Higher Learning. 1998-2005
Ecological Society of America, 1999-2016. Director, ASU SEEDS Program, 1999-2003. Faculty Advisor, ASU Campus Ecology chapter, 2003-2016.
National Association of African American Studies 2000-2016 * American Society of Veterinary Parasitologists

* Position held

AWARDS AND HONORS

American Men of Science, 1965
U.S. National Teaching Fellowship Award, 1972
Fellowship Award, Institute for Academic Deans and Business Officers, 1974
International Who's Who of Intellectuals, U.K., 1975
Who's Who in America, 1976

Letter of Commendation for Outstanding Service by the Nigerian Society for Parasitology, 1981.
Foundation Fellow of the Nigerian Society for Parasitology. (FNSP), 1983
Foundation Patron, Nigerian Venereal Disease Association, 1989
Fellow of the Nigerian Academy of Science, (FAS), 1992.
ASU Nominee for 1996 Research Achievement Award by National Association for Equal Opportunity in Higher Education (NAFEO)
ASU Nominee for 1999 Research Achievement Award by National Association for Equal Opportunity in Higher Education (NAFEO)
ASU Nominee for the U.S, Professor of the Year 2000 Award
Cited as one of 2000 Outstanding Intellectuals of the 21st Century, 2002, UK
Cited as a Great Mind of the 21st Century, 2002, USA Recipient of Universal Award of Accomplishment, 2002, USA
Appointed Member of Food Advisory Committee of the US Food and Drug Administration, 2002-2005; Consultant 2006-present
Cited as International Educator of the year 2003
Recipient of the Nigerian National Honors Award by the President of Nigeria of Officer of the Order of the Niger (OON), 2003.
Recipient of Life Achievement Award for Leadership and Devotion, World Owerri People's Congress, 2004
Recipient of Life Achievement Award in Parasitology and Microbiology by the Nigerian Academy of Science, 2004
Cited in Who's Who among America's Teachers, 2005
Recipient of Distinguished Service Award from US Food and Drug Administration (FDA) Advisory Committee, 2005
Recipient of Exceptional Service Award by Christ the King College Alumni Association (CKC-AAA), 2006
Included in America's Registry of Outstanding Professionals, 2006-2007
Nigeria's Who's Who
Men of Achievement, Illustrated

Recipient of the Mississippi Academy of Science Award for Distinguished Contribution of Science, Feb. 2012

SERVICE AND RECOGNITIONS

Member Governing Board of Imo State University, 1980-1983 Research, Kaduna *(Chairman, Research Program Committee)
1981-1983.
Member, National Committee for the Control of Malaria, Nigeria, 1982-1986.
Member, National Communicable Diseases Control Committee, 1982-1987.
Member, National Expert Committee for the Control of Sexually Transmitted Diseases (STDs), Nigeria—1990-92.
Chieftaincy Conferment, Dec. 24, 1992. (Title: Ogbuhoruzo I of Amaigbo and Awaka)
*Chair, Literature Committee, American Society of Parasitologists, 1994-2001.
Pro-Chancellor and Chairman of Governing Council, (Board of Trustees) Imo State Univ., Nigeria 1997-1999.
Council Member, World Federation of Parasitologists, 1998present.
Executive Board Member, World Federation of Parasitologists, 1998-2002; 2006-2014
President, Alcorn State University (ASU) Faculty Senate, 1999-2004.
Program Director, Strategies for Ecology Education, Diversity and Sustainability (SEEDS of Ecological Society of America) at ASU, 1999-2002.
Program Director, Ecology Education Workshop and Faculty Advisor, SEEDS Ecology Chapter, ASU 1999-2016
Founder/President and CEO, the Willy Ester Foundation, Inc. 2001 - present
Second Chieftaincy Conferment, Dec. 24, 2002. (Title: Ekwueme I of Ihitta Ogada and Awaka)

Third Chieftaincy Conferment Mar. 31, 2007. (Title: Omereoha)
Member, Governing Board of the Nigerian Institute for Trypanosomiasis Research, Kaduna. *Chair, Research Program Committee 1981-83
Editor-in-Chief, Advances in Science and Technology Journal, 2007-present.
Coordinator Research Training and Education, Center of Excellence in Minority Health and Health Disparities (NIH/NIMHD) School of Public Health, Jackson State University, Jackson, MS. 2010–present.

Some International Congresses Attended in Which Scientific Papers were Presented, 1985-2012

Nairobi, Kenya, 1985. International Congress of Protozoology
Brisbane, Australia, 1986. 6th International Congress of Parasitology.
Harare, Zimbabwe, 1987. 5th African Regional STD Conference.
Yaunde, Cameroon, 1989. 6th African Regional STD Conference.
Accra, Ghana, 1990. 2nd Congress of Pan-African Union for Science and Technology.
London, England, 1990. 35th General Assembly of International Union against Venereal Diseases and Treponematosis (IUVDT)
Lusaka, Zambia, 1991. African Regional STD Conference.
Izmir, Turkey, 1994. International Congress of Parasitology.
Chiba, Japan, 1998. 9th International Congress of Parasitology
Christchurch, New Zealand, 2005 20th International Conference of the World Association for the Advancement of Veterinary Parasitology
Glasgow (Scotland), United Kingdom, 2006. 11th International Congress of Parasitology
JeJu, South Korea 2008. International Congress of Tropical Medicine and Malaria.
Melbourne, Australia 2010 International Congress of Parasitology

Rio de Janeiro, Brazil 2012. XVII International Congress for Tropical Medicine and Malaria (Sep 23-27, 2012)
Mexico, Mexico City 2014 international congress of Parasitology

International Congress Attended

Vancouver, Canada, Aug. 2002. 10th International Congress of Parasitology

SUBJECTS TAUGHT

Integrated Science
Research methods and projects
General Biology
Invertebrate Zoology
Microbiology
Histology
Histological Technique
Human Anatomy and Physiology
Genetics
General Parasitology
Advanced Parasitology (graduate)
Mycology (graduate)
Ecology, Morphology and Taxonomy of Animals (graduate)
Medical Parasitology (Medical/Dental students, Midwife and Nursing students,
Master's in Public Health students, Medical Technology students and Resident Doctors)
Clinical Parasitology,
Techniques in Parasitology (graduate)
Host-Parasite Relationship, (graduate)
Topics in Parasitology, (graduate)
Advanced Medical Protozoology, (graduate)
Medical Entomology (graduate)
Environmental Science
Field Biology and Ecology (undergraduate and graduate)

Toxicology
Independent study
Advanced Invertebrate Zoology, (graduate)
Seminar (graduate and undergraduate)

RESEARCH SUPERVISION (graduate and undergraduate students)
I have supervised the research of many undergraduate and graduate students
(B.S., M.S., and Ph.D.).

MY OUTSTANDING CONTRIBUTION TO KNOWLEDGE IN SCIENCE:
I found, described, and named a total of 14 new species of parasites.

LIST OF PUBLICATIONS

Book Chapters

1. Acholonu, A.D.W. 1972. Guyana, Wildlife and Pollution in Guyana: A composite monograph. Inter Aner, University Press pp. 66-85.

2. Acholonu, A.D.W. 1981. Agents responsible for diarrhea diseases: Protozoal diarrhea. In GIAM (Global Impacts of Applied Microbiology) Eds. Emejuaiwe, S.O., Ogunbi, O and Sanni, S.O., p.435-445. Academic Press, Ibadan.

3. Acholonu, A.D.W. 1984. Training for Medical Research in Nigeria-Solution of Manpower Problems. In "Strategy for Medical Research, "University Press, Ibadan, pp. 261-265.

4. Acholonu, A.D.W. 1991. Various Health Schemes and Their Impact in Nigeria: Thirty years of Nationhood; Consolidation of National Independence, pp. 201-216.

Book Review

1. Acholonu, A.D.W., 1973. Annual Review of Ecology and Systematic.

2. Johnson, R.F., Frank, P.W., Michener, C.O., Eds. Palto Alto. Calif.: Annual Reviews, Inc. 1970. Revista Interamericana Review. 3 (1): 112-114.

Books and Booklets

1. Acholonu, A.D.W., 1989. Parasitosis and human health in Nigeria: Present situation and future needs. University of Lagos Press. Pp. 36

2. Acholonu, A.D.W. and Uzoma, K.C. 1991. Medical Laboratory Diagnosis: Collection, Handling, and Storage of Pathological Specimens for Laboratory Investigation. College of Medicine Press, University of Lagos, pp.62.

3. Acholonu, A.D.W., 1998. Trichomoniasis: A Little Recognized Sexually Transmitted Disease but with Grave Consequences. The Nigerian Academy of Science. pp.32.

Articles

1. Acholonu, A.D.W., 1963. Effectiveness of various media for culturing *Trypanosoma lewisi* and *Trypanosoma cruzi*. J. Colorado Wyoming Academy of Science, 5 (4):66.
2. _____.1964. Freshwater cercariae of northern Colorado together with a checklist of the species described in the United States and their molluscan hosts. Dessert. Abst. 25.

3. _____.1964. Life history of *Cotylurus flabelliformis* (Faust, 1917). (Trematoda: Strigeidae) J. Parasitol. 50 (3, Sect. 2): 28. (3, Sect. 2): 28-29.
4. _____.1964. Life history of two Notocotylids (Trematoda). J. Parasitol. 50 (3, Sect. 2): 28-29.
5. _____.1965. Contributions to the life history of *Cotylurus flabelliformis* (Faust, 1917) (Trematoda: Strigeidae). Proc. Helminth Soc. Wash. 32. (2): 138-140.
6. _____.1966. Occurrence of Haemogregarina (Protozoa) in Louisiana turtles. J. Protozool. 13 (Suppl.): 10.
7. _____.1966. Occurrence of *Porocephalus crotali* (Humboldt, 1808) (Pentastomida) in Louisiana turtles. Prog. And Abst. 41st Annual Meeting of the Amer. Society of Parasitologists. P.32.
8. _____.And O. Wilford Olsen, 1967. Studies on the Life History of two notocotylids (Trematoda). Proc. Helminth. Soc. Wash. 34(7): 43-50.
9. _____.1967. Studies on acanthocephalan parasites of Louisiana turtles. Bull. Wildl. Dis. Assoc. 3:40.
10. _____.1967. The spider, *Ctenus bryrrbus*, as a host of the hairworm, Neochordodes sp. (Gordiidae: Nematomorpha). Prog. 41st Annual Meeting Louisiana Acad. Sci. p.3.
11. _____.1968. Studies on the freshwater cercariae of Northern Colorado. Proc. Helm.Soc. Wash. 35(2): 259-271.
12. _____.1968. Studies on the digenetic trematodes of Louisiana turtles. Trans. Am. Micro. Soc. 87(1): 124-125.
13. _____.1968. A new host record for *Cercaria pteractinota* Miller. 1935 (Trematoda) Prog. 42nd Annual Meeting Louisiana Acad. Of Sci. p.6.
14. _____.1968. Neochordodes sp. (Nematomorpha) as a parasite of the spider (*Ctenus bryrrbus*) in Costa Rica. J. Parisit. 54. (6): 1233-1234.
15. _____.1968. Acanthocephala of Louisiana turtles with a redescription of Neoechinorhynchus *stunkardi* Cable and fisher 1961. Proc, Helminth. Soc. Wash. (362): 177-183.

16. _____.1969. Some monogenetic trematodes from Louisiana turtles. Proc. La. Acad. Sci. 32: 20-25.
17. _____.1969. Haemogregarina (Sporozoa) in ophididans from Louisiana. Progress in Protozoology, 3rd Intern. Cong. Protozool., Leningrad, USSR. p. 331.
18. _____.1969. A new record of turtle cestode in Louisiana. 44th Annual Meeting of the American Society of Parasitologists. p.75.
19. _____.1970. On *Proteocephalus testudo* (Magath, 1924) (Cestoda: Proteocephalidae) from *Trionyx spinifer* (Chelonia) in Louisiana. J. Wildlife Dis. 6: 171-172.
20. _____.1970. Studies on *Mesocoelium danforthi* Hoffman, 1935 (Trematoda: Branchycoelidae) and its distribution in the herpetofauna of the Greater Antilles. Proc. Second Intern. Cong. Parasitol., Washington, D.C., J. Parasitol. 56 (4): Sec. 11 Pt.2
21. _____.And Katherine Arny, 1970. Incidence of nematode parasites of Louisiana Turtles. Proc. La. Aca. 33: 26-43.
22. Haywood, M.J. and A.D. Acholonu, 1971. Some helminth parasites of Pennsylvania Turtles. Prog. Annual Wildlife Disease Conference. p.226.
23. _____.1973. Prevalence of human ascariasis and trichuriasis in San Juan and vicinity, Puerto Rico. J. Parasitol. 59: 460.
24. _____.And M.E. Acholonu, 1973. Avian hematozoa of southwestern Puerto Rico. Prog. In Protozool; 4th Intern. Cong. Protozool. Clemont-Ferrrand. France p.3.
25. _____.And Olivera, J. Finn, 1974. *Moniliformis* (Bremser, 1811) Acanthocephala in the cockroach: *Periplaneta ameri cana*, in Puerto Rico. Trans. Amer. Micro. Soc. 93: 141-142.
26. _____.1974. *Haemogregarina pseudemydis* n. sp. (Apicomplexa: Haemogregarinidae and *Pirhemocyton chelonarum* n. sp. in turtles from Louisiana. J. Protozool. 21: 659-664.
27. Mueller, J.F. and A.D. Acholonu, 1974. Sparganum growth factor in New World Spirometra sp. J. Parasitol. 60: 728-729.

28. Acholonu, A.D., 1974. The hooks of some pentasomes. Proc. Third Intern. Cong. Prarsitol., Munich, Germany. P. 1023-1024.
29. _____.1976. Helminth fauna of saurians from Puerto Rico with observation on the life cycle of *Lueheia inscripta* (Westrumb, 1821) and description of *Allopharnyx puertoricensis* sp. n. Proc. Helminth. Soc., Wash. 43(2): 106-116.
30. Fischthal, J.H. and Acholonu, A.D., 1976. Some digenetic trematodes from the Atlantic Hawksbill turtle, *Eretmochelyes imbricata imbricata* (L.) from Puerto Rico. Proc. Helminth. Soc. Wash. 43: 174-185.
31. Acholonu, A.D., 1977. Some hematozoa of reptiles from the Caribbean. 5th Inter. Cong. Protozool. New York, U.S.A. p. 399.
32. _____.1977. Some helminths of domestic fissipids in Ponce, Puerto Rico. J. Parasitol. 63: 757-758.
33. _____.1978. Some pentastomes in reptiles from Louisiana; U.S.A. Proc. Intern. Cong. Of Parasitol. Warsaw. Poland. Sec. 33 p.57.
34. _____.1978. *Raillietiella gehyrae* Bovien 1927 (Pentastomida: Cephalobaenidae) a new record in Nigeria with a summary of published records. 2nd Annual Conf. Nig. Soc. Parasitol. Bk of Abstr. p. 26.
35. _____.1979. A review of Human helminthiasis in Nigeria 1900-1978 1: Hookworm infection. 3rd Annual Conf. of Nig. Soc. Parasitol, Bk of Abstr. p. 24.
36. _____.1980. A review of Human helminthiasis in Nigeria 1900-1979: 11: Intestinal roundworms, with comments on their prevalence in two Southern states. Prog. And Abst. 5th Annual Meeting of the American Society of Parasitologists. p. 59-60.
37. _____.1980. Human helminthiasis in Puerto Rico: Prevalence in 14 localities with Comments on transmammary infection of hookworm in man. Carbi. J. Sci. 15 (3-4): 199-207.
38. _____.1980. Parasitic infectious diseases in children: Current trends in parasitic Infections covering

onchocerciasis, loiasis, and dracontiasis. Proc. XVI Intern. Cong. Pediat. Barcelona, Spain. p. 203.
39. _____.1980. A review of Human helminthiasis in Nigeria 1900-1970: 111: Filariasis and dracontiasis, with comments on their prevalence in Lagos and Imo States. Proc. and Abstr. 55th Annual Meeting of the Am. Soc. Parasitol. Berkeley, California. P. 39.
40. _____.1980. A review of trichonomiasis vaginalis in Nigeria with comments on its Prevalence at Lagos University Teaching Hospital. Nig. J. Parasitol. 1 (Special suppl.): 177-188.
41. _____.1980. Filarial infectionsepidemiology and pathophysiologyA review. Nig. J. Parasitol. 1(2): 157-164.
42. _____.1982. This wormy Nigeria. Nigerian Society for Parasitology *Presidential Address. Nig. J. Parasit. 3(1&2) 1-7.
43. _____.1982. Schistosomiasis in Nigeria with comments on its prevalence at Lagos University Teaching Hospital. Abstr. Of the 5th Intern. Cong. Parasitol., Toronto, Canada. p. 733.
44. _____.1982. Experimental Parasitology of Onchocerca. Proc. of the First National Conference on onchocerciasis, Kaduna, Nigeria. The Nigerian Institute for Trypanosomiasis Research, Kaduna Publication No. 1: 59-61.
45. _____.1983. Trichomoniasis in Imo State: A First Report. Nig. J. Microb. 3(1): 15-18; 1984 Af. J. STD. 1 (1): 27-28.
46. Anyiwo, C.E. and A.D. W. Acholonu, 1983. Cefotaxine (Cleforon) in the treatment of gonorrhea patients. Nig. J. Microb. 3(1): 1-5.
47. _____.1983. Mezocoellin in the treatment of male gonorrhea in Lagos. Proc. 3rd Af. Reg. Conf. on STD, p. 79.
48. Acholonu, A.D.W., and Nwobu, R.U. and Obi, J.C., 1983. Studies on Mycosis at Lagos, Nigeria. J. Microb. 3(2) p. 134-140.

49. _____, Green, M.F., and Oduche, B.A., 1983. Cockroach, intermediate host of *Moniliforms* (Acanthocephala) and *Raillietiella gehyrae* (Pentastomida) in Lagos, Nigeria. Prog. And Abstr. 58th Annual Meeting on Am. Soc. Of Parasitol. p. 42.
50. Igweh, A.C. and Acholonu, A.D.W., 1984. In vitro testing of the trypanocidal action of certain drugs and chemical agents. Nig. J. Microb 4: (1&2): 34-48.
51. Acholonu, A.D.W., 1984. Malaria in Amaigbo, Imo State, Nigeria. Nig. J. Microb. 4(1-2): 80-88.
52. _____.And Onubogu, U.L., 1985. The Epidemiology of Trichomonoiasis and candidiasis in Ikorodu, Lagos State, Nigeria with comments on the situation of gonorrhea. Nig. J. Microb. 5(1-2): 18-24.
53. Jaji, B.E. and Acholonu, A.D.W., 1985. Toxoplasmosis in Lagos, Nigeria: Antibodies determination and age distribution. Nig. J. Microb. 6(1-2): 18-24
54. Acholonu, A.D.W., 1986. Trichomoniasis and candidiasis in Amaigbo, Imo State, Nigeria as revealed from urine samples. Nig. J. Microb. 6 (1-2): 61-66.
55. Acholonu, A.D.W., 1987. The prevalence of *Trypanosoma Lewisi, stercorarian hemoflagellate*, in Lagos State, Nigeria. Nig. J. Microb. 7 (1-2): 102-104.
56. _____.1987. Trichomoniasis and candidiasis in Oguta, Imo State, Nigeria. Nig. J. Microb. 7 (1-2): 57-61.
57. _____.1988. Sero-epidemiology of amoebiasis in Lagos, Nigeria. Nig. J. Microb. 8 (1-2): 99-103.
58. Eng. G., Coddington, S.A., Stockton, L.L., Acholonu, A.D., 1989. Structure—Activity relations of organotin biocides on *Ceratocystis ulmi*. Pesticide Science 26: 117-121.
59. Acholonu, A.D.W., 1988. Antitoxoplasma antibodies in patients at the Lagos University Teaching Hospital, Lagos, Nigeria: A 53 months review. Nig. J. Microb. 8 91-2): 77.
60. _____.1989. Dracunculiasis in Nigeria: An epidemiologic review, 1900-1980. 1st Nat. Conf. on Dracunculiasis. Prog. And Abstr. p. 23.

61. _____.1989. Trichomoniasis and candidiasis in Abiokuta, Oguta, Nigeria. Annual Conf. Sci. Assn. Nig. Prog. And Abstr. p. 16
62. Acholonu, A.D.W., and Njunda, A. L., 1990. Intestinal parasitosis among school children in Ogun State, Nigeria. Annual Conf. Sci. Assn. Nig. Prog. And Abstr. p. 18.
63. Eng. G. and Acholonu, A.D.W, 1991 Tolerance of aggressive and non-aggressive isolates of *Ceratocystis ulmi* to organotin fungicides. Appl. Organometallic Chem. 5: 131-134.
64. Acholonu, A.D.W., Lushbaugh, W.E., Franzblau, S. and Udenya, L. 1994. Trichomonacidal action of some medical herbs on *Trichomonas vaginalis* in vitro. Intern. Cong. Parasitol., Izmir, Turkey, p. 216.
65. _____.1995. Human parasitic and mycotic infections in Mississippi. Prog. and Abstr. American Society if Parasitologists, Annual Meeting, Pittsburgh, Pa., p.169.
66. _____.White, J., Lushbaugh, W.B., Caeson, Z. and Lemos, 1995. Trichomoniasis in women from Mississippi. A five year retrospective review of Papanicolaou smears. Am. J. Trop. Med. Hyg. (suppl.): 171.
67. _____. and Williams, A., 1996. The occurrence of *Haemogregarina pseudemydis*Acholonu, 1974 (Apicomplexa: Haemogregarinidae) in turtles from Mississippi. J. Ms. Acad. Sci. 41 (1): 88.
68. _____. and Williams, l., 1996. Intestinal parasites of turtles from Mississippi: A preliminary report. J. Ms. Acad. Sci. 41(1): 88.
69. Ugo, H.C. And Acholonu, A.D.W., 1996. Concurrent Sexually Transmitted Diseases (STDs) in Acquired Immune Deficiency Syndrome (AIDS) patients from Northern Zimbabwe: A five year retrospective review. Amer. J. Trop. Med. Hyg. 55 (suppl.): 294.
70. Acholonu, A.D.W. and Williams, L. N., 1996. Intestinal parasites of turtles from Mississippi. Prog. Abstr. Am. Soc. Parasitologists, Tucson, Arizona p. 120

71. Acholonu, A.D.W. AND Anderson, Angela L 1997. Tricomoniasis in Claiborne and Jefferson counties, Mississippi, as revealed from urine samples. J. Ms. Acad. Sci. 42 (1): 48.
72. Acholonu, A.D.W., Stewart, T.J., Thibodeau, l. j., and Valsaraj, K. T., 1997. Benthic invertebrates of lake Yazoo and Yazoo river: A preliminary report. J. Ms. Acad. Sci. 42 (1): 86-87.
73. Acholonu, A.D.W. and Turner, C.W., 1997. Preliminary report on the hematoza of the catfish (*Ictaturus punctatus*) from Mississippi J. Ms. Acad. Sci. 42 (1): 87.
74. _____. Stewart, T.J., Thibodeaux, L. J. and Valsaraj, K.T., 1997. Benthic invertebrates of Lake Yazoo and Yazoo River with assessment and characterization of their substrates. Proc. WERC and HSRC Joint conference on the Environment. pp. 489-495.
75. _____. and Walker, T., 1998. Trichomoniasis surveillance in Mississippi, U.S.A. 1996-1997. Proc. 9th Intern. Congress Parasitol. Pp.713-717.
76. Acholonu, A.D.W. and Epps, c 1998. Prevalence of lice on pigs from Southwestern Mississippi. J. Ms. acad. Sci. 43 (1): 86.
77. _____,Wells. M., 1998. Lice infestation of goats from Southwestern Mississippi: A preliminary study. Prog. And Abstr. 73rd Annual Meeting of Am. Soc. Parasitol. p. 72.
78. _____., Bates, G.T., Williams, R., Swaringer, III, L.E., and Cooper, Quinton, 1999. Gastrointestinal parasites of swine Southwestern Mississippi. J. Ms. Acad. Sci. 44(1): 103-104.
79. _____., Stewart, T.J., Thibodeaux, L.J. and Valsaraj, K. T. 1999 An annotated checklist of benthic invertebrates of Lake Yazoo and Yazoo River, Mississippi J. Ms. Aca. Sci., 44 (4):230-234.
80. _____.2003. Trends in teaching Parasitology: the American situation. Trends in parasitol 19:6-9.
81. Phillips, I. and Acholonu, A. D. W. 2003. Examining Ayers vs. Musgrove: Expanding Higher Education Opportunities for African American. 2003. Education

Monograph Series, National Association of African American Studies and Affiliates, 423-432.
82. Acholonu, A.D.W. and Phillip I. 2003. Examining Ayers vs. Musgrove: Expanding Higher Education Opportunities for African Americans—An Update 2003 Education Monograph Series, National Association of African American Studies and Affiliates. 1-18.
83. Acholonu, A.D.W., Njoku, A and Opara, A. 2006. Trichomoniasis in Imo State, Nigeria with comments on its prevalence as compared to other sexually transmitted Diseases (STDs). Proceedings of 11th International Congress of Parasitology (ICOPAXI) Glasgow (Scotland) United Kingdom, 201-205.
84. _____., Harris Jr., Michael 2006. Comparative Study on the Water Quality of China and Mississippi, USA. Education Monograph Series, National Association of African American Studies and Affiliates, 1605-1617.
85. _____.2006. My Experiences as a Visiting Scholar in China. Education Monograph Series, National Association of African Americans studies and Affiliates, 394-413.
86. _____.and Jenkins, T.2007. Water quality studies on freshwater bodies in New Orleans, Louisiana one year after Hurricane Katrina. J. MS. Acad. Sci. 52(4): 289-294.
87. Acholonu, A.D.W., Njoku, A and Dunbar, A.2007. Prevalence of tuberculosis (TB) and HIV infection in Imo State, Nigeria. Education Monograph Series, National Association of African American Studies and Affiliates pp777-787.
88. Acholonu, A.D.W., Njoku, A and Dunbar, A. 2007. Prevalence of Tuberculosis (Tb) and HIV Infection in Imo State, Nigeria. Advances in Science and Technology. 3(1): 24-29.
89. Okorie, P and Acholonu, A.D.W. 2008. Water quality studies on River Nworie in Owerri, Imo State, Nigeria. J. MS. Acad. Sci. 53(4): 232-238.

90. Acholonu, A.D.W. and Epps, C. 2009 Lice infestation of swine from Southwestern Mississippi. J. MS. Acad. Sci. 54(2):153-156.
91. Opara, A.U. and Acholonu, A.D.W. 2010 The carrier rate of Newcastle Disease Virus in Pigeons in Owerri area of Imo State, Nigeria. Adv. Sci. Tech. J. 4 (1): 83-87.
92. _____.AU and Acholonu, A.D.W. 2010 The carrier rate of Newcastle Disease Virus in Ducks in Owerri Area of Imo State, Nigeria Advance Science Technology Journal 4(2): 144-147.
93. Acholonu, A.D.W. and Harris, M. 2011. Water Quality Studies on the Lower Mississippi River in Port Gibson, MS. J. MS. Acad. Sci. 56(2-3):185–189.
94. Acholonu, A.D.W., Culley, G., Shumaker, K., Grant, Y. and Morris, K. 2011. Water Quality Studies on the Big Sunflower and the Yazoo River. MS. Adv. Sci. and Tech J. 5(2): 113120.
95. _____.Culley, G., Shumaker, K., Grant, Y. and Morris, K. 2011. Water Quality Studies on the Big Sunflower and the Yazoo River. MS. Adv. in Sci and Tech J. 5(2) 113120.
96. _____.and Owens, L. 2012. Assessment of the Quality of Water Collected from the Surface Waters of Houston and Galveston, Texas One Year after Hurricane Gustav and Hurricane Ike. J. MS. Acad. Sci. 57(4): 257-263.
97. Okorie, P.U., Acholonu, AD.W and Ekwuruo, V.C.2012. Water Quality Studies of Okitankwo River in Owerri, Nigeria. J. MS. Acad. Sci. 57(4).
98. Okorie, P.U., Acholonu, AD.W and Onyemaechi, C.J. 2013. Water Quality Studies of Groundwater in Owerri, Nigeria. J. MS. Acad. Sci. 58(2-3):183–188.
99. Acholonu, ADW and Harris, M 2013. Comparative study on the water quality of China and Mississippi, USA. Adv. Sci. and Tech 7(1): 31–36
100. _____.Hopkins, R. 2014. Pollution Studies on the Lower Pascagoula River in Mississippi, USA. Adv. Sci. and Tech J. 8 (1): 43–46.
101. _____.2014. Landfill as a Method of Solid Waste Disposal: Advantages and Environmental Issue with

Comments on the American and Nigerian Situation. Adv. Sci. and Tech J. 8 (2): 85–93.

102. _____, Oduche A. B., 2014. The Parasites of Cockroach, *Periplaneta americana* (Insecta: Blattidae) In Lagos, Nigeria with Special Reference to Raillietiella Gehyrae Larvae (Pentastomida) and the Experimental Infection of Albino Rats with Cystacanths of Moniliformis. Adv. Sci. and Tech J. 8 (2): 64–72.

103. _____.Wells. M. 2014. Lice Infestation of Goats from South Western Mississippi, USA. J. MS. Acad. Sci. 59 (3-4): 417–421.

104. Hopkins, R. and Acholonu A.D.W. 2015. Assessment of Water Quality of two Lotic Bodies of Water in Jefferson County, Mississippi. J. MS. Acad. Sci. 60 (4): 339–347.

105. Acholonu, A.D.W. 2015. Introduction of Sweet Corn cultivation as an Alternative Energy Source at Awaka, Imo State, Nigeria. Adv. Sci and Tech J. 9 (1-2): 39–42.

106. _____. 2015. River Nworie in Owerri, Imo State, Nigeria: A Public Health Hazard? Adv. Sci. Tech. J 9(1 & 2): 34-38.

107. _____. And Vaughan, A.M. 2015. Pollution studies on the Big Black River in Mississippi, USA Adv. Sci. Tech. J 9(1 & 2): 34-38.

108. Acholonu, A.D.W. 2016. River Nworie in Owerri, Imo State, Nigeria, A health hazard? Proceedings of the Nig. Acad. Sci. 9:12-21.

109. Acholonu, A.D.W. 2016. The Quality and Disposition of Treated Wastewater at Alcorn State University, the use of Wastewater for energy production and other benefits Adv. Sci. Tech. J. 10(1 & 2): 26-35.

110. Acholonu, A.D.W. 2016. River Nworie in Owerri, Imo State, Nigeria: A Public Health Hazard? Adv. Sci. Tech. J. 10(1 & 2): 21-25.

111. Acholonu, A.D.W. 2017. Some facts about Ebola virus Disease and Comments on the Nigerian Situation and control measures taken. Adv. Sci. Tech. J. 11(1): 7-11

Magazine Articles

Acholonu, A.D.W. 2009. CKC, Onitsha—Memories are Made of Thee. The Amaka Gazette. A Journal of CKC—AAA, MC. (13TH Annual Convention17-19 July 2009, Chicago, IL) p. 43—45

Acholonu, A.D.W. 2010. Nnadozie: Redefining, Refocusing, and Repositioning Igbo Consciousness in the 21st century. A speech delivered to the world Igbo Congress during the 16th Annual Convention in Philadelphia, PA. September 2-5 2010. Community Voice Action Magazine.5 (6):3

Acholonu. A.D.W. 2011. Report on Free Medical Mission and HIV/AIDS Screening Conducted at Awaka in Owerri North Local Government Area (LGA) Imo, State, Nigeria on December 22–23, 2011. Community Voice Action. Magazine 5 (6): 4–7

Acholonu, A.D.W. 2012. Eulogy of late Sir Cyril Manuba Acholonu Community Voice Action Magazine 7 (8):16.

Acholonu. A.D.W. 2012. Conference Highlights: Annual Conference of the Mississippi Academy of Sciences (MAS) held from the 23RD to the 25TH of February 2012. Community Voice Action. Magazine 7 (8): 12–13

Acholonu. A.D.W. 2012. Some Facts about Diabetes: Questions and Answers. Community Voice Action. Magazine 7 (8): 14–15

Acholonu, A.D.W. 2013. Broadcast on water and health. Community Voice Action Magazine. 9(10): 12-13

Acholonu, A.D.W. 2014 Some facts about diabetes: Questions and Answers. Community Voice Action Magazine 8(9):14-15.

Acholonu, A.D.W. 2015. Broadcast on water and health. Community Voice Action Magazine 9 (10): 12-13

Acholonu, A.D.W. 2016. The Future of Ndi-Igbo. A speech delivered to the World Igbo Congress (WIC) on the occasion of the 12th Annual Convention in Boston, MA, U.S.A. ON August 31 to September 4, 2016. Community Voice Action Magazine 10(11):9—11.

Acholonu, A.D.W. 2016. Report on free medical mission and HIV/AIDS screening conducted in Owerri North LGA Imo State, Nigeria on May 21 2016. Community Voice Action Magazine 10 (11):4-7

Acholonu, A.D.W. 2016. River Nworie in Owerri, Imo State, Nigeria: A public health hazard? Adv. Sci. Tech. 10 (182): 21-25

Acholonu A.D.W. 2017. Management of Old Age: Questions and answers. Community Voice Action Magazine 12(13):7-8 Acholonu A.D.W. 2017. Health is Wealth: Questions and Answers. Community Voice Action. Magazine 12(13):5-6

Acholonu, A.D.W. 2017. The role of the Diaspora in nation building: A case study of Imo State. Community Voice Action Magazine 11(12):8-13

Acholonu, A.D.W. 2017. Chronic Kidney Disease (CKD): Questions and Answers. Community Voice Action Magazine13 (14): 11-12

News Paper Articles

Acholonu, A.D.W. 2003. Some important facts about HIV and AIDS. The New Times vol. II no 6, pages 1 and 10. Sept. 2003

Acholonu A.D.W. 2004. Ayers Case Settlement: What is in it for Faculty and Staff? Jackson advocate 66(21): 4A March, 11-17, 2004

Acholonu, A.D.W. 2007. Toxoplasmosis is a disease caused by a parasite. The New Times vol. 16 No 4, page 11a. April 2007. Acholonu, A.D.W. 2007. Toxoplasmosis: The Scourge of those afflicted with HIV/AIDS. The African Herald Vol. 18(3): 1, 29, 30, March 2007.

Acholonu, A.D.W. 2013. Essential information about life, living, flow of energy and good health. The African Herald 24 (7 & 8): 1 and 29.

Acholonu, A.D.W. 2013. Essential information about life, living, flow of energy and good health with questions and answers. African Harold; The Leader p. 14 and Aug. 25, 2013

Acholonu, A.D.W. 2017. Health is Wealth: Questions and Answers. The Leader LVIII (18): 4.

Acholonu, A.D.W. 2017. Heath is Wealth Questions and Answers. The African Herald 28 (6): 6-7.

Acholonu, A.D.W. 2017. Management of old age: Questions and Answers. The Leader. LVIII (19) 5

TV and Radio Broadcasts on Public Health

1. Broadcast and TV talk on *Pneumocystis carinii*
2. Broadcast and TV talk on Malaria
3. Broadcast and TV talk on Diabetes
4. Broadcast and TV talk on the management of Diabetes.
5. Broadcast and TV talk on Toxoplasmosis
6. Broadcast and TV talk on Cryptosporidiosis
7. Broadcast and TV talk on Sickle cell anemia
8. Broadcast and TV talk on Ascariasis
9. Broadcast and TV talk on Trichomoniasis
10. Broadcast and TV talk on Tuberculosis (TB)
11. Broadcast and TV talk on Typhus Fever
12. Life, living good health and the flow of energy
13. Management of old age (delivered to senior citizens)
14. Some facts about diabetes: Questions and Answers
15. Management of Diabetes
16. Water and Health
17. Management of Old age

ABSTRACTS OF SOME PAPERS PRESENTED TO SCIENTIFIC ORGANIZATIONS 1999-2017

1. Acholonu, A.D.W 1999. Gastrointestinal parasites of Goats from Southwestern Mississippi. Prog. And Abstr. Joint meeting of the American Society of Parasitology and Society of Nematologists, Monterey, CA p.79.
2. Acholonu, A.D.W., Stewart, T.J., Thibodoeaux, L.J., Valsaraj, K.T. and Gates, A.T. 1999. Organic and Inorganic Pollutants in Water and Sediment from the Yazoo River and Lake Yazoo, Mississippi. 84th Annual Meeting of the Ecological Society of America, Spokane, Washington p. 220.

3. Acholonu, A.D.W., Culley Gayle Grant Yolonda, and Shumker, Ketia 1999. Water Quality studies on the big sunflower River, Mississippi, MS Acad. Of Sci., 45 (1): 100.
4. Acholonu, A.D.W., Gates, Arther, Morris, Keturah, Valsarsaj, K.t. 1999. Analysis of Bed Sediments of the big Sunflower River in Mississippi for Polycyclic Aromatic Hydrocarbons. MS Acad. Of Sci., 45(1): 100-101.
5. Acholonu, A.D.W., Culley, G, Shumaker K., Grant Y. Morris, K., 2000, Water Quality Studies on the Big Sunflower River and the Yazoo River, Mississippi. Abstr. Annual Meeting of the Ecological Society of America, Snowbird, UT (Aug. 6-10, 2000) P 241
6. Acholonu, A.D.W. 2000. Gastrointestinal Parasites of Goats from Mississippi. Prog. And Abstr. Joint Meeting of the American Society of Parasitologists and the Society of Protozoologists, San Juan, Puerto Rico p. 93.
7. Acholonu, A.D.W., Neal, C., Durr, P, Love D., Shaw, R., Strong, J., Sullivan, K. H., and Thomas, E.N. 2001. Studies on the Habit Profiles of Eagle Lake and Lake Chotard in Warren County, Mississippi. Annual Meeting of the Ecological Society of America, Aug 2001, p. 247.
8. Neal, C.O. and Acholonu, A.D.W. 2002 Comparative Study of the seasonal distribution of pollutants in Eagle Lake and Chortard Lake in Warren County, Mississippi. J. MS Acad. Sci. 47(1): 88
9. Meeks, T. Acholonu, A.D.W. 2002. Assessment of water quality in three lentic bodies of water in the industrial areas of Warren County, Mississippi. 87th Annual meeting of the Ecological Society of America and 14th Annual International Conference of the Society for Ecological Restoration, Tucson, Arizona, p 392.
10. Neal, C.O. and Acholonu, A.D.W. 2002 Studies on the habitat profiles of Eagle Lake and Chotard Lake in Warren, County, Mississippi, Annual meeting of the Ecological Society of America, Tucson, Arizona, p 222.
11. Hopkins, R. and Acholonu, A.D.W. 2003. Assessment of Water Quality in two lotic bodies of water in Jefferson

County, Mississippi, A Preliminary Study J. MS. Acad. Sci. 48(1): 90
12. McKinney, T. and A.D.W. 2003. Preliminary studies on Anti-*Toxoplasma gandii* Antibody from Crystal Springs Mississippi, p 929
13. Russell, A., Acholonu, A.D.W., Dunbar, A and Bates, G. 2004 retrospective study on the prevalence of sickle cell anemia in Louisiana 1990-1995. J. MS, Acad., Sci. 49(1): 117
14. White, J. and Acholonu, A.D.W.2204. The Prevalence of Sickle Cell Anemia in Louisiana 1995-2003.J.MS. Acad. Sci. 49(1): 117
15. Acholonu, A.D.W and Todd, T 2004. The Prevalence of Sickle Cell Anemia in Texas, 1995-2003. J. MS. Acad. Sci. 49(1): 117
16. Carter, R and Acholonu, A.D.W. 2004. Prevalence of Sickle Cell Anemia in Mississippi 1995-2003 J. MS. Acad. Sci. 49(1): 117-118.
17. Payne, B Acholonu, A.D.W., Dunbar, A and Bates, G. 2004. Sero prevalence of *Toxoplasma gondii* infection in market weight pigs from Crystal Springs Mississippi. J. MS. Acad. Sci. 49(1): 118
18. Vaughan, A.M and Acholonu, A.D.W. 2004. Preliminary Studies on Water Quality of the Big Black River in Mississippi. (Pollution Studies) J. MS. Acad. Sci. 49(1):119
19. Coleman, Mary L., Acholonu, A.D.W and Dunbar, Abram. 2005. Seroprevalence of *Toxoplasma gondii* infection in pigs from southwestern Mississippi. J. MS. Acad. Sci. 50(1): 119-120.
20. Acholonu, A.D.W. 2005. HIV/AIDS in Mississippi and Nigeria. J. MS. Acad. Sci. 50(1): 120
21. Hopkins, Rosie and Acholonu, A.D.W. 2005. Assessment of water quality in two lotic bodies of water in Jefferson County, Mississippi. J. MS. Acad. Sci. 50(1): 120
22. Acholonu, A.D.W. 2005. HIV/AIDS in Nigeria: A workable plan for control. Science and Technology Conference Dividesforging partnerships with Nigerian Diaspora, Abuja, Nigeria. July 25-27, 2005.

23. Acholonu, A.D.W. and Harris, N. 2006. Comparative Study on the Water Quality of China and Mississippi, USA. J. MS. Acad. Sci. 51(1): 114-115.
24. Harris, M. Acholonu, A.D.W., Jenkins, T. Jones, A. and Jones, E. 2006. Water quality studies on the lower Mississippi River: A preliminary report. Prog. &. Abstr. 14th Biannual Research Symposium. Atlanta GA. p128.
25. Acholonu, A.D.W. 2006. Introduction of the cultivation of sweet corn at Awaka Owerri North LGA, Imo State, Nigeria. 1st Nigerian Diaspora Day and 2nd Science and Technology conference Abuja, Nigeria, July 25-28, 2006.
26. Acholonu, A.D.W., Jenkins, T., Kinnard, M., White, S., Phipps, T., and Williams, T. 2007. Water quality studies on freshwater bodies in New Orleans, Louisiana after hurricane Katrina. J.MS. Acad. Sci. 52(1):152
27. Acholonu, A.D.W., Njoku, A., and Dunbar, A. 2007 Prevalence of tuberculosis (TB) and HIV infection in two states, Nigeria. J. MS. Acad. Sci. 52(1):152.
28. Acholonu, A.D.W. and Okorie, P.U.2008. Water quality studies of Nworie River in Owerri, Imo Stare, Nigeria. J. MS. Acad. Sci. 53(1):118
29. Acholonu, A.D.W. Acholonu 2008. Prevalence of Tricomoniasis in Nigeria. J. MS. Acad. Sci. 53(1):119-120
30. Jones, C., and Acholonu, A.D.W 2008. Prevalence of Tricomoniasis in Zimbabwe. J. MS. Acad. Sci. 53(1):120
31. Addae, C and Acholonu, A.D.W 2008. Prevalence of trichomoniasis in Ghana. J. MS. Acad. Sci. 53(1):120
32. Wanyoike, M. and Acholonu, A.D.W 2008. Prevalence of trichomoniasis in Kenya. J. MS. Acad. Sci. 53(1):120
33. Alexander, J.S. and Acholonu, A.D.W 2008 Seroprevalence of *Toxoplasma gondii* in goats from Southwestern, Mississippi. Suppl. Am. J. Trop. Med. Hyg. 79(6):83
34. Acholonu,A.D.W and Opara,A2008 Prevalence of *Schistosma harmatobium* infection in Lake Basin of Anambra State, Nigeria Program and Abstr. XVIIth

International Congress for Tropical Medicine and Malaria, Jeju, Korea. P 61

35. Acholonu, A.D.W. and Okorie, P.U., Phipps, and Davis, K.L. 2008. Chemical profile of Nworie River in Owerri, Imo State, Nigeria. Meeting program. Ecological Society of America (ESA) 93RD Annual meeting, Milwaukee, W1.p.61.

36. Acholonu, A.D.W., Johnson, S and Humphrey, K. 2009. Prevalence of Cryptosporidiosis among HIV/AIDS individuals in Mississippi and Nigeria. J. MS. Acad. Sci. 54(1):117

37. Acholonu, A.D.W. and Antoine, D. 2009 Prevalence of Cryptosporidiosis among HIV/AIDS patients and nonHIV/ AIDS in Louisiana and Ghana. J. MS. Acad. SCI. 54(1):118

38. Acholonu, A.D.W. Drakes, D., Martin, R and Qwens, L.2009 Water quality studies on the Lower Mississippi River. J. MS. Acad. Sci. 54(1):119

39. Acholonu, A.D.W. and Fisher, T 2009. Prevalence of Cryptosporidiosis among HIV/AIDS individuals in Tennessee and Kenya. J. MS. Acad. SCI. 54(1):119

40. Acholonu, A.D.W. and Smith, D. 2009. Prevalence of Cryptosporidiosis among HIV/AIDS patients and nonHIV/ AIDS individuals in Georgia and Tanzania. J. MS. Acad. SCI. 54(1):119-120

41. Acholonu, A.D.W. 2010. Trends on the Prevalence of Malaria in Nigeria. J.MS. Acad. SCI. 55(1):145

42. Acholonu, A.D.W. and Owens, J. 2010. Trends on the Prevalence of Malaria in Kenya. J. MS. Acad. SCI. 55(1):145-146

43. Acholonu, A.D.W. and Smith, L. 2010. Trends on the Prevalence of Malaria in Shana. J. MS. Acad. SCI. 55(1):146

44. Acholonu, A.D.W. 2010. Trends on the Prevalence of Malaria in Zambia. J. MS. Acad. SCI. 55(1):146

45. Acholonu, A.D.W. and Brown, A. 2010. Assessment of pollutants in the Lower Mississippi River in the Area of Port Gibson. J. MS. Acad. SCI. 55(1):147

46. Acholonu, A.D.W. and Martin R. 2010. Assessment of Water Samples Collected from the Deep Waters of the Mississippi River in the area of Vicksburg. J. MS. Acad. SCI. 55(1):147
47. Acholonu, A.D.W. and Eubanks, M. 2010. Seasonal distribution of Contaminants in the Yazoo River in Yazoo City. J. MS. Acad. SCI. 55(1):140
48. Acholonu, A.D.W. 2010. *Seroprevalence of Toxoplasma gondii* infection in goats from two countries in Mississippi USA xiith International congress of parasitology. Melbone Australia page 598 Abstract No 713
49. Acholonu, A.D.W. 2011. A Retrospective Study on Human Parasitic and Mycotic Infections in Mississippi. J. MS. Acad. SCI. 56(1):136
50. Opara, A. and Acholonu, A.D.W. 2011. The Carrier Rate of New Castle Disease Virus in Ducks in Owerri Area of Imo State, Nigeria. J. MS. Acad. SCI. 56(1):137
51. Acholonu, A.D.W. and Garda, M. 2011. Water Quality Studies on the Lower Mississippi River in the Port Gibson Area, Mississippi during the winter of 2009. J. MS. Acad. SCI. 56(1):138-139
52. Acholonu, A.D.W. and Williams, J. 2011. Water Quality Studies on the Lower Mississippi River in the Port Gibson Area, Mississippi during winter of 2010. J. MS. Acad. SCI. 56(1):139
53. Acholonu, A.D.W., Dee, M., Howard, H., Shelton, A. and Drake, Jandrea. 2011. Water Quality Studies on the Lower Mississippi River in the Port Gibson Area, Mississippi during the fall, 2010. J. MS. Acad. SCI. 56(1):139
54. Okorie, P., Acholonu, A.D.W. and Ekwuruo, V. 2011. Water Quality Studies of Okitankwo River in Imo State, Nigeria. J. MS. Acad. SCI. 56(1):140
55. Okorie, P., Acholonu, A.D.W. and Onyemaechi, C. 2011. Assessment of Groundwater Quality in Owerri Municipality, Nigeria. J. MS. Acad. SCI. 56(1): 140
56. Acholonu, A.D.W. 2012. Prevalence of Toxoplasma gandii infection in chickens (Gallus domesticus) from

McComb, Mississippi, USA 18th International Congress for Tropical Medicine and Malaria Sept. 23-27. Brazil. P 159.
57. Acholonu, A. D. W., Hinton, T., Campbell, E., Smith, Y. 2013. Water Quality Studies of Mud Island Creek in Jefferson County, MS. J. MS. Acad. SCI. 58(1)
58. Erah, P., Benson, K.F., Beaman, J.L., Ou, B., Okubena, A., Okubena, O., Jensen, G.S., Acholonu, A.D.W. 2013. Antioxidant, Anti-inflammatory and Immune-Modulating Properties of Jobelyn Composed of a Southwestern Nigerian Sorghum Bicolor Leaf Sheaths. J. MS. Acad. SCI. 58(1)
59. Acholonu, A. D. W., Hopkins, R., Payne, D. 2013. Preliminary Studies on Helminth Parasites of Gastrointestinal Tract of Catfish (Ictalurus Punctatus and Buffalo Fish (Ictiobus Cyprinellus) From Lower Mississippi River. J. MS. Acad. SCI. 58(1): 143
60. Acholonu, A.D.W. 2014. Assessment of Water Quality of Two Lotic Bodies of Water in Jefferson County, Mississippi. J. MS. Acad. Sci.
61. _____. 2014. Studies on the Parasites of the Cockroach, *Periplaneta americana (Insecta: Blattide)* In Lagos, Nigeria. J. MS. Acad. Sci.
62. _____. 2014. A Comparative Study on the Habitat Profile of the Lower Mississippi River in Port Gibson Area and the Pond near the Front Gate of Alcorn State University (ASU) Campus during the fall of 2014. J. MS. Acad. Sci.
63. Acholonu, A.D.W. 2017. Trends on Prevalence of Malaria in Nigeria. Programs and Abstracts, Annual meeting of American Society of Parasitologists. San Antonio, TX June 27–July 1, 2017. p. 118 Abstract #162.
64. Acholonu, A.D.W. 2017. Trends in the Prevalence of HIV/ AIDS in the State of Mississippi: A five year review 20112015. Program and Abstracts of the 66th Annual Meeting of the American Society of Tropical Medicine and Hygiene Nov. 5-9, 2017.

Chapter Eleven

Some Relevant Congratulatory Messages and Tributes

This chapter is necessitated by the fact that it gives more meaning to my journey through life. The people who complimented me at every accomplishment, gave me the spunk, the impetus to continue to climb to greater heights, to continue achieving and not rest on my oars. They are words or messages of praise and encouragement. A person said "may your focus not be on what you have achieved but what you have yet to achieve".

They helped me to focus on what I have yet to achieve and add to my journey through life. This emphasizes the saying and my stated philosophy, "He who stops being better, stops being good."

Congratulatory message from Dr. Kenny Acholonu, President and CEO, Bioorganic Co, Lagos, Nigeria

Birthday Wishes from Eze Emmanuel Sonde Okoro

The Royal Palace of Eze Omenyi II
HRH Eze Emmanuel Sonde Okoro Eze Omenyi II of Emii

Goodwill Message to a Brother and Friend

My dear Prof.

Rejoice in the Lord, for he made you and have kept you till date. He has a purpose for all these. Therefore, do not slumber nor refuse to do what you have to do for the emancipation of the society and mankind in general. Our Good Lord does everything, and He is there for you—always.

I therefore felicitate with you on this auspicious occasion of the celebration of your 80th birthday, and pray God Almighty for more grace for you to continue the good works.

Congratulations and Happy Birthday

HRH Eze Emmanuel Sonde Okoro
Eze Omenyi II of Emii
Owerri–North LGA
Imo State of Nigeria

Georgia Institute of Technology

**Chief Dr. Augustine O. Esogbue,
FAAAS, FIEEE, FAS, FNAEng, NNOM**
The OZORKILOLO of IBUSA
Professor and Director Emeritus,
Intelligent Systems and Controls Laboratory
H. Milton Stewart School of Industrial and
System Engineering,
Georgia Institute of Technology

Atlanta, Georgia 30332-0205, USA
TEL: 404-894-2323 Fax: 404-894-2301
E-Mail: aseogbue@isye.gatech.edu Web: http://www.isye.gatech.edu/aesogbue

November 07, 2012

I am pleased to offer my most heartfelt congratulations
to a dear friend and respected colleague,

Chief Professor Alex D.W. Acholonu, FAS, OON, FNSP
The OGBUHORO UZO 1 of AMAIGBO and AWAKA,
The EKWUEME1 of IHITTA OGADA AND
AWAKA and The OMEREOHA

As you mark the attainment of a major milestone in your long and illustrious life, as we celebrate you on this memorable occasion which is resplendent with our deep respect for a life of remarkable longevity in our heritage, I am reminded of the statement credited to the famous black performer, athlete, and lawyer, Paul Roberson (1898-1976), "I have simply tried never to forget the soil from which I sprang." Indeed, throughout your sojourn abroad, amidst a brilliant and obviously eminently successful career, you have simply refused to forget your heritage.

Over the years, you have not only given freely and abundantly, but you continue to give to your fellow man simply because you care.

Through caring, you have changed the lives of so many people, in many lands of the universe and through a protracted period of time. The famous American lawyer and social activist, Marian Wright Edelman (1939) once said, "You really can change the world if you care enough" and you certainly do justice to that adage. This world is indeed a much better place because the likes of Chief Professor Alexander Dozie Wozuzu Acholonu, the Ogbuhoro Uzo 1 of Amaigbo and Awaka, The Ekwueme 1 of Ihitta Ogada and Awaka, and the Omereoha passed through it.

At 80, Chief professor Alex D.W. Acholonu is still educating, touching and changing lives, letting people, both young and old in Africa and America and indeed the world, drink from his bottomless fountain of knowledge, acquired through an uncommon dedication to diligence, science and love of discovery, cemented with disciplined scholarship. Indeed, from your continued display of unbridled enthusiasm, boundless energy and love of education, there is no evidence that this giant of a world scholar is about to pack up his academic wares for the village in Awaka any time soon. What a man, what a resource for humanity, what a mentor for us all but especially in present day generation of professionals characterized by a paucity of the desirable gem of longevity in the work place.

Enjoy your day in the sun of life for you are a shining light to your people and all that have the rare privilege of knowing you. May the rest of your sojourn on planet earth be filled with the fondest memories of a life well lived and may the thousands of lives you touched emulate and perpetuate the examples you have so diligently laid for them.

With admiration, love and utmost respect, my friend,

Professor Emeritus (Chief) Augustine O. Esogbue,
Ph.D. FAAAS, FIEEE, FAS, FNAEng, NNOM
The OZORKILOLO of IBUSA KINGDOM,
Oshimili North Local Government, Delta State, Nigeria.

Mississippi Academy of Science (MAS) Award for Distinguished Contribution to Science. He is first Professor in the history of Alcorn State University to receive this kind of award from the Academy

Prof. Acholonu receiving award from MAS President Dr. M. Ye with Dr. Kenneth Butler, Director and Award Committee Chairman of MAS looking

Prof. Voletta Williams Interim chair, Biology Department (left), Prof. Acholonu (middle) and Prof. Babu Patlolla, Dean, Arts and Science, ASU pose after MAS award

FEDERAL UNIVERSITY OF TECHNOLOGY
OWERRI, NIGERIA
OFFICE OF THE VICE-CHANCELLOR

Vice - Chancellor
Professor Celestine O.E. Onwuliri, KSJ, JP
B.Sc., Ph.D (Nigeria), C. Biol., M.I. Biol. (London),
FBSN, FNSP, ALOHA,

P.M.B 1526, Owerri, Nigeria
Tel/Fax: 083-233734, 083-233931
e-mail: vc@futo.edu.ng

FUT/VC/GEN.52   March 18, 2007

Chief Prof. Alex. D.W. Acholonu, FAS, OON

My dear Prof. A.D.W.

CONGRATULATORY MESSAGE

It is with great delight that I write on behalf of the Senate, staff and students of the Federal University of Technology, Owerri, to congratulate you on the conferment of your third Chieftaincy title by HRH Eze Emmanuel Sonde Okoro, Eze Omenyi of Emii.

This recognition did not come to me and indeed the entire FUTO community as a surprise given your excellent track records of achievement in academics, administration, research productivity, philanthropy, trado-cultural involvements etc. Indeed, you very well deserve this honour.

It is also gratifying to acknowledge the good things you have done and are still willing to do for the Federal University of Technology, Owerri.

I pray that God will continue to grant you wisdom, excellent health and courage in the service of mankind.

Once again, accept my congratulations on this major recognition.

With kindest regards

18/03/07

Professor C.O.E. Onwuliri, KSJ, JP
Vice-Chancellor

Technology for Service

Congratulatory message on the conferment of my third chieftaincy tittle as "Omereoha" from Prof. C.O.E Onwuliri

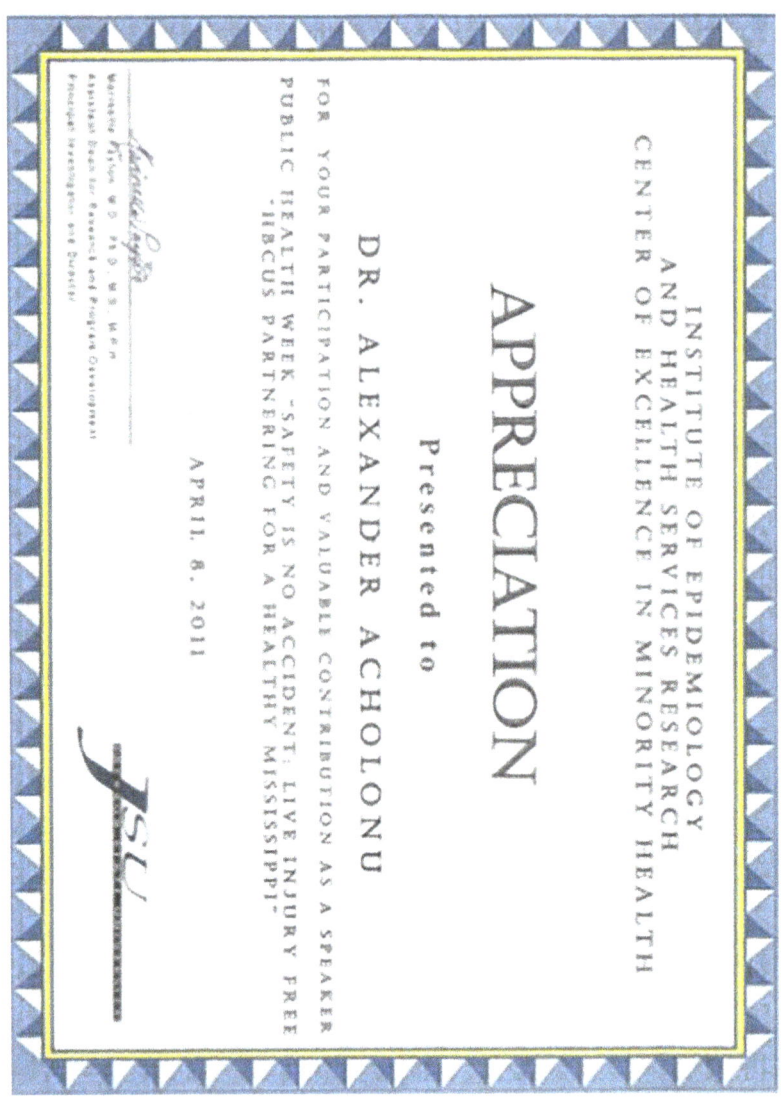

A certificate of appreciation from April 2011

Dr. Marinelle Payton, Principal Investigator and Director Center of Excellence in Minority Health and Health Disparities, Jackson State University, Jackson, MS

Chidi Emmanuel Akujor, KSC Ph.D., Dip. (sp valicana) MASN, FRAS, FNIP,

Professor of Physics and Space Science
and Member Governing Council,
Federal University of Technology Owerri, Nigeria.

Our dearest Prof.

May I on behalf of my wife Lady Jane and children wish you a happy birthday celebration. You deserve all the accolades you are getting because you have paid more than your dues in academics and service to humanity.

We are glad to share your joy this period and pray that the almighty God continues to shower His blessings and grace on you and your family.

Happy birthday sir!

Birthday Wishes from Nick Udumaga

Chief (Dr.) Alexander Wozuzu Acholonu

"Prof—Prof," my beloved in-law, simply marvels me! At the eve of his 80th birthday, he called me by about 7:30 AM, as he was about to go and teach a class at Alcorn University, Mississippi, at 8:00AM! I dare anyone to beat that! We should all rejoice and celebrate this illustrious son of the land, and not envy and detract him, for he has worked and is still working very, very hard to achieve and earn all he has achieved.

Since behind every successful man, there is a woman, let me also seize this golden opportunity to salute his beloved wife, and my most beloved cousin, Lolo Mary Ekeoma Acholonu. Kudos coz!

I will fondly call them Chief and Lolo Mkpuruakom, of Awaka. Also, to Chief Acholonu's official title of "The Ogbuhoro Uzo 1, of Awaka," I will add, "The Omeogo," and "The Okwaibo," of Owerre. I take off my hat in salute, sir!

Happy birthday and many happy returns!

God bless.
Nick I. Udumaga

Birthday Wishes from Udokamma and Family

My wife and family congratulate you on your 80th birthday. It is a great milestone. I also take this opportunity to thank you for opening the door to the USA and success for us all. We appreciate you, love you, I wish we were there to celebrate this great day with you and the rest of the family. I want you to know that I love you and I'll be there in spirit with you. May God continue to bless you and keep you for many years to come.

Happy Birthday.

Love,

Udokamma, Scholar, and Family
Doctoral Candidate
Learning Sciences & Technology Design
Stanford University School of Education.

Congratulatory Message from the Felix Acholonu Family

Ndaa Alex,

Congratulations for the honor being bestowed on you. The fact that this is the third time you are receiving this honor shows that after you received the first and the second, you continued to do the work God set apart for you to do. Receiving honor for hard work does not mark the end of performing the necessary activities we are called to do nor does it mark the end of achieving.

We all wish you long life and good health. May you continue to help your people and may God bless you in all that you have done and all that you will continue to do.

Affectionately,

Dr. & Mrs. Felix Acholonu & Family

Congratulatory Message from the Wilfred W. Acholonu, Jr. and Family

My Dear brother, Alex,

It is my pleasure to acknowledge and accept your invitation to your 80th birthday celebration. It seems unbelievable that 57 years have gone by since you came to the U.S.A. You are truly the trail blazer for the family. You are like the Acorn, which, when planted in a fertile ground, developed into forest of oak trees. The family will remain indebted to your goodwill in opening the way of success to all. In addition to your 80th birthday celebration, your academic, professional, family accomplishments, and the 2012 Thanks Giving Ceremony by the whole family, will also be celebrated in your honor.

Success, says Dr. Deepak Chopra, can be defined in many ways including, but not limited, to good health, emotional stability, fulfilling relationship, material abundance and peace of mind. His favored definition of success resonates most is the continued expansion of happiness and progressive realization of worthy goals. Many of the goals you have set for yourself, including opening the way to U.S.A for our family, are worthy goals, and their realization is the call for this celebration.

My wish for you on your 80th birthday, therefore, is a continued expansion of happiness and a progressive realization of worthy goals.

Your affectionate brother and family,

Wilfred W. Acholonu, Jr. Pharm.D, BCPP
Pharmacy Residency Program Director
Clinical Pharmacy Specialist, MHC/PSYCH
North Florida/South Georgia VHS Gainesville, FL 32608

My father has taught me so many things in life. I admire him  tremendously for his strength, wisdom, compassion for the poor and needy, his willingness to help people and his willingness to teach and be taught. When I reflect on my life today, I am grateful for how my father was relentless in teaching us, thereby creating the solid foundation on which I have grown to be who I am today.

God gave me to my dad so that my dad can raise me according to His perfect will; my dad has done as God commanded him to do.

At a very early age, my dad taught my siblings and me how to pray. Being raised as Catholics, he taught us The Lord's prayer, Hail Mary, and how to pray the rosary. He taught us about what sin was, how to keep from sinning and how to confess and apologize to God when we have sinned. All these things helped set the foundation on how I would live my life in the future; In fact, that Christian foundation is what helped me get a good husband.

Some of the things I will never forget about my dad are his famous quotes which I use today to coach and/or mentor my employees at work. Some of those sayings are:

- What is worth doing, is worth doing well
  - To encourage my employees to produce quality products
- There's nothing so certain as the certainty of change
  - To help them adjust to organizational change which is inevitable
- Look before you leap and think before you talk
  - To encourage wisdom when dealing with customers or their peers
- The definition of insanity is doing the same thing over and over again, yet expecting different results.

- ○ To get them to change tactics for problem analysis and resolution
- ➤ Leave footprints in the sands of time
  - ○ I say this to them selfishly so they don't keep intellectual property in their mind, and rather document them. This enables their knowledge to be used in the future as needed
- ➤ Don't burn the bridge behind you
  - ○ To encourage them to maintain relationships for future endeavors

I'm very proud of the fact that my father named my first son Omenichekwa after him; he named all my kids and their names are all reflections of his wisdom. He named my second son Onyekurukeya and named my daughter Ahumonyehurum.

My dad is a fun loving man. We used to take annual trips to Bar Beach in Lagos or to Badagry beach. He used to teach us how to enjoy the water without putting ourselves in danger. He would tell us to dig our feet in the sand to stabilize ourselves then wait for the water to wet us. It was so much fun.

My dad is a great dancer and he loves to sing and loves entertainment. I always loved watching him and my mom do the 4-step, fox trot and the boogie woogie dance of the 60s and 70s. He used to act like he was Andy Williams or Bing Crosby and sing along with them, in baritone, to their music from our 8-track player—remember those? Fun times. He would play Oriental brothers or Oliver De Coque on our record player and he would call us to come and dance for him. He also encouraged us to come up with our own entertainment and he and my mom would sit and watch us. He always encouraged family time and considered them very important—no matter how tired he was when he came home after driving for hours in Lagos traffic.

My dad is also very athletic. He used to play tennis with my mom very often, unfortunately as he got busier travelling, he eventually stopped. However, he still exercises first thing every morning.

My dad is extremely loving and kind. He never makes a promise which he can't keep. When he makes a commitment, he sticks to it.

This is evident in how he helped his brothers and relatives as much as he could to bring them over to the United States or helped to pay their school tuition or helped them find jobs. Some Acholonu family members in Awaka helped to put money together for him to come to the United States; he made a commitment to them that he would help them or their children in return. He kept his promise and went above and beyond expectations. He definitely deserves the title Ogbuhoro Uzo 1 and Ekwueme 1. He values relationships; he would hardly be the first to break a relationship, the other party will have to act first and he will react as necessary.

My dad being a very studious man also taught us to always have something to read while we were on long distance travels. If we happened to forget a book to read, he would stop and buy a newspaper and have us keep ourselves busy reading it. My father used to train us on note-taking by making us sit down every night and listen to NTA News at 9 o'clock. We would have to sit and listen to the news, write down what we heard and then read it back to him after the news ended. Since he listened along with us, he could tell if we wrote down the right information or were making things up so that we could quickly go to bed. If we didn't write down the correct information, we would have to stay for the 11 o'clock news to listen again and correct our mistakes. By this, we learned very quickly how to get it right the first time. This really helped me with note taking while I was in college and I still use these skills to take down notes in meetings which I attend so that I do not forget what was discussed.

My dad always tells me that the sky is the limit and that he does not want me to be like him; he wants me to be greater than him. With that, I strive to do the best that I can do and be the best that I can be. I really appreciate him for who he is and all he has done to raise his kids and be a supporting husband to my mom.

Lolo Engr. Mrs. Leslie O. Acholonu-Okere,
B.Sc., MS, CAPM, Certified ITIL
Lead IT Oklahoma Gas and Electric Co. Delivery Manager

Congratulatory Message from High Chief and Lolo Kennedy Okere

On behalf of the board of directors of Horizon International Medical Mission, Inc., USA, and the Okere family, we wish you, Chief Sir Prof Alex D.W. Acholonu and Lolo Mrs. Mary E. Acholonu God's Blessings on your third chieftaincy honor.

Daddy, Your life is a challenge to many of us, your children. Your hard work is worth emulating. Today your chieftaincy honor bears witness that there is a reward for those who genuinely work hard in this society. It indeed befits you.

Mom, congratulations and thank you for your everlasting support to daddy all these years. You are a model of a true Lolo. I love and appreciate you and strive to perform as you have been doing supporting my husband as well. Thank you for being my role model.

My in-laws, continue to leave footprints in the sands of time and we shall continue to follow your footprints. Congratulations Omereoha of Emii.

High Chief Dr. Kennedy Okere, MD
Aka Ji Ogwu I of Owerri West LGA
President & Founder, Horizon International Medical Mission, Inc., USA
Director of Family Medicine, Variety Care Foundation
Clinical Professor of Family Medicine, Medical College of Georgia & Mercer School of Medicine, USA

Lolo Mrs. Leslie Okere (nee Acholonu)
Director of Technology and Development, Horizon International Medical Mission, Inc., USA
Lead IT Service Delivery Manager
Vendor Management Office
Oklahoma Gas and Electric

I am very proud to be the daughter of Chief Professor Alexander D. W. Acholonu. I admire and respect him. He inspires me in many ways.

He is a Philomath, one who enjoys learning new facts and acquiring new knowledge, and he believes that one should never stop learning. Furthermore, although he is a professor by profession, he is a teacher at heart. He loves to share the knowledge he acquires.

He prides himself in being a disciplinarian; although he doesn't care for corporal punishment. In fact, his preference is to discipline in a manner that promotes education.

He is benevolent. He lives up to his name, Dozienze, and believes in taking care of less fortunate people. He believes that God blesses people so they can be a blessing to others, not so they can store up treasures for themselves.

My Dad is a faithful Christian. He takes his Christian believes very seriously and using his God-given responsibility of being a father, he instilled Christian values in all his children, to the best of his ability. He taught us to believe in God and to pray to Him, and he ensured that we learned more about God by taking us to church and catechism classes.

He is very wise and has foresight, and he is always willing to forgive anyone who offends him. All you have to do is apologize and he forgives.

He is very confident and handsome. You see it in the way he carries himself, in his swag, and in his smile. He loves music and one of his favorite pastimes is dancing.

We cannot pick our family members, so I owe great thanks and praise to God for making Chief Professor Alexander D.W. Acholonu my father. I could not have asked for a better father.

Esther Eberegbulam Acholonu Streete, *Esq, CPA, LLM*
Principal/Partner McNamee Hosea, Annapolis, MD

TRIBUTE FROM STUDENTS

Dear Chief Professor Acholonu,

It has been a pleasure to work with you as your research assistant. I have learned a lot from you. Please continue to inspire me and other students. Congratulations on the Conferment of a third Chieftaincy title on you by His Royal Highness, Eze Emmanuel Sonde Okoro, Eze Omenyi II of Emii.

Kimberly A. Maxwell
Research Assistant and Biology Major
Alcorn State University, Mississippi

I am grateful to Chief Dr. Alex D.W. Acholonu. I have learned so much from him during this course, spiritually, academically, culturally, and most of all as a person. Being a nontraditional student in his class made me feel like I blended in with my classmate. Chief Acholonu classroom manner made me feel respected and of seniority in a positive way. He is a great man of knowledge. I will never forget Chief. Dr. Alex D.W. Acholonu. He is an inspiration to me of continued education. God Bless.

Mrs. Venessia King
Introduction to Environmental
Biology/Ecology Class, ASU

Some Relevant Congratulatory Messages and Tributes

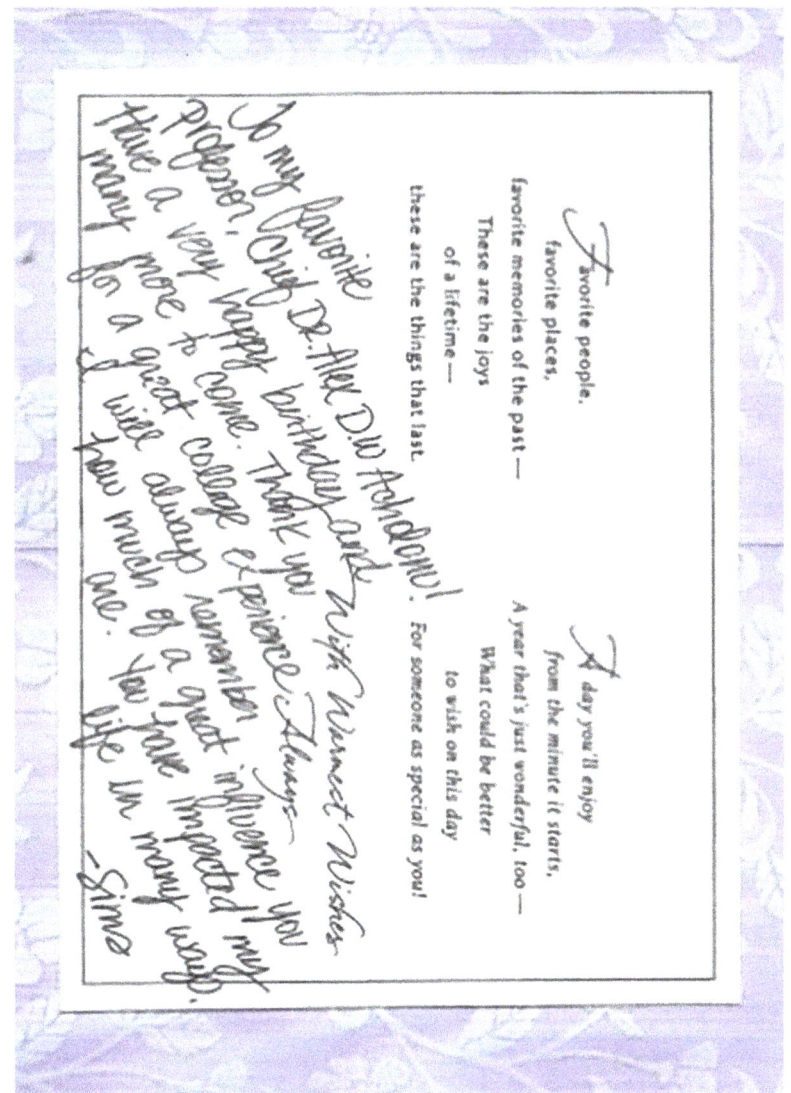

Kieurra Sims
General Parasitology Class

I want to thank and acknowledge you, Chief Prof. Alex D. W. Acholonu for being the most humble, tenacious and most kind fellow I have met in the world. To be a student of a great teacher like yourself is a great honor. You have taught me discipline, patience, and how to make excellence not just a habit but a lifestyle. I have had the privilege of being a student in several of your classes at Alcorn State University, all in the Biological Sciences Department. I also had the privilege of being your student research assistant in the past few years. I have learned that you are a man of many parts and with an endless will to give and improve people in this world we all inhabit, both near and far. Your humility and compassion for the greater good of the needy and poor are some qualities that inspire me daily to be the best that I can be and strive to selflessly give back to the world. You stand for truth, kindness, achievement, knowledge, culture, wisdom and service. As one of your pupils, I have learned to appreciate the life I have been given and to take advantage of all forms of knowledge and wisdom it offers. "Success patiently waits for anyone who have the determination and the strength to seize it," is one of the many quotes of wisdom I have been blessed to learn from you. Chief Prof. Acholonu, I will always remember and honor you. You may not know how deeply your presence and teachings have influenced me. I cherish you for all that you do and all that you are. There may never be another as memorable to me as you in my life.

Sharkiesha Jackson
Biology Major and Research Assistant

Some Relevant Congratulatory Messages and Tributes

Congratulations

to

Chief Sir Prof Alex D.W. Acholonu
Oguhoruzo, Ekweme, Omereoha

Members of the Department of Biological Sciences
Faculty & Staff, Alcorn State University

TO: Chief Dr. Alexander D.W. Acholonu
             Professor of Biological Sciences

FROM: Dr. Bettaiya Rajanna
             Professor & Chairman
             Faculty and Staff

Congratulations!

The Department of Biological Sciences wish to express our warmest congratulations to you on your attainment of 80 years of age! You are blessed! As a faculty member and colleague, we all are proud of you and wish that God will grant you a longer time to possibly become a centenarian.

Best to the Best! I congratulate and esteem you to the highest! You're admired by Alcorn State University and in every area of academia and research. It is truly an honor to have worked with, and witnessed the knowledge, wisdom, structure, humor, as well as the rigidity you've received accolades of all kinds and made numerous contributions that are well noted across the globe. You've helped transform the world of science and medicine. You're highly respected community servant, a scholar in the classroom, and prolific research scientist. "If" I was the president of the United States, you would receive the Nobel Prize. Again, congratulations and thank you for ALL of your contributions as well as you love support for the Department of Biological Sciences, Alcorn State University and the global community!

Wishing you all the best,

Voletta P. Williams
Prof. and Chair,
Dept. of Biological Sciences

My Dear Esteemed Colleague Professor Alex D. W. Acholonu

It gives me great pleasure to know that you are in the process of writing your Autobiography. I am honored and equally thrilled to write this tribute for such a brilliant and unbelievable person. You certainly immersed yourself in your calling and carrying out at your best every single day for the half century yet to realize your full potential. You have reached the heights that many of us cannot even dream of. As a colleague at Alcorn State University, I have all praise for your commitment. You have shown plenty of times that you are the man for the job. You worked hard and never left anything to chance. Your work ethic, your determination, and pride in representing Alcorn is unparalleled.

By receiving the 'Distinguished Contribution to Science Award' and 'Contribution to Health Disparities Award' from the Mississippi Academy of Sciences, you rose to a different pedestal not just as a Professor at Alcorn State University but also as a shining light that shone brightly throughout the research world. You distinguished yourself being the first and the only Alcorn State University professor to receive those awards, you made all of us at Alcorn proud. You had a glittering career and you had amass number of awards in science and humanity. You are well known for your devotion for community service and its wellbeing. You are associated with a number of charities and service organizations on a voluntary basis.

Personally, every time I talked to you I learned something new and noticed that you are always trying to improve your skills. You answer questions with utmost respect and enthusiasm and you never lost your temper and composure. At times, even when you said casually 'thanks for your support' it felt surreal to say the least. With your colleagues you are friendly, respectful, and highly cooperative. Some are genuinely afraid of you because of how strictly you follow your tenets. People may know about your tremendous love for the scientific field but few know of the extraordinary love you have for your students. You enforce high academic and professional standards keeping the best interest of students as your priority. It was a privilege to work with you. May God Bless you with many more accolades and awards. May you achieve everything that your heart desire.

Best regards,

Babu P. Patlolla, *Ph.D.,*
Professor of Biology and
Dean, School of Arts and Sciences

Alcorn State University

Napoleon Moses
Vice President for Academic Affairs
Alcorn State University
Mississippi, USA

Chief Alexander Acholonu, Professor of Biology

Best Wishes from Alcorn State University's Faculty and Students.

Alcorn State University is aware of your accomplishments and your national and international recognitions. The Conferment of a third chieftaincy title is a praiseworthy addition to your already long list of achievements. Please continue the good work.

Hearty Congratulations!

Napoleon Moses
Vice President for Academic Affairs,
Alcorn State University
Mississippi, USA

On behalf of the Provost Office, I extend best wishes to you on your 80th birthday and want you to know how much we appreciate you as a scholar and professor in the Department of Biological Sciences at Alcorn State University. I value all our employees, but a few, like you, have distinguished themselves by continued excellence. Your work is esteemed more than you know. Were you not so indispensable, we might have managed to give you the day off! However, since you have reached a new milestone; one that I may say very much deserves a celebration, you are hereby granted "leave" to party the night away.

Congratulations and much success!

Samuel L. White, Ph.D.
Executive Vice President/Provost

Some Relevant Congratulatory Messages and Tributes

Dr. Acholonu, what a pleasure it has been to work with and interacted with you for the many years you have been in the employ of Alcorn State University. You began your tenure at this distinguished institution as an outstanding professor, and the accolades have continued to follow you throughout your career. A consummate professional, you have always been a vociferous advocate for your students. You have always given your student the very best of yourself.

You are a devoted teacher whose enthusiasm is only excelled by your commitment. You always have the interest of your students at heart. You motivate them, do research with them, and publish your research findings with them thus making them authors so early in their lives. They love and respect you because they see love and respect in you. They work hard for you because they know that you work hard for them.

Your work has also been recognized by the distinguished presidents of Alcorn State University. I recall when you were acknowledged by our late President, Dr. Clinton Bristow during one of our faculty and staff beginning of the academic year workshops. He announced that you and another instructor (Mr. Darryl Grennell, now retired and is the current Mayor of Natchez, Mississippi), were recognized by students as the best instructors in the Department of Biological Sciences. The current, and nineteenth president of Alcorn State University, Dr. Alfred Rankins, Jr., noted your achievements at the meeting of the Board of Trustees of State Institutions of Higher Learning (IHL). Your teaching, publications, and honors and awards have brought distinction not only to yourself, but also to the University. It is understandable why even presidents have publicly noted your accomplishments.

You have excelled not only in the field of teaching and research but you are also a prolific writer. You have been continuously publishing your research findings and other scholarly works. You have, as a result of these, received many accolades and recognitions from different bodies, societies, and governmental agencies, including being the first Alcorn State University professor to receive the **Distinguished Contribution to Science Award** from the Mississippi Academy of Sciences in 2012; and another, **Contribution to Health Disparity Research Award**, from the same Society in 2016. You have really made Alcorn proud.

Apart from teaching, research, and writing, you have held many national and international positions of leadership as your curriculum vitae shows. You were a member of the Executive Council of the World Federation of Parasitologists. You served as a member of the Advisory Committee of the United States Food and Drug Administration, the Chairman of the Healthcare Disparity Committee of MAS, a position you have held since 2012 and currently the Chairman of Zoology and Entomology division of MAS, the President of Africa Assembly of the American Society of Tropical Medicine and Hygiene, Chairman, U.S. Department of Agriculture Grant Award Review Panel and several others.

Dr. Acholonu, you have rendered outstanding services to Alcorn State University since joining the faculty of the institution in 1991. Among other positions, you served as the President of the Faculty Senate for a period of six years and became one of the outstanding Faculty Senate Presidents. You conducted annual Earth Day Celebration on campus for many years. You also chaired the Environmental Biology Program for many years.

Dr. Acholonu, at the age of almost 85, you are still active in teaching, research, and service to Alcorn State University and outside groups. Alcorn State University is proud of you for your achievements and distinguished service to the University and pays high tribute to you for what you are, what you have accomplished, and what you have yet to accomplish. Alcorn State University wishes you well and above all, wishes you success in all of your future endeavors.

Dr. Donzell Lee,
Provost and Executive Vice President for Academic Affairs
Alcorn State University
Lorman, MS, 39096

TO THE FAMILY AND FRIENDS OF DR. ALEX D.W ACHOLONU:

One of my joys of being the 18th President of Alcorn State University is the privilege of recognizing the awesome students, alumni, faculty and staff of this great institution.

Today, we pay tribute to Dr. Alex D.W. Acholonu, professor in the Department of Biological Sciences and director of the Ecology Education Program at Alcorn on his 80th birthday. He also served as chair of Zoology and Entomology division for Mississippi Academy of Sciences.

We eagerly acknowledge what his life and work has meant to us understanding that at the age of 80 many of us would have retired already. What makes Dr. Acholonu give of himself?

Dr. Acholonu's passion for research and scholarship, but most of all his desire that every student will discover their true calling and go beyond what they could have ever imagined.

His accomplishments include leading environmental education at Alcorn, undertaking research in parasitology, spearheading annual Earth Day on campus, leading the K-12 Teachers Ecology Education Workshop, conducting research and publishing papers on HIV/AIDS in Mississippi and water quality research on the lower Mississippi River.

Dr. Acholonu also received a prestigious award from Mississippi Academy of Sciences for his outstanding contributions to science. Recently, he participated in the 3rd Federal University of Technology International conference on Renewable and Alternative Energy held in Nigeria where he served as an invited speaker and presented a paper entitled "Issues in Nuclear Energy Production and Usage."

Like a true servant leader, Dr. Acholonu inspires others to believe in themselves. On his 80th birthday, his Alcorn family celebrates how BRAVE he has been over the years and wishes him good health and long life to continue sharing his wisdom with us.

Always Alcorn,
M. Christopher Brown II

May 14, 2012

Chief Dr. Alex Acholonu
Professor of Biology and Director of Ecology
 Education Program
Alcorn State University
1000 ASU Drive
Alcorn State, MS 39096

Dear Chief Acholonu:

    On behalf of the Alcorn State University family, we congratulate you on your receipt of the science award by the Mississippi Academy of Sciences on February 23, 2012 for your outstanding contributions to science. We appreciate your hard work and dedication to Alcorn State University and your Department.

Always Alcorn,

M. Christopher Brown II
President

MCB2:krs

cc: Dr. Samuel L. White, Provost/Executive Vice President
      Dr. Norris A. Edney, Interim Dean, School of Arts & Sciences

Office of the President | 1000 ASU Drive 359 | Alcorn State, MS 39096-7500
Phone: 601.877.6111 | Fax: 601.877.2975 | www.alcorn.edu

Some Relevant Congratulatory Messages and Tributes

We sincerely appreciate your dedication and contributions to the success of Alcorn State University. Best Wishes for a Wonderful Birthday!

President and First Lady Rankins

18th President

Appreciated Birthday wishes from the 19th President of Alcorn State University for my 85th Birthday, Nov. 30, 2017

Dr. Alfred Rankins Jr.

Conclusion

My journey through life

I have painstakingly and as objectively as possible recorded the good, the bad and the ugly in my life.

How so true it is that life is like a roller coaster. Sometimes you are up and sometimes you are down – the ups and downs of life, the vicissitudes of life. No condition is permanent. How so true it is that often times the people you help most become the ones to seek your downfall; to show hatred or jealousy towards you or ingratitude. This, generally speaking, has been my fate. It is the main reason why I named my beloved fourth daughter, Barr. (Attorney), Mrs. Esther Acholonu Streete, "EBEREGBULAM" (that is, may being helpful to people, especially my relations, not kill me). *C'est la vie* (that is life).

Even so, faith in God, hope (hope for the best while prepared for the worst) and love (disinterested love), conquer all. Someone said: "Accept the challenges so that you may feel the exhilaration of victory."

**Chief Sir Prof. Alex D. Wozuzu Acholonu,
Ph.D., FNSP, FRAES, FAS, OON**

My Journey Through Life

Behind a Successful Man, there is a Supporting Wife

Appendix

My Firsts

Cambridge School Certificate or Secondary School Certificate	First in Acholonu family
B.S. Degree	First in Acholonu family
MS	First in Acholonu family
Ph.D	First in Awaka
Full Professor	First in Awaka
Pro-Chancellor of a University and Chairman, Governing Council (Imo State University)	First in Awaka
Rector of Institution (Rector Amaigbo College of Technology)	First in Awaka
OON (Officer of the Order of the Niger)	First in Awaka
Chieftaincy Title	First in Acholonu family
Member of Governing Council of a University (IMSU)	First in Awaka
Chairman Awaka Constitution Drafting Committee Under Eze Oshimiri David Osuagwu (late)	First in Awaka
Sponsored the Training and Ordination of 1st Awaka Priest (Rev. Fr. Valentine Acholonu)	First in Acholonu family and Awaka
Fellow of Nigerian Academy of Science (FAS)	First in Awaka and Alaenyi
Construction of biggest Commercial house in Awaka	First in Awaka
Most wildly travel person in Awaka	First in Awaka

Countries Visited

1. Australia
2. Austria
3. Barbados
4. Belgium
5. Brazil
6. Bulgaria
7. Cameroon
8. Canada
9. Canary Islands
10. China
11. Democratic Republic of Congo
12. Denmark
13. Dominican Republic
14. Egypt
15. England
16. Ethiopia
17. France
18. French Guyana
19. Gabon
20. Germany
21. Ghana
22. Guinea
23. Guyana
24. Haiti
25. Holland
26. Hong Kong
27. India
28. Italy
29. Jamaica
30. Japan
31. Kenya
32. Martinique
33. Mexico
34. New Zealand

35. Philippines
36. Poland
37. Puerto Rico
38. Russia
39. Senegal
40. South Africa
41. South Korea
42. Spain
43. Surinam
44. Tanzania
45. Trinidad
46. Turkey
47. USA (46 States of 50)
48. Venezuela
49. Virgin Islands
50. Zambia
51. Zimbabwe

Total: 51

Positions of Leadership Held

1950	Vice-Captain, St Michael's House, Christ the King College, Onitsha, Anambra
1957	Vice President, Newman Catholic Club, Howard University, Washington DC
1957	Chairman, Social Committee, Pan African Union, Washington, DC
1968 – 1969	President, Sigma Xi Scientific Honor Society, Southern University, Baton Rouge, Louisiana
1970 – 1972	Chairman, Department of Biology, Inter American University, San Juan, Puerto Rico
1972 – 1973	Chairman, Research and Development Committee, Catholic University of Puerto Rico, Ponce, Puerto Rico
1973 – 1977	Dean of Liberal Studies (Arts and Sciences), State University of New York, Oneonta, New York
1979 – 1980	Vice President, Nigerian Society for Parasitology
1980 – 1981	President, Nigerian Society for Parasitology

Appendix

1979 – 1982	Head, Department of Medical Microbiology and Parasitology, College of Medicine, University of Lagos, Lagos, Nigeria
1981 – 1983	Chairman, Research Program Committee, Governing Board of the Nigerian Institute for Trypanosomiasis Research, Kaduna
1983 – 1984	Rector, College of Technology, Amaigbo (now School of Health Sciences) Imo State
1982 – 1990	Editor, Nigeria Journal of Microbiology
1987 – 1991	Vice President, African Union Against Venereal Diseases and Treponematosis
1994 – 2001	Chairman, Literature Committee, American Society of Parasitologists
1999 – 2002	Program Director, Strategies for Ecology Education, Diversity and Sustainability of the Ecological Society of America
1999 – 2004	President, University Faculty Senate, Alcorn State University, Mississippi
1999 – 2016	Director, Ecology Education Workshop Program, Alcorn State University Mississippi
2001 – Present	President and CEO, Willy-Esther Foundation

2002 – 2005; 2017	Chair, Zoology and Entomology Division, Mississippi Academy of Sciences
2012 – Present	Chair, Healthcare Disparity Committee, Mississippi Academy of Sciences
2014 – Present	President, Africa Assembly, American Society of Tropical Medicine and Hygiene (ASTMH)
2016 – Present	Editor-in-Chief Community Voice Magazine
2017 – Present	Editor-in-chief, Advances in Science and Technology Journal

Awaka Constitution as Prepared by My Committee and I in 1984

INTERIM REPORT OF THE AWAKA CONSTITUTION DRAFTING COMMITTEE 16TH JULY 1984

OBJECTIVE

To prepare a durable and well thought out Constitution for the governance of the Ancient Town of Awaka.

The committee has had several meetings since the assignment given to it and has collected many pertinent reference documents to use.

It deliberated on a number of issues and decided to, first and foremost, construct an organogram which will show the governance structure of Awaka.

The following is what the committee has designed and proposed for adoption.

1. THE ORGANOGRAM SHOWING THE PROPOSED ORGANISATIONAL OR GOVERNANCE STRUCTURE OF AWAKA

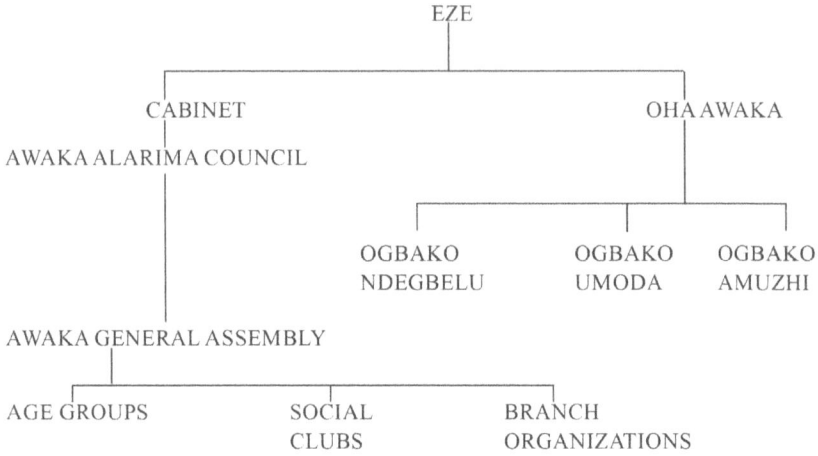

2. ORGANISATIONAL OR GOVERNANCE CATEGORIES

   A   EZE AWAKA: The committee was informed that there exist an instrument for the selection and recognition of the Awaka filed and registered with the Government of Imo State, containing among other things mode of selection, deposition and code of conduct for the Eze. Based on this information the committee decided to defer further deliberation on the Eze to future date pending the production and perusal of the registered document.

   B   CABINET:
   Composition:
   (i) The Eze shall have the prerogative of selecting members of his cabinet.
   (ii) In selecting the members of his cabinet the Eze shall take into consideration the geographic spread of Awaka town.
   (iii) The membership of the cabinet shall not exceed twelve.

Qualification:
(i) For person to qualify to be appointed as a cabinet member, he/she must be able to read and write in English Language.
(ii) The person must be known to be honest and proven good character with the interest of Awaka at heart.

Functions:

(i) The cabinet shall be an executive body with several members having definite portfolios.
(ii) The cabinet shall meet at the request of the eze.
(iii) The cabinet shall consult with the Eze when there is the need for a meeting and may do so individually or in a group.
(iv) The cabinet shall serve in an advisory capacity to the Eze in all matters referred to it by the eze.

C. OHA AWAKA:

Composition:
(i) Oha Awaka shall be made up of 19 members.
(ii) One member shall come from each of the kindreds in Awaka.

Qualification: To qualify as an Oha, a person must be the oldest surviving member of each kindred.

Functions:

(i) Settlement of disputes
(ii) Custodians of customs and traditions of Awaka

Burial Rites: The Oha awaka shall have the discretion to determine and provide the manner and requirements for the burial of a deceased member.

Power: The Oha shall have the power to discipline any recalcitrant member and protect the dignity and respect of the office.

Vacancy: where a vacancy occurs, and after one year the Okoro-oha does not take the necessary steps to be initiated as Oha, the Oha Awaka shall have the powers to take disciplinary action against that Okoro-oha and shall in addition appoint the next in line or oldest member of that kindred as Okoro-Oha and action Oha.

Initiation of Oha: The procedure and requirements for initiation into Oha Awaka. (see attached document).

C. OKORO-OHA
Qualification:
(i) He shall be the second oldest member of his kindred.
(ii) He shall be presented to the Oha Awaka by his kindreds in cabinet Oha.

Initiation of Okoro-oha: The procedure and requirements for the initiation into Okoro-oha (see attached document).

D. OGBAKO OF EACH VILLAGE
Composition: Made up of every taxable adult in each of the villages of Awaka.

Functions: Shall have a strong administrative structure for the maintenance of peace, order and settlement of disputes.

References

Acholonu, A.D.W. 1968. Studies on the freshwater cercariae of Northern Colorado. Proc. Helm Soc. Wash 35(2): 259-271

_____.1989. Parasitosis and human health in Nigeria: Present situation and future needs University of Lagos Press. pp 36.

_____. and Uzoma, K.C. 1991. Medical Laboratory Diagnosis: Collection, Handling and Storage of Pathological Specimens for Laboratory Investigation. College of Medicine Press, University of Lagos pp 62

_____. 2009. CKC Onitsha *Memories are made of thee*: the Amaka Gazette. A journal of CKC-AAA Inc. Thirteenth Convention Edition pp. 43-45.

Clinton Bill (2004). *My life:* An autobiography of the former president of the United State. Knopf Publishing Group (Random House). pp. 1008.

Castro, F and Ramonet, I. (n.d.). 2008. *Fidel Castro: My Life.* London: Peguin books pp.724

Duante A. 1995. Health Alternatives (tape).

http://www.howard.edu/Jexploreehistory.htm

Holy Trinity Catholic Church Awaka 2012. The Hub of Catholic Missionaries (Catholic Missionary Stations: Onitsha to Nebuku to Awaka to Ulakwo to Awaka to Emekuku, 1912.

Njoku, A. O. 1995. Owerre man is not an Owere man. PaJob Enterprises Owerri. pp. 15

Nwulu, V.C. 2004. The Bridge Across Time: The Biography of Sir Cyril Manuba Acholonu. Simon Printers Ltd. Yaba, Lagos pp120.

Obaze, O. H. 2015. Regarscent Past: A collection of poems. A Solonnes Consult Publication in association with Ben Bosah Books pp 81

Index

A

Academic Administrative Experiences 248
Academics and Professional Development xviii, 115
Acholonu family xxx, xxxi, xxxii, xxxiii, 5, 6, 10, 51, 108, 137, 206, 219, 220, 221, 222, 225, 251, 252, 298, 321
Acholonu Nwokoro 5, 82
akpiri mba 8
Alaenyi clan 2
Ala-Ukwu Awaka 1
Alcorn State University xxxiv, 115, 123, 124, 127, 129, 154, 182, 183, 185, 242, 244, 249, 256, 257, 259, 273, 282, 288, 301, 304, 305, 306, 307, 309, 310, 311, 312, 313, 314, 317, 325
Alexandra Kaonyeuyoaso Acholonu 71, 72, 77, 96, 212
Alfred Ugwuegbula Acholonu 5, 205, 224
Alganish 66, 86, 87
Alma mater 30, 122, 224, 251
Alternative Energy Society of Nigeria 152, 154
Alvan Ikoku College of Education 118, 147
Ama Ibeanana 1
Amaigbo College of Technology 121, 135, 136, 137, 138, 208, 209, 248, 321
Amaigbo people 121, 135, 136, 138, 139
America xiii, 36, 47, 48, 49, 50, 51, 55, 56, 59, 61, 63, 65, 66, 67, 68, 72, 87, 110, 115, 137, 149, 153, 168, 172, 188, 199, 200, 201, 202, 210, 220, 221, 236, 241, 243, 245, 248, 251, 252, 253, 257, 258, 259, 276, 277, 280, 287, 325
American Society of Parasitologists 116, 151, 257, 259, 265, 266, 277, 282, 325
American Society of Tropical Medicine and Hygiene (ASTMH) 151, 257, 282, 312, 326
Anderson Ukachi Acholonu 70, 97, 230
Anthony Omeni Njoku 212, 228
Association of America 153, 245
Atlanta University 115
Autobiography xxix, xxx, xxxi, xxxiii, xxxv, xxxvi, 51, 212, 331
Awaka autonomous community 12
Awaka Club 2, 13, 153, 223, 251, 252
Awaka community 7, 12, 223, 251
Awaka Mbutu 2, 3
Awaka vocalist 189, 214
Award 54, 149, 154, 179, 186, 187, 198, 211, 244, 245, 249, 252, 288, 315

B

Bachelor of Science degree 57
Baptized 11
Barr. Ihekwoazu 140
Baton Rouge, Louisiana 66, 69, 70, 242, 256, 324
Best ballroom dancers 31
Blessed Alexander vii, 6, 28
Bona fide Town 8
Brigadier General Ike Nwachukwu 121, 135
British colonial government 23

C

Cambridge School certificate Examination 30
Catholic Missionary 10, 331
Catholic University of Puerto Rico Ponce, Puerto Rico 242
Cercaria alganishi 67, 86
Chief Innocent Ugwuegbulam 232
Chief Olusegun Obasanjo 198
Chief Prof. Alex Acholonu 114, 127, 171, 180, 193
Chief Prof. Augustine O. Esogbue 211
Chief Sam Mbakwe 120, 135
Chieftaincy 136, 143, 145, 152, 155, 156, 157, 159, 160, 161, 162, 163, 164, 165, 244, 253, 259, 260, 301, 321
Christianity 10, 14, 225
Christianity in Awaka 10
Christopher Columbus 108, 137
Christ the King College (CKC) 29, 30, 41, 44, 153, 237, 241, 245, 247, 250, 251, 252, 324
CKC-AAA (Christ the King College Alumni Association) 153, 154, 245, 252, 258, 331
College Librarian 33
College of Medicine University of Lagos 51, 136
College of Technology Amaigbo, Imo State, Nigeria 243
Colonel T.K. Zubairu 123, 130
Colorado State University 57, 66, 115, 151, 247, 254
Curriculum Vitae (CV) 139, 151, 154, 312
Cynthia Acholonu xxxvi, 72, 85, 95, 117

D

Degree Knight of Columbus 153, 166
Dennis Memorial Grammar School 32, 35
District Officer 23
Dr. Alfred Rankins 311, 317
Dr. Benedict Njoku 27, 92, 241
Dr. Ham. Benghuzzi 178
Dr. Ira Jones 116
Dr. John Njoku 27
Dr. John Nnadi 222, 236
Dr. Kenneth Butler 179, 288
Dr. Kenny Uzoma Acholonu 113
Dr. Laz Ihekwoazu 139
Dr. Lewis White 92, 115
Dr. Louis Scott 115
Dr. Mordecai Wyatt Johnson 53
Dr. Nicholas Onyewu 52, 67, 87
Dr. Nnamdi Azikiwe 48, 63, 64, 207
Dr. Ofonagoro of Amaigho 141

E

Early Days of My Life xii, 23
Education xxix, xxxii, 4, 26, 27, 28, 29, 47, 48, 49, 53, 61, 63, 75, 76, 77, 85, 118, 120, 188, 209, 210, 219, 220, 222, 244, 251, 253, 287, 300, 302, 314
Egbu and Naze 2
Egbu people 7, 8, 9, 141, 222
Ekeamma day 6
Ekeamma market 6
Ekemma Elementary School 12
Ekpudo 2
Ekwem Oha 2
Ekwueme 1 of Ihitta Ogada 142, 159, 161, 251, 287
Emekuku Comprehensive School 210
Emekuku Parish 14, 206
Engineering School 115
Engineer Uchenna Acholonu 87, 118
England 36, 47, 48, 50, 66, 67, 150, 221, 248, 260, 322
Engr. Gregory Okafor 62, 68
Esther Eberegbulam Acholonu 96,

300
Esther Rose Acholonu 83, 84, 223, 247
Ethiopian lady 66
Eze Mitchell Egbukole 141
Eze Okoro 144, 232

F

Federal Ministry of Works 55
Fellowship of the Nigerian Academy of Science 152
Food and Drug Administration 154, 249, 258, 312
Fr. Anselem 12
Freeman Catholic Church 56
Fr. Valentine Acholonu 142, 224, 235, 244, 321

G

Godwin Etoh Achodo 11
Government College Umuahia 30

H

Hazlehurst City 184, 185
Health Disparity Research 178, 245, 312
His Royal Highness Eze Christopher David Osuagwu 10
His Royal Highness Eze W.C. Nwosu 136
His Royal Highness (HRH) Eze Okoro 232
Holy Ghost College 206
Holy Trinity Catholic Parish 11, 12, 17, 18, 233
Hon. Darryl Grennell 186
Hon. Mayor Henry Banks 180, 245
Hon. Raymond Amanze Njoku 48, 209
Howard University 47, 53, 54, 56, 57, 61, 63, 115, 122, 123, 150, 207, 222, 236, 241, 242, 243, 247, 254, 324
Human Anatomy 116, 261

I

Igbo Community Association of Mississippi 153
Ihitta-Ogada 1
Ikedi Ohakem 12
Imo Diaspora award 154
Imo State Congress of America (ISCA) 153, 172, 252
Inter American University 116, 208, 242, 248, 324
International Congress of Parasitology 9, 260, 261, 271
Invertebrate Zoology 116, 261, 262

J

Jaja of Opobo 138

L

Law School 47, 51
Leslie xxxv, xxxvi, 72, 76, 77, 85, 95, 98, 99, 171, 298, 299
Local Government Area (LGA) 1, 2, 24, 139, 247, 274
Lolo Lady Mary Ekeoma Acholonu xxxv, 70, 253

M

marriage 2, 66, 68, 71, 73, 74, 75, 77, 199
Mbaise 2, 3
Medical Mission 189, 212, 225, 227, 228, 229, 230, 274, 299
Minister of Commerce and Industry 48, 59
Ministry of Agriculture 4
Mississippi Academy of Science 154, 179, 244, 245, 259, 288
Motherless Babies Home 239, 250
Mount Camel Catholic Church 206,

239
Mr. Alfred U. Acholonu 10, 14
Mr. Anthony Manuba 36
Mr. Columbus Obihara 36
Mr. Derryl Grennell 245
Mr. Ezeoke 33
Mr. George Mbara 48
Mr. Goodman 56
Mr. Herbert Emezi 145, 146
Mr. John Eme 4
Mr. Murphy 56
Mrs Paulina Okpechi 221
Mrs. Philomena Osuji 49, 221
M.V. Aureol 52
My American Experience xiii, 47
My Family xiv, 65, 157
My Titles, Affiliations and Laurels 135

N

Nathan Ejiogu 209, 217
Ndegbelu 1, 6, 15, 48, 145, 146, 147, 206, 241
Ndum Oha 2
New York 51, 52, 53, 56, 60, 67, 72, 107, 117, 138, 208, 220, 243, 248, 255, 266, 324
Nigeria-Biafra 4, 6, 199, 201
Nigerian Academy of Science 152, 154, 169, 170, 249, 258, 263, 321
Nigeria Television Authority (NTA) 141
Nkwere people 121, 136

O

Obu Omumu xxxv, 6, 15, 16, 144
Officer of the Order of the Niger 153, 154, 249, 258, 321
Ogbuhoruzo I of Amaigbo 244, 259
Omereoha I of Emii 143
Orlu Senatorial zone 135

Oshimiri Christopher David Osuagwu 145
Otamiri River 8, 222
Otula Ukwu Awaka 3
Our Lady's School 26, 27, 28, 29, 50, 54, 210, 247

P

Parasitology 9, 51, 57, 115, 119, 152, 154, 174, 211, 242, 243, 248, 249, 250, 255, 256, 258, 260, 261, 267, 270, 271, 276, 303, 324, 325
Parasitology and Public Health Society of Nigeria 152, 174, 256
Phi Beta Sigma Fraternity 56, 252
Philadelphia 116, 125, 126, 274
philanthropy 211
Physiology 116, 261
Political Science 53
Prairie View A & M University 57, 242
President Andrew Johnson 53
Priest, Rev. Fr. Anukanti 10
Prof. Anya O. Anya 64, 207, 211
Prof. Babu Patlolla 177, 288
Prof. Bart Nnaji xxx, xxxv, 211
Prof. Chidi Akujor 212, 228
Prof. C. Onwuliri 238
Professional Accomplishments and Recognitions 248
Prof. Jibril Aminu 152
Prof. Peter Okorie 212
Prof. Ransome Kuti 152
Prof. Voletta Williams 177, 288

R

Rev. Fr. Daniel Walsh 11
Rev. Fr. Valentine Acholonu 224, 235, 244, 321
Rev. Martin Luther King 56

Rev. Sister Mary Joy Haywood 116, 125, 126
Rochas Okorocha 12

S

Sciences xxxvi, 115, 116, 118, 124, 152, 177, 208, 248, 249, 250, 254, 255, 257, 274, 293, 304, 305, 306, 307, 308, 310, 311, 312, 314, 315, 324, 325, 326
Security in Awaka 12
Service to Nigeria 250
Southern University 55, 66, 67, 69, 92, 115, 116, 242, 256, 324
St Joseph Catholic Church 167
St. Patrick's College 29, 32, 34

T

Teacher Training Schools 29
Texas 56, 57, 242, 247, 254, 272, 278
the Acholonu family xxx, xxxi, xxxii, xxxiii, 5, 10, 108, 137, 206, 219, 220, 221, 251, 252
The Igbos xxiv, 199, 205
Traditional Titles 135
Treasury Ministry 36

U

Umuodu 1, 2, 3, 145, 206
University of Lagos (UNILAG) iv, xxxv, 51, 118, 119, 120, 122, 136, 207, 208, 211, 243, 244, 248, 250, 263, 325, 331
University of Maiduguri 55
University of the District of Columbia Washington DC 243
Uratta 1, 2, 9, 36, 219, 239

V

Victoria Awani 67
Vigilante group 12
Virginia Lodge 54, 61

W

Washington, DC 47, 53, 54, 56, 63, 122, 143, 324
Water 7, 8, 9, 128, 222, 244, 251, 272, 274, 277, 278, 297, 315
Willy-Esther Foundation 20, 223, 224, 225, 227, 228, 229, 231, 232, 244, 245, 251, 325
Willy-Esther Foundation Diagnostic Laboratory 20, 231
Willy Wozuzu Acholonu 6, 7, 19, 20, 243
Willy Wozuzu Acholonu Memorial Mansion 6, 19, 20, 243
World Federation of Parasitologists 152, 179, 249, 259, 312
World Owerri People's Congress, (WOPC) 153, 258

Z

Zinc building 11, 50

About the Author

Chief Sir, Prof. Alexander D. Wozuzu Acholonu is a professor of Biology at Alcorn State University, Mississippi. He was born at Awaka in Owerri North Local Government Area (LGA) of Imo State, Nigeria, on November 30, 1932. He got his secondary education at Christ the King College, Onitsha, Anambra State, in 1952, his Ph.D. degree from Colorado State University, Fort Collins, Colorado, in 1964, and a Continuing Education Certificate in Tropical Medicine and Hygiene from Tulane University, Louisiana in 1994. He is a professor of Biology with diverse experience in Medical Microbiology and Parasitology, Environmental Biology, Ecology, and in fact, Human Anatomy and Physiology. Dr. Acholonu has not allowed his career in academics to prevent him from carrying out community services. He was a Board Member of former Owerri Community Bank in Imo State of Nigeria and which he helped to establish. For more than five decades, professor Acholonu instructed various aspects of Biological Sciences to various students at various levels and various institutions at various places. The Eze (Traditional Ruler) of Amaigbo conferred on him, a chieftancy title, Ogbuhorouzo 1 of Amaigbo, which means the first PATHFINDER. The Eze of Ihitta Ogada also gave him chieftaincy title of Ekwueme 1 of Ihita Ogada. The Eze of Emii equally in recognition of his academic, professional, organizational and community developments contributions conferred on him the third title of Omereoha (The caregiver of all). This title, more than anything else, synchronizes with the visons of his Willy-Esther Foundation. He is a true philanthropist. His adroitness in the field of Biology and his enormous contributions to scholarship, especially in Medical Microbiology and Parasitology, earned him a remarkable place in the world of Science. As a result of this, he was admitted into the fellowship of Nigeria Academy of Science in 1992. Equally, many other academic and professional bodies in the field of Medical, Natural, and Applied Sciences have recognized his contributions to Science.Professor Acholonu's career in academics is interspersed with administrative responsibilities. He travelled far and wide (up to 51 countries) doing research, acquiring and imparting knowledge. He has served in several academic positions in the USA and his country of birth, Nigeria. Amongst several positions, Acholonu has served as Departmental Chair, College Dean, Faculty Senate member, and also Faculty Senate president. He was the first and only Rector of the defunct College of Technology, Amaigbo, Imo State Nigeria now called the School of Health Sciences. He served on the Governing Council of old Imo State University (IMSU) when it was located at Uturu and he later became the Pro-Chancellor and Chairman of Governing Council of IMSU. He is also the founder and the president of the Willy-Esther Foundation, and also a member of a number of community-based organizations.Professor Acholonu has numerous publications especially in the area of public health and has engaged in many radio and television programs. He is currently the Editor-in-chief of Advances in Science and Technology Journal. Prof. Acholonu is a recipient of numerous professional, academic, and service excellence awards and accolades. He not only belongs or belonged to many academic and social organizations but held positions of leadership in many of them. Chief Sir, Prof. Alexander D. Wozuzu Acholonu is married to Lolo Mary Ekeoma Acholunu (MS). They have seven grown-up children and 16 grandchildren.

www.ingramcontent.com/pod-product-compliance
Lightning Source LLC
Chambersburg PA
CBHW041125110526
44592CB00020B/2687